Maimonides
On
Prophecy

Maimonides On Prophecy

A Commentary
on Selected Chapters
of *The Guide of the
Perplexed*

David Bakan

Jason Aronson Inc.
Northvale, New Jersey
London

Production Editor: Bernard F. Horan
Editorial Director: Muriel Jorgensen

This book was set in 11/13 Goudy Old Style
by Lind Graphics of Upper Saddle River, New Jersey
and printed and bound by Haddon Craftsmen of Scranton, Pennsylvania

Library of Congress Cataloging-in-Publication Data

Bakan, David.
    Maimonides on prophecy: a commentary on selected chapters of The
Guide of the Perplexed / David Bakan.
      p.   cm.
    Includes bibliographical references and index.
    ISBN 0-87668-692-7
    1. Maimonides, Moses, 1135-1204. Dalālat al-ha 'irīn.
2. Philosophy, Jewish. 3. Philosophy, Medieval. 4. Judaism-
Doctrines. 5. Maimonides, Moses, 1135-1204—Views on Prophets.
6. Bible. O.T. Prophets—Criticism, interpretation, etc.
I. Title.
BM545.D35B25 1991
181' .06—dc20   90-21726

Manufactured in the United States of America. Jason Aronson Inc. offers books and
cassettes. For information and catalog write to Jason Aronson Inc., 230 Livingston Street,
Northvale, New Jersey 07647.

Contents

Preface and Acknowledgments

T he essential goal of this study is to explain text, and for Maimonides the primary text is Scripture. The Mishnah explains Scripture, as do the texts of the Sages. In *The Guide of the Perplexed* Maimonides explains the prophetic texts in Scripture. This presentation seeks to explain some portions of *The Guide of the Perplexed*.

My father gave me a copy of the *Guide* when I was a youth, and I have been reading in it all of my life. While it would be hard to specify exactly all the ways, the book has been a major influence on me in all of my intellectual work. Two recognitions, that the book has a structural center in Chapter II:31, the chapter on the Sabbath, and that the book's essential project is to explain the dreams and visions of the prophets, rose to prominence in my mind some years ago. With this came a sense that the full usefulness of the *Guide* in connection with both religion and psychology was yet to be realized. My hope is that this study of the *Guide* might contribute to such a realization.

I would like to take the occasion of the publication of this study to memorialize one of my teachers, Rabbi Moishe Weintraub, who opened important windows for me in my youth. I want to express my gratitude for the few contacts that I had with Leo Strauss when we were colleagues at the University of Chicago. This work builds on his. I want to express my gratitude to York University for the spirit of academic freedom that prevails in it, and for the support it has given me for many years. I want to express my thanks especially to my two study companions in this work, Dr. Mildred Bakan, professor of philosophy, and Dr. David S. Weiss, psychologist and rabbi. Without them this work could not have been completed.

Reader's note: The quotes from *The Guide of the Perplexed* that pertain to the chapter under discussion appear in **boldface** type; all other quotes from Maimonides and references to specific pages in *The Guide* are set in regular type. The edition of *The Guide of the Perplexed* to which I refer was translated by Shlomo Pines and published by the University of Chicago Press in 1974.

David Bakan
Toronto
November 25, 1990

Introduction

T he purpose of this commentary is to explicate Maimonides' *The Guide of the Perplexed.*

Three observations should be made at the beginning to provide a perspective:

1. The subject matter of the book is prophecy.
2. The book is continuous with Maimonides' earlier writings, the *Commentary on the Mishnah* and the *Mishneh Torah,* in his aim of clarifying the connections between Scripture and the Mishnah.
3. The book aims to clarify the connections between Scripture and the Mishnaic law that begins "One is not to expound upon. . ." (*Hagigah* 11b).

Since the Mishnaic law begins with "One is not to expound upon . . . ," Maimonides is obliged to defer to it in his exposition of the topics that are so constrained. Maimonides thus writes on those topics in hints, flashes, and allusions, after he has completed his work on all the rest of Jewish law.

The Mishnaic law imposes constraint on exposition with respect to three topics: sexuality, the creation of the universe, and a third

thing – whatever it is that is the subject of the vision of Ezekiel. They
are the *Ariyot* (nakednesses), *Maaseh* (account or work of) *Bereshit*
(beginning), and *Maaseh* (the account or work of) *Merkabah*. *Merkabah* is characteristically translated as "chariot." However, we refrain
from translating it because the very identification of the meaning of
that term is a critical feature of the exposition.

According to the Mishnaic law, the nakednesses, understood as the
scriptural constraints on sexual acts, may not be expounded to three,
that is, not more than two at a time. The *Maaseh Bereshit* may not be
expounded to two, that is, not more than one at a time. And the
Maaseh Merkabah may be expounded not even to one unless he were
wise and understanding of his own knowledge.

Maimonides states that the constraint of the Mishnaic law extends
to writing a book, since a book is read by many people. However, he
finds a license to write a book that is at least overtly about the second
and the third topics. He finds that license in the indication in the
Talmud that exposition of the third topic is to be restricted to "chapter
headings." He takes that to mean intimation in a more general sense.
He takes it that writing a book in "chapter headings" is not in violation
of the Mishnaic law.

The results of this study are presented in the following pages in the
form of ad locum commentary to several selected parts of *The Guide of
the Perplexed*.

The first is to the Introduction to Part I of the *Guide*. The second is
to Chapter II:30, which is the most explicit exposition Maimonides
makes in the book of the *Maaseh Bereshit*. The third is to Chapter
II:31, on the Sabbath. As we will note, the first Sabbath is, for
Maimonides, the divider between the *Maaseh Bereshit* and the *Maaseh
Merkabah*. We have also joined to that a commentary on Chapters
I:67–70, four chapters in the book in which Maimonides deals most
explicitly with God. The fourth is to the Introduction to Part III, and
to Chapters III:1–7 following, which is Maimonides' most explicit
exposition of the *Maaseh Merkabah*.

In the course of this study, speculation was aroused that Maimonides had composed a prior and more explicit version of *The Guide of
the Perplexed* for himself in preparation for writing a version for the
eyes of others. One might imagine it to have been something like the
succinct characterization he made of Aristotelianism [*Guide*, pp.
235–239].

Under any circumstances, while ad locum commentary has certain expository advantages, it is desirable to try to state clearly what we take Maimonides to be saying:

1. The essence of God and the existence of God are to be distinguished.
2. Knowledge of the existence of God is available to all human beings, Jew and Gentile alike, by virtue of the universally possessed rational faculty, the faculty whereby human beings can be said to be in the image of God.
3. The essence of God is creation out of nothingness.
4. Jews hold the creation out of nothingness as a matter of Law.
5. Aristotle does not accept the creation out of nothingness, and is therefore barred by his assumption from being able to reach toward God's essence.
6. Philosophy's natural and divine sciences bear on the existence, not the essence, of God.
7. Prophecy is to be distinguished from philosophy.
8. Prophecy reaches toward the essence of God.
9. The patriarchs, Moses, and the other prophets knew natural science and divine science in connection with their knowledge of the existence of God before those sciences were known to the Greek philosophers.
10. Moses' prophetic mode, out of which the commandments arose, is different from the prophecy of other prophets. The author does not intend to deal with Moses' prophetic mode in *The Guide of the Perplexed*.
11. The reach to God's essence is not available to the rational faculty alone, except in the case of Moses.
12. The prophecy of prophets other than Moses occurs only in visions and dreams.
13. The prophetic visions and dreams of the prophets other than Moses are not real in the sense of actual historical events.
14. The prophetic visions and dreams of the prophets other than Moses result from the combined action of the rational and the imaginative faculties, both being excellent.
15. Philosophers are deficient in the imaginative faculty.
16. The prophetic visions and dreams of the prophets other than Moses are constructed by the imaginative faculty from content

provided to it by the rational faculty, using combinations, substitutions, and word, letter, and number play. The interpretation of prophecy takes that into account.

17. Perplexity and heartache are associated with interpreting visions and dreams in their external senses. Apprehension of the internal meanings produces relief.

18. The scriptural texts of the *Maaseh Bereshit* and the *Maaseh Merkabah* are mainly the opening texts of Genesis and Ezekiel, respectively.

19. The first Sabbath divides the *Maaseh Bereshit* from the *Maaseh Merkabah*.

20. The creativity of God prior to the first Sabbath is represented in the *Maaseh Bereshit*.

21. The *Maaseh Bereshit* is of two creations. First, *beriyah*, the creation out of nothingness of a tripartite universe, consisting of Elohim, heaven, and earth, and second, *assiyah*, the unfolding of the established forms in the second to sixth days of creation.

22. *Elohim* are the forces in the universe. They correspond to the angels of Jewish tradition and the intellects of Aristotle.

23. The creativity of God after the first Sabbath is *yetzirah*, and is represented in the *Maaseh Merkabah*.

24. The work of the second day of creation was left unfinished to allow a place for *yetzirah* after the first Sabbath.

25. The *Maaseh Merkabah* apprehension of prophets other than Moses is of the ensoulment of human beings in the imagery of sexual intercourse.

26. The most detailed scriptural text of the *Maaseh Merkabah* in prophecy is found in the description of the vision of Ezekiel. The most laconic scriptural text of the *Maaseh Merkabah* in prophecy is found in Isaiah 6:1.

27. The principle of Rabbi Akiva, which is to be applied to the interpretation of prophecy, is to recognize the sexual imagery in Scripture and to take it as metaphorical.

It is of value to note some of the main features of the historical context surrounding *The Guide of the Perplexed*.

Maimonides was born in the city of Córdoba in Spain in 1135. He and his family were forced to leave Spain when he was a young man. After some wandering, they settled in Egypt. He had a fine education in both religious and secular matters. When his family fortunes failed, he undertook to make a living as a physician and became the physician to the Egyptian royal household. He was a personal leader in his local Jewish community, and his opinions were respected throughout the Jewish world.

Maimonides is regarded as significant in the history of the Jews primarily for his extraordinary contribution to Jewish law. His main contribution was to show clearly the connections between the Written and the Oral Law, and to provide a topical organization of the law as a whole.

The Written Law comprises the 613 commandments to be found in Scripture. The Oral Law, taken as the "explanation" of the Written Law of Scripture, is traditionally understood to have been transmitted orally down the generations from Moses. It was given final written form by Judah Ha-Nasi in the third century. It consists of a series of paragraphs, each of which is referred to as a *mishnah*. The whole of it is also called the *Mishnah*.

The Talmud, consisting of the *Mishnah* and extensive commentary added ad locum to the paragraphs, developed after Judah Ha-Nasi. The Talmud exists in two forms, the Palestinian and the Babylonian. The latter is taken as the more authoritative by Maimonides. There is a vast associated literature.

The major aim of Maimonides' literary efforts was to make Jewish law accessible. The culmination of his work is the *Mishneh Torah*. In it the commandments from Scripture are organized by topic and joined with the laws from the Mishnah and selected material from the commentaries. In the introduction, Maimonides tells the reader that with the *Mishneh Torah* in his possession, he need consult no other work except Scripture. With the *Mishneh Torah* in hand, all necessary Jewish law, oral and written, is made readily accessible, comprehensible, and learnable.

This claim caused some chagrin to some in the Jewish community. Nonetheless, the *Mishneh Torah* had great social significance. Young adults could rarely achieve reasonable mastery of Jewish law before this work became available. People could thus rarely assume full leadership roles in the Jewish community until late in life. With the publication of the *Mishneh Torah*, reasonable competence in Jewish law could be achieved by early adulthood. For this and other reasons the *Mishneh Torah* became a major factor in shaping the Jewish community in the centuries that followed.

Maimonides does deal with the "One is not to expound upon . . ." Mishnaic law in his earlier writings. However, his presentations are extremely laconic. The fuller treatment is left for *The Guide of the Perplexed*, which substitutes intimation for laconism to defer to the Mishnaic law.

One of the major historical questions is why *The Guide of the Perplexed* has remained, as Leo Strauss puts it, "sealed with many seals" [*Guide*, p. xiii] for almost eight centuries. While the topic would require extensive investigation, we venture but two speculations here. Both speculations are suggested by the content of Leo Strauss's Introduction to the *Guide*. Leo Strauss is the major contemporary commentator to highlight the esoteric character of *The Guide of the Perplexed*. From a historical perspective, although Strauss is hardly to be identified as associated with the Jewish mystical tradition, he is its contemporary representative, for mystics too saw *The Guide of the Perplexed* as a document of concealed content. The first speculation is associated with the extensive discussions of Greek philosophy to be found in the pages of *The Guide of the Perplexed*. The second speculation is associated with the sexual nature of the concealed content.

Most thinkers in history, for various reasons, conceive of Judaism and Greek philosophy as a priori alien to each other. In *The Guide of the Perplexed* Maimonides devotes a considerable amount of positive attention to Greek philosophy. If one approaches *The Guide of the Perplexed* with the assumption that Maimonides understood Judaism and Greek philosophy to be a priori alien to each other, the book becomes extraordinarily difficult. If one does begin thus, the book tends to become either a book of defection or a book of reconciliation, and then a knot.

Some have taken the book as evidence of a kind of intellectual and spiritual disorder in Maimonides in his later years, as evidenced by his friendliness to the Greek thinkers. Others take Maimonides to have sought to put Jewish—or even Judeo-Christian—thought together with the Greek thought. But all who deal with him find knots that do not unravel. Indeed, there has arisen a tendency among some writers simply to declare that Maimonides deliberately introduces substantive contradictions, and that explains the knots. However, as will become evident in our study, Maimonides does not intend to do that.

There is, however, a historical line of thought going back at least to the third century B.C.E. in which the claim is made that Greek thought had a Jewish origin. The fact is that the knowledge and wisdom characteristically associated with Greek thought *was taken by Maimonides* to have been possessed by the patriarchs, Moses, and the other prophets long before the time of Aristotle. His theory of prophecy takes the existence of this knowledge among the prophets as fundamental. The knowledge identified as Aristotelian is, for Maimonides, Jewish in the first place. Thus, he characterizes Abraham's teaching as follows: "Thus Abraham taught the people and explained to them by means of speculative proofs that the world has but one deity . . ." [*Guide*, p. 379].

This statement about Abraham is parallel to the way Maimonides speaks of Aristotle when he presents the Aristotelian premises. He describes these Aristotelian premises as: "The premises needed for establishing the existence of the deity . . . and for the demonstration that He . . . is one . . ." [*Guide*, p. 235].

Our point may be demonstrated by two consecutive sentences from Strauss. He writes first: "One begins to understand the *Guide* once one sees that it is not a philosophic book—a book written by a philosopher for philosophers—but a Jewish book: a book written by a Jew for Jews" [*Guide*, p. xiv].

This is certainly right in the sense that the book is, as Maimonides states, a book intended to explicate the prophecy of prophets he identifies as Jewish.

But then, as though Strauss may have had a key in his hand and dropped it, he states: "[The book's] first premise is . . . that being a Jew and being a philosopher are two incompatible things" [*Guide*, p. xiv].

This is not Maimonides' premise. Accepting this as Maimonides' premise makes it virtually impossible to open the door.

The second speculation is about forbearance concerning speaking publicly about sexuality. There is a normal and proper forbearance based on the possibility that open speech about sexuality can have damaging effects, especially on the immature. It is reasonable to suppose that the possibility of causing damage by speaking publicly about sexuality was the ground for the Mishnaic law itself. We must, however, take note of the great decline in the necessity for and even desirability of such forbearance in the last century.

We have to assume there have been many people in history who were able to discern the sexual content that is intimated in *The Guide of the Perplexed*. We can also assume that they felt constrained from writing about it. The interesting thing, of course, is that there is a great exception. It is in the Jewish mystical tradition that followed after Maimonides, which was less forbearing with respect to sexual imagery than the common social norm. Some of the Jewish mystics even claimed that their inspiration came from *The Guide of the Perplexed*.

Strauss is significant on this point as well. Strauss published his Introduction in 1963. By 1963, the norm was down. By 1963, Strauss was not so forbearing as not to say anything. He writes that for Maimonides, the scriptural indication that man is made in the image of God

> . . . might be thought to mean that man is the image of God because he is bisexual or that the Godhead contains a male and a female element that generate "children of God" and the like. . . . Maimonides does not discuss the implication which was stated, for it is one of the secrets of the Torah and we are only at the beginning of our training. [*Guide*, p. xxviii]

This image of a male and a female element generating the children of God is, as we will note, the major feature of the *Maaseh Merkabah* for Maimonides. The quote above patently demonstrates that Strauss had recognized the concealed content as sexual in the thought of Maimonides. We must assume that many others had also noted it but were more constrained than Strauss was in 1963, when the above was published.

I

A Commentary on the Introduction to the First Part

After completing the Mishneh Torah, Maimonides turned to the composition of The Guide of the Perplexed. The Mishneh Torah opens and deals briefly with the commandments concerning belief and affect with respect to God. That is, it opens and deals briefly with the commandments enjoining belief in God's existence and unity, and with the commandments to love God and to fear God. The bulk of the Mishneh Torah, however, deals with overt conduct.

The Guide of the Perplexed is a work on the apprehension of God, or at least the reach toward Him, by the prophets other than Moses as recorded in Scripture. For Maimonides, all the commandments of overt conduct were associated with the prophecy of Moses. Having completed the task of explicating them in the Mishneh Torah, he turned to the explication of the prophecy of prophets other than Moses.

What that becomes in Maimonides' hands is an essay on creativity, which we take The Guide of the Perplexed to be. On the one hand, it deals with cosmic creativity. On the other hand, it deals with the creativity of human beings.

The Guide of the Perplexed opens with

CAUSE ME TO KNOW [Guide, p. 5]

13

The Introduction to the first part of *The Guide of the Perplexed* opens with the citation of three biblical verses: "Cause me to know the way wherein I should walk, For unto Thee have I lifted my soul" (Psalms 143:8). "Unto you, Ishim, I call, And my voice is to the sons of man" (Proverbs 8:4). "Incline thine ear, and hear the words of the wise, And apply thy heart unto my knowledge" (Proverbs 22:17).

Maimonides indicates the transition from *halakhah*, traditional law, to prophecy, the topic of *The Guide of the Perplexed*. The first line of the first citation alludes to *halakhah*, literally "walking." The second line, "unto Thee have I lifted my soul," alludes to that which happens in connection with the apprehension of the prophets. The limited promise of *The Guide of the Perplexed* to the reader is to help him come to understand the meaning of prophecy. There is, however, a spiritual promise as well.

Ishim is one of the names of the angels. It is the name associated with the tenth angel in the scheme Maimonides accepts. That tenth angel corresponds to the Active Intellect, the angel associated with the earth, that which is below the sphere of the moon. The Active Intellect allows that which is potential to become actual, that which is not apprehended to be apprehended, that which is not minded to be minded. It is also the agent of prophecy.

When Maimonides enumerates the premises of Aristotle in what appears to the modern reader as a forbidding scholastic exercise [*Guide*, pp. 235–241], he makes the Active Intellect the eighteenth premise, and marks it with a special indication, "Understand this."

[18] The eighteenth premise: Everything that passes from potentiality to actuality has something other than itself that causes it to pass, and this cause is of necessity outside that thing. For if that cause were that thing and there were no obstacle to prevent this passage, the thing would not have been for a certain time in potentia but would have always been in actu. If, however, the cause of the passage from potentiality to actuality subsisted in the thing, and if there was at the same time an obstacle to it, which was subsequently removed, there is no doubt that the factor that put an end to the obstacle is the one that caused that potentiality to pass into actuality. Understand this. [*Guide*, p. 238]

Maimonides enumerates the ten ranks of angels in the *Mishneh Torah*:

> *Hayoth hakodesh* . . . , *Ophanim, Erelim, Hashmalim, Serafim, Malakhim, Elohim, Bene Elohim, Cerubim* and *Ishim*. . . . The form of those called *Ishim* are of the tenth rank. And these are the angels that speak with the prophets and make them envision the visions of prophecy. They are called *Ishim* because their rank is so close to that of the human intellect. [*Yesodei Hatorah* II:7]

The second citation indicates the generation of the prophetic message. The third citation indicates the human participation in prophecy.

For Maimonides, the critical verse in Scripture bearing on prophecy is: "If there be a prophet among you, I the Lord do make Myself known to him in a vision, I do speak to him in a dream" (Numbers 12:6).

Hearing in dreams is a lesser degree of prophecy than the apprehension of a vision. Maimonides devotes a chapter (Chapter II:46) to explaining the degrees of prophecy, the lower degrees being associated with hearing, and the higher degrees being associated with vision. We take the last citation as an allusion to the degrees of prophecy.

Although prophecy for Maimonides is that which is apprehended in dreams and visions, prophecy is a higher degree of apprehension than philosophy. For in prophecy God's "I do make myself known . . ." can be realized. Prophecy entails a kind of knowledge that is higher than any other knowledge, and is beyond the exercise simply of the rational faculty. Indeed, the thing that makes it superior is that it also entails the imaginative faculty. Maimonides expresses this idea in the form of a parable almost at the end of *The Guide of the Perplexed*:

> The ruler is in his palace, and all his subjects are partly within the city and partly outside the city. Of those who are within the city, some have turned their backs on the ruler's habitation, their faces being turned the other way. Others seek to reach the ruler's habitation, turn toward it, and desire to enter it and to stand before him, but up to now they have not yet seen the wall of the habitation. Some of those who seek to reach it have come up to the habitation and walk around it searching for its

gate. Some of them have entered the gate and walk about in the antechambers. Some of them have entered the inner court of the habitation and have come to be with the king, in one and the same place with him, namely, in the ruler's habitation. But their having come into the inner part of the habitation does not mean that they see the ruler or speak to him. For after their coming into the inner part of the habitation, it is indispensable that they should make another effort; they will be in the presence of the ruler, see him from afar or from nearby, or hear the ruler's speech or speak to him.

Now I shall interpret . . . this parable. . . . Those who are outside the city . . . have no doctrinal belief, neither one based on speculation nor one that accepts the authority of tradition. . . . Those who are within the city, but have turned their backs upon the ruler's habitation, are people who have opinions and are engaged in speculation, but who have adopted incorrect opinions. . . .

Those who seek to reach the ruler's habitation and to enter it, but never see the ruler's habitation, are the multitude of adherents of the Law, I refer to the *ignoramuses who observe the commandments.*

Those who have come up to the habitation and walk around it are the jurists who believe true opinions on the basis of traditional authority . . . but do not engage in speculation concerning the fundamental principles of religion and make no inquiry whatever regarding the rectification of belief.

Those who have plunged into speculation concerning the fundamental principles of religion have entered the antechambers. . . . If . . . you have understood the natural things and have understood divine science you have entered . . . into the inner court and are with him in one habitation. This is the rank of the men of science . . .

There are those who set their thought to work after having attained perfection in the divine science, turn wholly toward God . . . , renounce what is other than He, and direct all the acts of their intellect toward an examination of the beings with a view to drawing from them proof with regard to Him, so as to know his governance of them in whatever way it is possible. These people are those who are present in the ruler's council. This is the rank of the prophets. . . . [*Guide*, pp. 619–620]

We take the latter in the sense of "apply thy heart unto my knowledge." We must note that this is a form of knowledge that is higher than that of the "rank of the men of science" and that there are ways of knowing which are beyond the rational forms of knowing of those who are not yet inside the ruler's council.

Maimonides seeks to explain this last kind of knowledge in *The Guide of the Perplexed*. Such a notion is also found in Plato's *Timaeus*, a work that Maimonides evidently had on his desk as he wrote *The Guide of the Perplexed*. Maimonides cites Plato variously, as we will note, and actually mentions the *Timaeus* by name [*Guide*, p. 283]. What we find in the *Timaeus* that converges with what is found in Scripture, and that plays so important a role in Maimonides' thought concerning prophecy, is the following: "No man, when in his wits, attains prophetic truth and inspiration; but [may receive] the inspired word [when] his intelligence is enthralled in sleep? . . ." (*Jowett*, p. 71).

We will presently mention some considerations concerning the relationships between Greek and Jewish thought in connection with Maimonides.

THE FIRST PURPOSE OF THIS TREATISE. [*Guide*, p. 5]

The Introduction to the First Part begins, after these citations, by saying,

THE FIRST PURPOSE OF THIS TREATISE IS TO EXPLAIN THE MEANINGS OF CERTAIN TERMS OCCURRING IN BOOKS OF PROPHECY. [*Guide*, p. 5]

This is followed soon by a statement that:

THIS TREATISE ALSO HAS A SECOND PURPOSE: NAMELY, THE EXPLANATION OF VERY OBSCURE PARABLES OCCURRING IN THE BOOKS OF THE PROPHETS. [*Guide*, p. 6]

The declaration of purpose is clear and simple. It is to explain prophecy.

While a review of the vast literature in connection with Maimonides is beyond the scope of this commentary, it is important to point out that a great deal of the literature does not seem to take Maimonides at his word, that the explication of prophecy is his main purpose.

We must at this point put in a brief note concerning the use of the word "prophecy." Usage often tends to take the word in the sense of divination or foreknowledge. This is not the sense in which Maimonides uses the word. For Maimonides, there is a relationship between such divination or foreknowledge and prophecy. According to Maimonides the faculty of divination, including foreknowledge, exists in all people but is especially strong in prophets. It is, however, something to be mentioned both to indicate its ubiquity, and to indicate it as a precondition for prophecy, rather than prophecy itself. A prophet must have two faculties that are very strong as the precondition for prophecy. One of these is courage, and the other is divination. Like courage,

> . . . the faculty of divination exists in all people, but varies in degree. It exists especially with regard to things with which a man is greatly concerned and about which his thought turns. Thus you will find in your soul that so and so spoke or acted in such and such a manner in such and such an episode, and the thing is really so. You will find among people a man whose conjecturing and divination are very strong and habitually hit the mark, so that he hardly imagines that a thing comes to pass without its happening wholly or in part as he imagined it. The causes of this are many—they are various anterior, posterior, and present circumstances. But in virtue of the strength of divination, the mind goes over all these premises and draws from them conclusions in the shortest time, so that it is thought to happen in no time at all. In virtue of this faculty, certain people give warnings concerning future events. [Guide, p. 378]

We take note of the fact that Maimonides says that in the Guide, his attention is on the books of prophecy, in the sense of the classical division of Scripture into Tanak (Torah), Neviim (prophecy), and Ketuvim (other writings). Thus, Maimonides deals with the books of Ezekiel, Isaiah, and so on.

Maimonides' writing on the books of prophecy after having finished his Mishneh Torah is then in quite orderly progression. For in the Mishneh Torah he essentially dealt with Torah; the Mishneh Torah is organized around the 613 commandments that are to be found in the five books of Moses. Having finished that, he then goes on to writing, in *The Guide of the Perplexed*, about *Neviim*, about the material to be found in the second category.

This, however, is too narrow. For Maimonides focused on the commandments in the books of Moses in his composition of the *Mishneh Torah*. There is, however, considerable narrative material as well that he did not deal with in the *Mishneh Torah*, including the narrative of the creation, and the narratives of Moses and the patriarchs, who are regarded by Maimonides as prophets. In *The Guide of the Perplexed* the narrative material, such as the material on the lives of Abraham and Jacob, as well as the narrative material in the books of prophecy, such as that found in Ezekiel, also fall under the heading of prophecy.

The narrative material is of considerable importance to Maimonides in the sense that the presumptive narratives, insofar as they are prophecy, must satisfy the criterion that Maimonides takes from: "If there be a prophet among you . . . I the Lord do make Myself known to him in a vision, I do speak to him in a dream" (Numbers 12:6). Thus, for Maimonides the prophetic narratives are not veridical accounts, but are rather visions or dreams of the prophets.

In Maimonides' recital of the degrees of prophecy, he exemplifies the highest degree of prophecy of prophets other than Moses, the eleventh, by the account of Abraham and the binding of Isaac. Thus, he writes: "The eleventh degree . . . consists in the prophet's seeing an angel who addresses him as in a vision as Abraham at the time of binding" [*Guide*, p. 402].

Since Abraham heard speech, it had to be in a dream, in accordance with "I do speak to him in a dream." Maimonides explains: "One could . . . say that every vision in which you find the prophet hearing speech was in its beginning a vision, but . . . became a dream. . . . All speech that is heard . . . is heard only in a dream; as the text has it: *I do speak to him in a dream* [*Guide*, pp. 402–403].

Scripture does not need to explain that the narratives concerning visions, and dreams

> . . . are not real actions, actions that exist for the external senses. Some of them are set forth in the books of prophecy without qualification. For since it is known that all these things occur in a vision of prophecy,

Scripture in the recounting of these details of the parable may dispense
with reiterating that they happened in a vision of prophecy. Similarly
a prophet may say, *And the Lord said unto me*, without the need to state
explicitly that this happened in a dream. [*Guide*, p. 404]

Maimonides indicates that it can be a mistake to think otherwise,
albeit,

. . . the multitude think that these actions, transportations, questions,
and answers occurred all of them in a state in which they could have
been perceived by the senses. . . . God is too exalted than that He
should turn His prophets into a laughing stock and a mockery for fools
by ordering them to carry out crazy actions [or] ordering them to
commit acts of disobedience. Only those [who are] weak in syllogistic
reasoning fancy with regard to all this that the prophet was ordered to
do certain things and hence did them. . . . [T]here remains no room for
obscurity as to any of these things having real existence. . . .

. . . Everything that is said concerning . . . a vision – for instance that he
acted in it or heard or went out or went in or spoke or was spoken to or
stood or sat down or went up or went down or made a journey or asked
a question or was asked – all of it happens in a vision of prophecy. And
even if such actions should have had a long duration and should have
been attached to certain times, to individuals that are indicated, and to
places, you should – as soon as it has become clear to you that the
action in question is a parable – have certain knowledge that it occurred in a vision of prophecy. [*Guide*, pp. 406–407]

Maimonides' notion of prophecy entails two things further: first, a
theory of how visions and dreams are generated; and second, corresponding methods of determining the meanings in these scriptural
prophetic accounts.

Prophecy for Maimonides comprises the processes that were identified as the "dream-work" in Freud's *The Interpretation of Dreams*.

Maimonides identifies two critical human faculties: the first is the
rational or speculative faculty, and the second is the imaginative
faculty. Maimonides provides us with a view of the dynamics of the
generation of visions and dreams of prophecy, as follows: "Know that
the true reality and quiddity of prophecy consist in its being an

overflow overflowing from God . . . through the intermediation of the Active Intellect, toward the rational faculty in the first place and thereafter toward the imaginative faculty" [*Guide*, p. 369]. The action is best when the prophet is asleep:

> [The] greatest and noblest action [of the imaginative faculty] takes place only when the senses rest and do not perform their actions. It is then that a certain overflow overflows to this faculty . . . and it is the cause of the veridical dreams. This same overflow is the cause of prophecy. [*Guide*, p. 370]

This agrees with what we have cited above from Plato's *Timaeus*. When the imaginative faculty is most perfect, then what has been produced appears as external: ". . . the imaginative faculty achieves so great a perfection of action that it sees the thing as if it were outside, and that the thing whose origin is due to it appears to have come to it by the way of external sensation" [*Guide*, p. 170]. It is in this ability that the prophet is superior to the philosophers. He possesses what the philosophers possess: "True prophets indubitably grasp speculative matters." [*Guide*, p. 377]. However, the prophet can, by further engaging the imagination in the process of apprehension, come to apprehend what the philosopher cannot apprehend: "by means of his speculation alone, man is unable to grasp the causes from which what a prophet has come to know necessarily follows. [Prophets give] information regarding matters with respect to which man, using only common conjecture and divination, is unable" [*Guide*, p. 377].

What then is this information? It is information that reaches toward the *essence* of God. The philosopher reaches only to the *existence* of God.

It is dangerous to teach essence. It is safe to teach existence. "It is . . . harmful to make clear the meaning of the parables of the prophets" [*Guide*, p. 70]. This is especially the case for those who are young or deficient:

> . . . It behooves . . . to educate the young and to give firmness to the deficient in capacity according to the measure of their apprehension. . . . Now it is not within their power to understand these matters as they truly are. Hence . . . the mind [of such persons] is led toward the

existence of the objects of these opinions and representations but not toward grasping their essence as it truly is. [*Guide*, I:33; pp. 70–71]

Maimonides elaborates on the distinction between essence and existence. Referring back to his making the distinction, Maimonides explains: "We have mentioned in one of the chapters of this Treatise that there is an immense difference between guidance leading to a knowledge of the existence of a thing and an investigation of the true reality or the essence and substance of that thing" [*Guide*, p. 97]. One can know of "the existence of [a] King through the fact that matters in a city proceed in an orderly fashion [while] there is nothing to give an indication of the ruler's essence" [*Guide*, p. 98]. One can teach of the one without the other: "The reason is that guidance leading to the knowledge of the existence of a thing can be had even if that should be through the accidents of the thing or through its acts or through a relation–which may be very remote from the thing–existing between the latter and things other than itself" [*Guide*, p. 97].

What is the potential harm? The prophets–the prophets other than Moses–are bound to use figurative language in their indications concerning that which they apprehended. The harm is the exposure of children to the sexual. Maimonides states this very succinctly. If we allow that the essence of God is that God is the Creator, then the prophets represent God as engaging in sexual intercourse because "we have no intellectual cognition of . . . bringing somebody . . . to existence except through sexual intercourse" [*Guide*, p. 99].

As far as the harm is concerned, there is warning of this with respect to the book of Ezekiel in the Talmud: "The Rabbis taught: There was once a child who was reading at his teacher's house the Book of Ezekiel, and he apprehended . . . whereupon a fire went forth . . . and consumed him. So they sought to suppress the Book of Ezekiel" (*Hagigah* 13a).

While Maimonides does not cite this in the *Guide*, he cites from this page in the Talmud at least seven times, and from the section of the Talmud in which this appears at least twenty-three times (see *Guide* index, p. 655).

The distinction between existence and essence corresponds to the human faculties, as we have already noted. That is, existence is apprehended through the rational faculty. Essence is apprehended through both the rational faculty and the imaginative faculty. The former characterizes philosophy, the latter characterizes prophecy.

Maimonides also brought these considerations to bear on the commandments themselves. Of the 613 commandments, Maimonides identified the commandments concerning the existence and unity of God as having a special status different from the other commandments in being associated with the rational faculty. While the bulk of the commandments were mediated through Moses, the commandments concerning the existence and unity of God were given directly to the people. Maimonides interprets this as meaning that the existence of God is a matter of demonstration by the rational faculty.

Explaining the nature of the communication that took place at Mount Sinai, Maimonides says: "Moses [was] the one who heard words and reported them to them. This is the external meaning of the text of the Torah and of most of the dicta of the Sages" [Guide, p. 364]. Maimonides goes on to qualify this with respect to the commandments concerning the existence and the unity of God: "However, [the Sages] also have a dictum . . . : They heard 'I [am the Lord thy God. . . .' (Exodus 20:2)] and 'Thou shalt have [no other gods before Me . . .' (Exodus 20:3)] from the mouth of the Force." Maimonides interprets this to mean direct communication and that, in turn, to mean the exercise of the rational faculty. First he says: "They mean that these words reached them just as they reached Moses . . . and that it was not Moses . . . who communicated them to them." And he follows that up immediately with: "For these two principles, I mean the existence of the deity and His being one, are knowable by human speculation alone" [Guide, p. 364].

This has extraordinary significance for removing much of the mystery that has been associated with The Guide of the Perplexed. It clearly separates the question of existence from the question of essence. It reserves essence to the prophets. On the other hand, it opens the question of existence to all peoples. By making it a matter addressed to all the people, and not necessarily involving Moses, it became linked to the exercise of the rational faculty. The rational faculty is, in Maimonides' view, not only something general to all humankind, in addition to the Israelites, but is, indeed, the essential feature of the human being that makes the human being human.

Many pages of *The Guide of the Perplexed* are devoted to the ideas of non-Israelites concerning the existence and unity of God, but not to the essence of God. With respect to the existence of God, there is no difference between Israelite and non-Israelite; there is only a difference between those who are not sufficiently developed in their rational faculty to appreciate it and those who are.

Maimonides accepted the traditional notion that Abraham was the first to have discovered the existence of God and taught it to others, and that from Abraham it reached the Greek philosophers. However, the critical thing for Maimonides is that the existence and unity of God was rationally demonstrable. There would be no reason for not entering into an engagement with non-Jews, even as Abraham did not hesitate to do.

It is interesting to consider one of Maimonides' favored epigraphs, an epigraph he places in *The Guide of the Perplexed* three times. It precedes each of the three major sections: the opening Epistle Dedicatory [*Guide*, p. 3], the Introduction to the Second Part [*Guide*, p. 235], and the Introduction to the Third Part [*Guide*, p. 415]. It is a verse from Scripture: "In the name of the Lord, God of the World" (Genesis 21:33).

It is significant in that it is from an account of Abraham making a covenant with the non-Jew Abimelech, who patently accepts the existence of Abraham's God: "And it came to pass at that time that Abimelech . . . spoke unto Abraham, saying: God is with thee in all that thou doest. Now therefore swear unto me here by God that thou wilt not deal falsely with me. . . . And Abraham said I will swear. . . . So they made a covenant. . . . And Abraham . . . called there *In the name of the Lord, God of the World*" (Genesis 21:22–33).

The commandments bearing on the existence and unity of God are part of the whole of the 613 commandments Maimonides attempted to order in the *Mishneh Torah*. The Jew is commanded with respect to the *existence* of God. But there are the two further things. First, the existence and unity of God are rationally demonstrable. And this is evident in the work of the philosophers. Second, the essence of God is not commandment in the same sense. However desirable it is to reach toward essence – indeed, however important it may be especially for one who has become perplexed – it is not obligatory. It is contingent on special excellences that only a few may possess. These excellences are possessed by the prophets who, excellent in both the rational and the imaginative faculties, can, in visions and dreams, reach toward the essence of God.

> SOME OF THESE TERMS ARE EQUIVOCAL; HENCE THE IGNORANT ATTRIBUTE TO THEM ONLY ONE OR SOME OF THE MEANINGS IN WHICH THE TERM IN QUESTION IS USED. OTHERS ARE DERIVATIVE TERMS; HENCE THEY ATTRIBUTE TO THEM ONLY THE ORIGINAL MEANING FROM WHICH THE OTHER MEANING IS DE-RIVED. OTHERS ARE AMPHIBOLOUS TERMS, SO THAT AT TIMES THEY ARE BELIEVED TO BE UNIVOCAL AND AT OTHER TIMES EQUIVOCAL. [*Guide*, p. 5]

There is a certain basic principle of interpretation that is taught in connection with all disciplines. This principle needs to be made explicit. For to appreciate what Maimonides does in connection with prophecy in *The Guide of the Perplexed* it is necessary to see how that principle is negated in connection with prophecy as he understands it. The principle to which we refer is that *meaning is determined by context*. The usual rule is that we take the meaning of a term to be consonant with the context in which the term occurs.

For Maimonides, this principle must be turned around completely for the understanding of prophecy. Followers of the principle are ignoramuses for Maimonides.

A fundamental methodological principle in connection with the interpretation of prophecy is the deliberate violation of context as a way of coming to appreciate the true meaning of the text. The assumption is that the role of context is to conceal the deeper meaning. This method of interpreting prophecy involves the identification of alternative meanings that might be suggested by the terms that are used.

For such an interpretive exercise, a lexicon providing various meanings a word may suggest in different contexts could be useful. Maimonides obliges by providing such a lexicon in the first of the three parts of *The Guide of the Perplexed*. His lexicon consists of a series of chapters on selected terms to be found in what Maimonides takes to be prophetic texts, and enumerating various meanings the terms may have.

The meaning of a word may even be ascertainable on the assumption of remote connections by wordplay and anagrams. In one chapter of *The Guide of the Perplexed*, Maimonides provides some scriptural foundation for this approach, as well as some interesting examples. In one of these examples Maimonides indicates that the prophet may see something in a dream or a vision. That thing suggests a word. That word suggests another thing. It is the latter that is intended by the former. He provides an example in the prophet who saw the rod of an almond tree. The word for almond is *shaqed*. *Shaqed* is like *shaqad*, to watch over. Thus the rod of the almond tree represents divine oversight:

> For instance the intention of the dictum of Jeremiah concerning *maqqel shaqed* (a rod of almond tree) is an indication based on the equivocality of the term *shaqed* (almond). Scripture accordingly proceeds to say: *Ki shoqed ani*, and so on (For I watch over) (Jeremiah 1:11–12). Thus in this case the intention of the parable did not concern the notion of rod or that of almond. [*Guide*, p. 392]

Maimonides even allows the interpretation of a word in terms of the meaning of an anagram of that word:

> [Scripture states that] He set up *hoblim* (ravagers). . . . In addition the prophet inferred . . . from . . . *hoblim* the repugnance of God. . . . However, this meaning can only be derived from *hoblim* through changing the order of the (*heth*), (*beth*), and (*lamed*). . . . Accordingly it changed the order of *habol* and transformed it into *bahol* (repugnance). [*Guide*, p. 393]

IT IS NOT THE PURPOSE OF THIS TREATISE TO MAKE ITS TOTALITY UNDERSTANDABLE TO THE VULGAR OR TO BEGINNERS IN SPECULATION, NOR TO TEACH THOSE WHO HAVE NOT ENGAGED IN ANY STUDY OTHER THAN THE SCIENCE OF LAW – I MEAN THE LE-GALISTIC STUDY OF THE LAW. FOR THE PURPOSE OF THIS TREATISE AND ALL LIKE IT IS THE SCIENCE OF THE LAW IN ITS TRUE SENSE. [*Guide*, p. 5]

We take note of the fact that Maimonides has four categories of possible readers in mind. There are three categories which he excludes. They are the vulgar, those who are only beginners in philosophy or speculation, and those who are legalistic students of Jewish law.

We take this as an allusion on the part of Maimonides to the story of the four who entered PaRDeS, the garden, or Paradise, from the Talmud, to which he variously refers in his writings.

> Our Rabbis taught: Four gathered in PaRDeS, Ben Azzai and Ben Zoma, Aher and Rabbi Akiva. Rabbi Akiva said to them: When you reach near the stones of pure marble, do not say "Water, water." For it is said: *Whoever speaks lies will not be gathered near my fountain* (Psalms 101:7). Ben Azzai glanced [at it] and died. Of him Scripture says: *Precious is the death of His saints at the fountain of the Lord* (Psalms 116:15). Ben Zoma glanced [at it] and was touched [became demented]. About him it is written: *Have you found honey? Eat what is sufficient, lest you be filled and throw it up* (Proverbs 25:16). Aher cut down seedlings. Rabbi Akiva came out in peace. [*Hagigah* 14b]

Entering PaRDeS is a metaphor for studying the esoteric content. PaRDeS is an acronym for the four levels of interpretation, *peshat* (literal meaning), *remez* (hint, as through *gematria*), *derash* (homily), and *sod* (secret, or mystery).

Ben Azzai and Ben Zoma represent degrees of preparation that are still insufficient for the study of the esoteric content. The Talmud indicates that neither was ordained. It is interesting, however, that both are distinguished in the Talmud for their opinions in connection with sexuality. Ben Azzai gave the opinion that abstaining from procreation was the same as shedding blood (*Yebamot* 63b), albeit he himself never married. Ben Zoma offers an opinion in connection with castration and with the possibility of women becoming impregnated without sexual intercourse (*Hagigah* 14b–15a).

Maimonides allows that Ben Zoma had reached philosophy enough to have studied logic and mathematics. He states toward the end of *The Guide of the Perplexed*: "Know, my son, that as long as you are engaged in studying the mathematical sciences and the art of logic, you are one of those who walk around the house searching for its gate, as [the Sages] . . . have said resorting to a parable: *Ben Zoma is still outside*" (*Hagigah* 15a) [*Guide*, p. 619]. Thus Ben Azzai is the vulgar, and Ben Zoma is the beginner in speculation, at least having learned mathematics and logic.

After those two there are Elisha ben Abuya, referred to as Aher, and Rabbi Akiva. Both are distinguished figures. Aher studied philosophy: "Greek song did not cease from his mouth. It is told of Aher that when he used to rise [to go] from the schoolhouse, many heretical books used to fall from his lap" (Hagigah 15b). Thus certainly Aher is one of those who has engaged in study other than the science of the law. Indeed, the story of Aher may be regarded as having provided Maimonides with the fundamental orientation, albeit in a negative sense, for the composition of The Guide of the Perplexed. For in Elisha ben Abuya—or Elisha Aher as Maimonides refers to him—Maimonides was presented with one who was both a great legal scholar and teacher as well as one who had been exposed to Greek thought. The story of Aher is told in great detail in the Talmud.

There can be little doubt that the story of Aher impressed Maimonides: for the extensive account of Aher in the Talmud represents the Talmud's response to someone who had been exposed to Greek culture. And it is a response that is provided precisely in the context of the Talmud's discussion of the study of esoteric matters. It represented a challenge in connection with the assessment of the relative place of the esoteric teachings and the Greek teachings in conjunction with the consideration of Jewish law.

It states that Aher cut down seedlings. It is manifestly a metaphor, or a participation in a metaphor. It allows the presence of seedlings in this place where the four of them gathered. We will presently indicate the significance of the esoteric tradition with respect to the understanding of the generation of human souls. While we have yet to demonstrate this, we bring it to bear on the imagery of Aher cutting down the seedlings. The Talmud then states in its commentary on the story: "Aher cut down the seedlings. Of him Scripture says: *Suffer not thy mouth to bring thy flesh into guilt*" [Ecclesiastes 5:5] (Hagigah 15a).

What does it refer to? Among the unmentionable things associated with the odious Greek tradition was its tolerance for and even celebration of homosexuality. There is, for example, the argument in Plato that those who are homosexual are the ones who are most suitable as statesmen (Jowett, p. 192). Homosexuality is suggested in the verse *Suffer not thy mouth to bring thy flesh into guilt*. There are other indications suggestive of homosexuality. In another place in the Talmud we find:

> Now what happened in connection with Aher? Some say that he saw the tongue of Huzpith the Interpreter rubbing a *davar ahar* (literally something else, something not to be named, a euphemism used in connection with unchaste conduct, sexual intercourse, sodomy, etc.; also swine). He said, the mouth that speaks pearls licks dust. He [Aher] then went out and sinned. [*Kiddushin* 39b]

Aher is the only one of the four the content of whose apprehension is described.

> He saw that permission was granted to Metatron (an angel of whom it is said that his name is similar to that of his Master, for it is written, *For my name is in him* [Exodus 23:21]—the numerical value of Metatron, equaling 314, is equal to that of Shaday, SHDY, 300, 4, 10 also equaling 314—[*Hagigah* 15a] [*Sanhedrin* 38b]) to sit and write down the merits of Israel.

The figure of Aher was certainly not insignificant in the thought of Maimonides even before his composition of *The Guide of the Perplexed*. In a negative way, he singles him out as significant. Thus in Maimonides' *Commentary on the Mishnah*, in the introduction to Seder Zeraim, he presents an enumeration of 128 sages who are mentioned in the Mishnah. He then proceeds to make special mention of *not* having included Elisha Aher, saying that: "We do not enumerate Elisha Aher with all these pure ones because of that which is well known about him."

Aher deviated in conduct. He states:

> "Since I have been driven forth from the other world, let me go forth and enjoy this world." So Aher went forth into evil enterprises. He went forth and found a harlot and demanded her. She said to him: Are you not Elisha ben Abuyah? When he plucked a radish on the Sabbath and gave it to her, she said: It is Aher. [*Hagigah* 15a]

But even after his apostasy, Aher's knowledge of Torah is still valued. Thus:

The rabbis tell a story of how Aher was once riding a horse on the Sabbath [in violation of the Law of the Sabbath], and how Rabbi Meir followed after him on foot to learn Torah as it would come from his mouth. [Aher] said to him: Meir, turn back. I have already measured by the paces of my horse that the distance here is the Sabbath limit [beyond which it is forbidden to walk on the Sabbath]. [Rabbi Meir] replied: You go back too. [Aher] answered him: Haven't I already told you that I have already heard from behind the Veil: *Return ye backsliding children* — [applies to everyone] except Aher? [*Hagigah* 15a]

The knowledge of Torah on the part of Aher is rendered by three food metaphors.

R. Meir ate the date and threw the kernel away. . . .

Why are scholars compared to a nut? To teach you that just as with a nut, though it be spoiled with mud and dung, yet what is inside is not repulsive, so with a scholar, although he may have sinned, yet his Torah is not repulsive . . .

Rabbi Meir found a pomegranate; he ate what was inside and threw the peel away. [*Hagigah* 15b]

R. Meir is, according to the narrative of the Talmud, a student of both R. Akiva and Aher. The Talmud indicates that there is something to learn from both of them. They are both distinguished in scholarship. While one of them apprehends and becomes an apostate, the other of them emerges in peace.

There is an error in *The Guide of the Perplexed*. The error appears in Chapter 5 of Part III, where a citation from the Talmud is given incorrectly. What it says is: "Rabbi Meir says . . ." [*Guide*, p. 425]. In point of fact what the text that Maimonides is citing says is: "Rabbi [Judah HaNasi] says . . ." (*Hagigah* 13a). We will consider this in detail below. But at this point in the discussion we include it to suggest that Maimonides identifies himself with Rabbi Meir, in that he would take from both the learning of Aher and the learning of Rabbi Akiva, without falling into the catastrophic mental condition of Aher. For Rabbi Meir was a student of both. The learning of Aher was great, albeit he did not manage himself properly after his exposure to the

Greek sources. Rabbi Akiva, on the other hand, went in and came out in peace. As we will presently note, Rabbi Akiva had a great formula for dealing with that which is involved in entering the mysteries, one that was clearly not available to Aher. One of the main aims of *The Guide of the Perplexed* is to explicate the path of Rabbi Akiva as a solution to the problem that confronted Aher. Thus Maimonides, at this most critical point of *The Guide of the Perplexed*, as we will explain, puts in the mark of R. Meir, the sage who even managed to study with Aher after his apostasy without falling into apostasy himself.

What is this formula of Rabbi Akiva, that he could thus go in and come out in peace? We note two things in connection with Rabbi Akiva. The first is the opinion that Rabbi Akiva is said to have held with respect to the *Song of Songs*. That work is certainly among the most prurient in Scripture. The Mishnah reports that Rabbi Akiva held that

> All the writings are Holy. But the *Song of Songs*
> is the Holy of Holies. [*Yedaim* 3:5]

The second is an exchange involving Rabbi Akiva and some of the other sages as reported in the Talmud. The stimulus is the seeming contradiction in a verse representing the vision of Daniel.

> Till thrones were placed,
> And one that was ancient of days did sit:
> His raiment was as white as snow,
> And the hair of his head like pure wool;
> His throne was fiery flames. . . .[Daniel 7:9]

The Talmud discusses this as follows:

> In one case it says: His *throne* was fiery flames;
> and the other case it says: Till *thrones* were
> placed. . . . [*Hagigah* 14a]

This is followed by citing what we take to have been the key for Maimonides for the interpretation of prophecy, the opinion of Rabbi Akiva on prurience and its interpretation:

> There is no contradiction: one [throne] is for
> Him, and the other for [His] beloved (dod).
> [Hagigah 14a]

Here we have what appears as the dreaded divine dualism, especially as male and female, for Judaism differs from other ancient religions in characteristically refraining from attributing sexuality to the divine.

Rabbi Akiva's answer elicits an angry reaction from one of the sages:

> Rabbi Jose the Galilean said to him: "Akiva,
> how long do you intend to profane the
> Shekhinah?"

Rabbi Jose the Galilean lets it be known that the second occupant is the Shekhinah, the divine presence.

Rabbi Akiva provides the critical answer, that it is metaphorical and not literal:

> But [says Rabbi Akiva] it means one is for justice
> and one is for grace.

The Talmud then raises the question as to Rabbi Akiva's source and authority for this opinion. It is asked:

> Did he receive this or did he not receive this?

That is, is this Kaballah or is it not Kaballah? And the answer is that it is not Kaballah:

> Come and hear. "One is for justice and one is
> for grace," are the words of Rabbi Akiva.
> [Hagigah 14a]

Thus we have the two-stage formula for interpretation of prophecy from Rabbi Akiva. The prophetic apprehension may be prurient in

MAIMONIDES ON PROPHECY 33

the first place, but it is to be interpreted as a metaphor in the second. This principle of Rabbi Akiva becomes Maimonides' key.

We take this as the reason why Rabbi Akiva could enter upon the esoteric topics and come out in peace, as contrasted with Ben Azzai, Ben Zoma, and Elisha ben Abuya. On apprehending what appeared to them as prurient, one died, the other went mad, and the last became an apostate. We take it that Maimonides understood it in this way.

Maimonides devotes a great deal of attention in *The Guide of the Perplexed* to the matter of ascription of human characteristics to God. Understanding God literally in terms of these human characteristics is strongly rejected by him. Nonetheless, he does not reject it completely, for he has a forbearing attitude toward such anthropomorphism because of the limitations of the intellectually immature. He recognizes the role of such anthropomorphism in their beliefs and devotions. He repeatedly cites, "The Torah is written in the language of men," the defense of the anthropomorphic language in which God is spoken of in Scripture.

Yet this cannot be allowed to go so far as to ascribe sexual characteristics to God—as, say, the Greeks did. And thus there is a need for secrecy. Yet that barrier is broken in the dreams and visions of the prophets. The task of explaining prophecy is to in some way both bring the reader to apprehend the prurient in the dreams and visions of the prophets and at the same time have the reader be immediately prepared to recognize that as metaphorical.

OR RATHER ITS PURPOSE IS TO GIVE INDICATIONS TO A RELIGIOUS MAN FOR WHOM THE VALIDITY OF OUR LAW HAS BECOME ESTABLISHED IN HIS SOUL AND HAS BECOME ACTUAL IN HIS BELIEF—SUCH A MAN BEING PERFECT IN HIS RELIGION AND CHARACTER, AND HAVING STUDIED THE SCIENCES OF THE PHILOSO-PHERS AND COME TO KNOW WHAT THEY SIGNIFY. [*Guide*, p. 5]

Consider the sequence of Jewish law and philosophy. What is represented here is a pedagogical sequence. The notion is that the person is well educated in Jewish law first, and then moves to the study of philosophy. It is important to highlight that idea and to mark it as pedagogical and not substantive. It is the learning sequence that takes place in the reader; it is not the sequence in connection with the generation of prophecy. In prophecy, the prophet is knowledgable about philosophy first. The prophet prophesies through the exercise of the rational faculty, excellent and cultivated in the first place, and then through the exercise of the imaginative faculty, in the second place. The prophet is able to come closer to the essence of God through the exercise of both faculties.

In our attempt to understand Maimonides on this point, it is necessary that we become very conscious of the contemporary view of history that regards religion as older and more primitive than philosophy and science, and recognize that Maimonides did not share this view. We have to put Maimonides in the class of those who believed that those who have not yet come to understand that God exists, the discovery of Abraham, were the primitive. Maimonides is to be understood as being in the tradition of those Jewish thinkers of the Hellenistic period who maintained that even Greek philosophy derived from the patriarchs and Moses (Droge, 1984).

THE HUMAN INTELLECT HAVING DRAWN HIM ON AND LED HIM TO DWELL WITHIN ITS PROVINCE [Guide, p. 5]

There is an impedance in connection with the pedagogical sequence in which one starts with Torah.

HE MUST HAVE FELT DISTRESSED BY THE EXTERNALS OF THE LAW. [Guide, p. 5]

Maimonides here mentions distress, distress due to the absence of awareness. He introduces the idea of there being two levels of meaning in Scripture, the external and the internal. The distress is indicated in the very title of his book, *The Guide of the Perplexed*. It is to be relieved by coming to understand the internal meanings in the accounts of the dreams and visions of the prophets.

AND BY THE MEANINGS OF THE ABOVE-MENTIONED EQUIVOCAL, DERIVATIVE, OR AMPHIBOLOUS TERMS [Guide, p. 5]

A term may have different meanings. The internal meaning may be associated with a meaning alien to the context in which the term appears. The term may be connected in some derivative way, even as an anagram, with some other term, that other term being intended. The term may itself be doubtful and of no clear meaning, such as the word *hashmal* that occurs in the prophecy of Ezekiel (1:27; 8:2).

AS HE CONTINUED TO UNDERSTAND THEM BY HIM-SELF OR WAS MADE TO UNDERSTAND THEM BY OTH-ERS. [*Guide*, p. 5]

The external meanings are the commonplace ones, the ones he would come to understand by himself. There is a clear intimation here of a need for a special type of guide or teacher, one who himself has an appreciation of the alternate, yet intended, meanings of terms.

HENCE HE WOULD REMAIN IN A STATE OF PER-PLEXITY [*Guide*, p. 5]

The state of perplexity is identified with a condition of rigidity, reading literally, of staying with the external meaning of the terms.

AND CONFUSION AS TO WHETHER [*Guide*, p. 5]

There are choices to be made. We have already noted the four options for Maimonides. He has left behind the two options associated with Ben Azzai and Ben Zoma, both of which are associated with inadequate readiness. There are two choices left, Aher or Rabbi Akiva.

HE SHOULD FOLLOW HIS INTELLECT, RENOUNCE WHAT HE KNEW CONCERNING THE TERMS IN QUES-TION, AND CONSEQUENTLY CONSIDER THAT HE HAS RENOUNCED THE FOUNDATIONS OF THE LAW. [*Guide*, p. 5]

This is the choice of Aher. Maimonides presumes that his reader has not yet made that choice; rather, he presumes that the reader is stopped at the point of choice and is suffering in it. He has not moved into apostasy, but is engaging in a piety that has lost its ground for him and not moving ahead intellectually.

OR HE SHOULD HOLD FAST TO HIS UNDERSTANDING OF THESE TERMS AND NOT LET HIMSELF BE DRAWN ON TOGETHER WITH HIS INTELLECT, RATHER TURNING HIS BACK ON IT AND MOVING AWAY FROM IT, WHILE AT THE SAME TIME PERCEIVING THAT HE HAD BROUGHT LOSS TO HIMSELF AND HARM TO HIS RELIGION. [*Guide*, pp. 5–6]

This is, in a sense, another option, not the options of Ben Azzai or Ben Zoma or Aher or Rabbi Akiva. It is a rigid hanging on to not understanding Scripture and willful blindness. The result is that:

HE WOULD BE LEFT WITH THOSE IMAGINARY BELIEFS TO WHICH HE OWES HIS FEAR AND DIFFICULTY AND WOULD NOT CEASE TO SUFFER FROM HEARTACHE AND GREAT PERPLEXITY. [*Guide*, p. 6]

Maimonides needs a license whereby to write *The Guide of the Perplexed*. Note that Maimonides here adds "heartache" to "perplexity." Our explanation of this is that, in the Talmud, where the question is raised as to whom esoteric matters may be taught, it says: "The headings of the chapters [dealing with the esoteric matters] may be transmitted only to the head of a court and to one whose heart is anxious within him. Others say: Only to one whose heart is anxious within him" (*Hagigah* 13a). We will presently note the significance of "the headings of the chapters" to Maimonides in connection with the composition of *The Guide of the Perplexed*.

THIS TREATISE ALSO HAS A SECOND PURPOSE: NAMELY, THE EXPLANATION OF VERY OBSCURE PARABLES OCCURRING IN THE BOOKS OF THE PROPHETS, BUT NOT EXPLICITLY IDENTIFIED THERE AS SUCH. [*Guide*, p. 6]

This refers to narrative portions of Scripture, to the general themes involved in them, to the meanings contained in them that are beyond the particular characters and the particular settings and even beyond the particular events being described.

HENCE AN IGNORANT OR HEEDLESS INDIVIDUAL MIGHT THINK THAT THEY POSSESS ONLY AN EX-TERNAL SENSE, BUT NO INTERNAL ONE. [*Guide*, p. 6]

Maimonides is here referring to the compelling, but not necessarily valid, claim to truth associated with scriptural narrative. Narrative is strongly contextual and thus gives force to the external meanings:

HOWEVER, EVEN WHEN ONE WHO TRULY POSSESSES KNOWLEDGE CONSIDERS THESE PARABLES AND IN-TERPRETS THEM ACCORDING TO THEIR EXTERNAL MEANING, HE TOO IS OVERTAKEN BY GREAT PER-PLEXITY. [*Guide*, p. 6]

And this is not true only of the ignorant and the heedless. The acceptance of the external meaning for anyone, no matter what his general level of knowledge may be, leads to great perplexity. The internal meaning must be specifically identified, and its meaning must supersede the external meaning. Thus, he says,

BUT IF WE EXPLAIN THESE PARABLES TO HIM [*Guide*, p. 6]

so that he knows the internal meanings

OR IF WE DRAW HIS ATTENTION TO THEIR BEING PARABLES [*Guide*, p. 6]

so that he may discount the external meanings

HE WILL TAKE THE RIGHT ROAD AND BE DELIVERED FROM THIS PERPLEXITY. THAT IS WHY I HAVE CALLED THIS TREATISE "THE GUIDE OF THE PERPLEXED." [*Guide*, p. 6]

Having made his claim that he is going to remove perplexity, and the associated heartache, and having indicated that there is a path —

which we take to mean the path of Rabbi Akiva, noting the sexual and understanding it as metaphorical–Maimonides seeks to qualify the expectation he may have engendered:

I DO NOT SAY THAT THIS TREATISE WILL REMOVE ALL DIFFICULTIES FOR THOSE WHO UNDERSTAND IT. [*Guide*, p. 6]

He is aware that *The Guide of the Perplexed* will be misunderstood by some who read it. Thus the removal of difficulties is partly associated with those who read it. As for that which is intrinsically indicated in the book:

I DO, HOWEVER, SAY THAT IT WILL REMOVE MOST OF THE DIFFICULTIES, AND THOSE OF THE GREATEST MOMENT. [*Guide*, p. 6]

There is, however, a limit to how much can be communicated:

A SENSIBLE MAN THUS SHOULD NOT DEMAND OF ME OR HOPE THAT WHEN WE MENTION A SUBJECT, WE SHALL MAKE A COMPLETE EXPOSITION OF IT, OR THAT WHEN WE ENGAGE IN THE EXPLANATION OF THE MEANING OF ONE OF THE PARABLES, WE SHALL SET FORTH EXHAUSTIVELY ALL THAT IS EXPRESSED IN THAT PARABLE. AN INTELLIGENT MAN WOULD BE UNABLE TO DO SO EVEN BY SPEAKING DIRECTLY TO AN INTERLOCUTOR. [*Guide*, p. 6]

And then Maimonides expressed some despair at the thought of those who would criticize without understanding:

HOW THEN COULD HE PUT IT DOWN IN WRITING WITHOUT BECOMING THE BUTT OF EVERY IGNO-RAMUS WHO, THINKING THAT HE HAS THE NECES-SARY KNOWLEDGE, WOULD LET FLY AT HIM THE SHAFTS OF HIS IGNORANCE? [*Guide*, p. 6]

We need to keep in mind that Maimonides' object at this point is to comment on texts which are common in the Jewish community, and about which one can presume virtually complete prior reading or at least exposure. Furthermore, the texts on which he is commenting have been the object of endless commentary already. What Maimonides is doing in *The Guide of the Perplexed,* as a commentary on prophecy in Scripture, is indicating internal meanings, in defiance of the history of the extant scholarship at the time and of the plain meanings of the texts.

At this point, Maimonides makes reference to his earlier legal writings:

WE HAVE ALREADY EXPLAINED IN OUR LEGAL COMPI-LATIONS SOME GENERAL PROPOSITIONS CON-CERNING THIS SUBJECT AND HAVE DRAWN ATTEN-TION TO MANY THEMES. THUS WE HAVE MENTIONED THERE THAT THE *MAASEH BERESHIT* (ACCOUNT OF THE BEGINNING) IS IDENTICAL WITH NATURAL SCI-ENCE, AND THE *MAASEH MERKABAH* (ACCOUNT OF THE CHARIOT) WITH DIVINE SCIENCE. [*Guide,* p. 6]

The *Maaseh Bereshit* is, in the first place, the scriptural account of the creation. The *Maaseh Merkabah* is, in the first place, the scriptural account of the vision of Ezekiel. All the transmitted teachings in connection with these two topics were collectively called Kabbalah, the esoteric tradition.

The esoteric tradition within the history of Judaism is grounded in the following mishnaiclow:

One is not to expound on the Nakednesses (the injunctions against sexual misconduct in Leviticus 18:6–23) to three [at a time], nor the *Maaseh Bereshit* (the account of creation in Genesis 1:1ff) to two [at a time]; nor the *Maaseh Merkabah* (the account of the vision of Ezekiel to be found in Ezekiel 1, 8, and 10) even to one [at a time], unless he were wise and understanding of his own knowledge.

As for anyone who should attempt to discern the meaning of [the following] four terms, pity him, for it were as though he had not come into the world.

[These are] What is above? What is below? [Ezekiel 1:27]

What is to the front? What is behind? [Exodus 33:17–23]

As for anyone who is not forbearing with respect to the glory of his maker, pity would have been shown to him had he not [been allowed to] come into the world. [*Hagigah* 11b]

Three special dichotomies of contemporary Jewish thought need to be highlighted as we move to consider the twelfth-century Maimonides. These dichotomies have greater significance for the time after the twelfth century, and we misconstrue history if we project them backwards without giving them special attention. The first is the sharp distinction between the rational and the mystical, with Maimonides characteristically being assigned to the rational. The second is the historical division between rabbinic and mystical Judaism, with Maimonides being assigned completely to the rabbinic side. The third is the division between religion and philosophy, with the modern question of how it could be that Maimonides could be both the major legal scholar of Jewish history, on the one hand, and committed to philosophy, as he appears to be in the first four chapters of the *Mishneh Torah* and in *The Guide of the Perplexed*, on the other.

These dichotomies are reflected in the work of a number of writers. For example, let us consider some of the views of Gershom Scholem. Scholem is particularly interesting because of his great achievement in providing a modern scholarly approach to the history of Jewish mysticism.

For Scholem, Maimonides is "the great rationalist" for whom

> ... the affinity of ... mystic[s] with the great
> rationalist [is] astounding. .... [Scholem, p.
> 126]

It is only from a modern provincial point of view that the connection between rationalism and mysticism should be astounding. In some of its earliest forms, such as among the Pythagoreans, mysticism and rationalism were integrally related. Plato is certainly a rational mystic. This is especially so in the *Timaeus*, perhaps the most Pythagorean of the Platonic dialogues, which Maimonides explicitly cites in

The Guide of the Perplexed by name, and identifiably alludes to in its pages.

With respect to the division between Jewish mysticism and philosophy, Scholem dutifully describes Abulafia's connection to *The Guide of the Perplexed*. Abulafia was one of the founding figures of the mysticism that developed from the thirteenth century onward. Scholem says:

> For him [Abulafia] there was no antithesis between mysticism and the doctrines of Maimonides. He rather considered his own mystical theory as a final step forward from the "Guide of the Perplexed" to which he wrote a curious mystical commentary. . . . According to him, only the "Guide" and the "Book of Creation" together represent the true theory of Kabbalism. [p. 126]

Scholem reports similarly concerning Moses de Leon, who—even as Scholem himself has argued so splendidly—is the author of the *Zohar*, the work that became the major resource for all later Kabbalism:

> There can be no doubt that Moses de Leon . . . began as a follower of Maimonides. . . . we have the clearest documentary proof in the form of a manuscript—described in the autographed catalogue of the Guenzburg collection of Hebrew manuscripts in Moscow—of the Hebrew translation of Maimonides' "Guide of the Perplexed," which was written in 1264 "for the erudite . . . Rabbi Moses de Leon." [Scholem, p. 194]

It is his view, however, that Moses de Leon only later became attracted to the study of Kabbalism, and that this represents a falling away from Maimonides.

And last, with respect to the presumptive tension between Jewish law and philosophy, Scholem writes:

> It is a remarkable fact that . . . Maimonides . . . prefaces [the *Mishneh Torah*] by [an attempt] to extend the Halakhah to matters which, strictly speaking, lie beyond its province. . . . [He provides] a philosophic and cosmologic preface in which the ideas of Aristotelian

enlightenment are introduced as elements of Halakhah . . . [T]he attempt . . . failed. [p. 95]

Maimonides . . . fail[s] entirely to establish a true synthesis of the two elements, Halakha and philosophy. . . . The synthesis of the spheres remains sterile, and the genius of the man whose spirit moulded them into a semblance of union cannot obscure their intrinsic disparity. [pp. 28–29]

What then are the connections among rationalism and mysticism, rabbinic Judaism and Jewish mysticism, and Halakhah and philosophy? We have to look at the nature of Maimonides' lifelong literary project, and especially at the relentless textualism of his approach. This textualism is based on his great conviction of the essential truth contained in the Torah; and his conviction—again coming from Rabbi Akiva—that every detail, including seeming peculiarities of the text, had significance.

Maimonides' lifelong project was to bring order to Jewish law and to make it accessible. Virtually all of his writing was directed toward this end. His project was exposition of Torah. But the Mishnaic law cited above placed an extraordinary obstacle in his path. For this Mishnah begins with "One is not to expound on . . ." and proceeds to give indications of topics and constraints with respect to them. The topics under constraint clearly indicated the injunctions with respect to sexual conduct in Leviticus, the story of creation in Genesis, and the vision of Ezekiel, especially verses 1:27 and 8:2. In the last, the words *above* and *below* occur. The Mishnaic law attaches *behind* and *in front*; also intimating the account in Exodus 33 of how Moses asked to see the glory of God, how it was refused, and how it was permitted for him to see *behind*, but not *in front*.

Maimonides' *Mishneh Torah* is a coherent and accessible compendium of Jewish law. It was virtually complete except for the constraint placed on him by the Mishnaic law we have cited. After providing an outline of the history of Jewish law, Maimonides ends his introduction to the *Mishneh Torah* as follows:

On these grounds I . . . bestirred myself and . . . intently studied these works with the view of putting together the results obtained from them in regard to what is permitted, clean or unclean, and the other rules of the Torah—all in plain language and in terse style . . . so that all the rules shall be accessible to young and old . . . so that no other work should be needed for ascertaining any of the laws of Israel. . . . A person who first reads the Written Law and then this compilation, will know from it the whole of the Oral Law without having occasion to consult any other book between them.

It is to the first four chapters of the *Mishneh Torah* that Maimonides is alluding when he refers to his treatment of the topics of the *Maaseh Bereshit* and the *Maaseh Merkabah*, when he states

WE HAVE ALREADY EXPLAINED IN OUR LEGAL COMPI-LATIONS [*Guide*, p. 6]

For there he explicitly states at the end of the second chapter: "What has been said . . . in these two chapters forms the *Maaseh Merkabah*" (*Yesodei Hatorah* II:11). And in the fourth chapter he states: "The exposition of the topics dealt with in the third and fourth chapters is termed *Maaseh Bereshit*" (*Yesodei Hatorah* IV:11).

In the *Mishneh Torah* Maimonides identifies that which is entailed in this Mishnaic law of constraint on exposition as the foundation for all of Jewish law. This Mishnaic law is the explanation in the Oral Law of five commandments of the Written Law, the three commandments concerning the existence and unity of God: to know that God exists (Exodus 20:2, Deuteronomy 5:6), not to allow the thought to rise in the mind that there is any other God but the Lord (Exodus 20:3), that he is one (Deuteronomy 6:4), and the two further commandments to love Him (Deuteronomy 6:5) and to fear Him (Deuteronomy 6:13, 10:20). It is for this reason that he places the discussion at the very beginning, albeit clearly indicating that the contents are under expositional bans.

However, while this Mishnaic law is a foundation in a systematic sense, it is not pedagogically primary. For while Maimonides opens with a declaration of the existence of God as the foundation: "The foundation of foundations and the pillar of all wisdoms is to know that there is a First Being, and that he brings into existence all that exists" (*Yesodei Hatorah* 1:1), yet he cites the Mishnaic law:

The meaning of the *Maaseh Merkabah* is not to be expounded even to one, unless he happens to be wise and understanding of his own knowledge, to whom only the chapter headings are indicated. And the meaning of the *Maaseh Bereshit* is taught singly, even to one who does not understand his own knowledge. [*Yesodei Hatorah* IV:11]

In *The Guide of the Perplexed* Maimonides explicitly undertakes to deal with two of the four topics indicated or intimated in the Mishnaic law. At one point he states—and we take it that he has in mind the Mishnaic law regarding that which is contained in Exodus 33—that:

> . . . the prophecy of Moses . . . is distinguished from the prophecy of the other prophets. . . . It does not enter into the purpose of this Treatise. I will let you know that everything I say on prophecy in the chapters of this Treatise refers only to the form of prophecy of all the the prophets who were before Moses and who will come after him. As for the prophecy of Moses . . . I shall not touch upon it in these chapters with even a single word, either in explicit fashion or in a flash. [*Guide*, p. 367]

Theological writings often characterize God in terms of His creativity, providence, and redemptiveness. It is valuable to identify Maimonides' task in *The Guide of the Perplexed* in terms of these categories.

We take note of the two things that Maimonides predicates of God in the first sentence of the first chapter of the *Mishneh Torah* cited above. God is the First Being; and God is the Creator of that which exists. We refer back to the distinction Maimonides draws between existence and essence. God as the First Being is an allusion to the Aristotelian argument for the existence of God. However, in addition God is the Creator.

Thus we note the Mishnaic law and its topics: first, human sexuality, which provides the imagery for prophetic representation of God's creativity; second, something about Moses of which we cannot speak; third, the *Maaseh Bereshit*; and fourth, the *Maaseh Merkabah*.

In order to be able to appreciate what Maimonides is driving at in *The Guide of the Perplexed*, it is essential that we look to the true end of the treatise. For Maimonides declares the treatise completed at the end of Chapter III:7. That is, it is the end of his discourse on God's creativity. The rest of the book, from Chapter III:8 onward, is a discussion on providence and redemption.

The duality of the *Maaseh Bereshit* and the *Maaseh Merkabah* for Maimonides is the duality between God having created the universe in the first instance, and His ongoing role in connection with the creation of human souls in the second instance.

It will be of some value to look ahead to how Maimonides ends the discussion of God's creativity in Chapter III:7. A major clue is provided by Maimonides at the beginning of Chapter III:7 in the form of hints to the solution of a riddle, which he takes the opening of Ezekiel to be. The text to which he alludes is as follows: "Now it came to pass in the thirtieth year, in the fourth month, in the fifth day of the month, as I sat among the captives by the river Kebar, that the heavens were opened, and I saw visions of God" (Ezekiel 1:1). Concerning this, Maimonides says:

> To the whole of things requiring investigation belongs the tying of the apprehension of the Merkabah to a year, a month, and a day, and also to a place. This is something the significance of which ought to be sought. It should not be thought that this is a matter without significance. [*Guide*, p. 428]

The riddle is solved by two things. First, conversion of the numbers to the corresponding letters, and recognizing that they make a word, *ledah*, the Hebrew word for birth. Second, by taking one of the anagrams of Kebar we have *kerub*, meaning cherub. If we add to this the explanation "Now cherub designates a human being of tender age" [*Guide*, p. 417], the vision of Ezekiel is of the birth of the cherubim, or the generation of human souls.

We are also provided with an understanding of why the *Maaseh Merkabah* is called that. For it, too, is subject to the same anagrammatic construction and becomes *Maaseh Mekrubah*, or the account, or work, of childing, the making of children. And one name which we might have for God, as Maimonides intimates in Chapter I:63, could be *Shekbar*, taken in the anagrammatic sense as *Shekerub*, the "one who cherubs" [*Guide*, p. 153]. Thus the *Maaseh Merkabah*, for Maimonides, corresponds to God's ongoing creative role in the universe, generating the souls of human beings, and represented in the visions of the prophets in sexual imagery.

This is all in accordance with Maimonides' belief that

> . . . we have no intellectual cognition of our
> bringing somebody other than us to existence
> except through sexual intercourse. [*Guide*, p.
> 99]

And such intellectual cognition of God's bringing human beings into existence in the course of history is represented within the dreams and the visions of the prophets, created within them by a process whereby their imaginative faculties rework that which they have apprehended with their rational faculties.

Consider now the identification Maimonides makes of that which is referred to in the Mishnah and the Aristotelian natural science and divine science, essentially the contents of Aristotle's *Physics* and *Metaphysics*, respectively:

SOME GENERAL PROPOSITIONS CONCERNING THIS SUBJECT. [WE] HAVE DRAWN ATTENTION TO MANY THEMES. THUS WE HAVE MENTIONED THERE THAT THE *MAASEH BERESHIT* IS IDENTICAL WITH NATURAL SCIENCE, AND THE *MAASEH MERKABAH* WITH DIVINE SCIENCE. [*Guide*, p. 6]

The reference is to the first four chapters of the *Mishneh Torah*, the first two chapters on the *Maaseh Merkabah*, and the next two chapters on the *Maaseh Bereshit*.

It is important for the reader not to be misled by this identification of the *Maaseh Bereshit* and the *Maaseh Merkabah* with the Aristotelian natural and divine sciences, respectively. The reader might, at this point, take Maimonides to be saying that Aristotle's presentation has made the prophetic writings anachronistic, with Aristotle having written much more clearly and forthrightly that which the prophets and sages, who were bound by the tradition of secrecy with respect to these matters, could express only through intimation. Thus, if one were interested in the meaning of the *Maaseh Bereshit* and the *Maaseh Merkabah*, one would be better advised to find copies of Aristotle rather than proceeding another page in *The Guide of the Perplexed*. If one were pious, one would henceforth refrain from encouraging any attention to Aristotle on the grounds that he spoke openly concerning that which should not, by Jewish law, be spoken of openly. If one were a religious scholar, one would look upon Maimonides' *The Guide of the Perplexed* as, at best, of some antiquarian interest, but in no serious way advancing the religious enterprise in the way in which Maimonides' *Mishneh Torah* — omitting the first four chapters — did. But all such approaches overlook the fact that Maimonides intends to throw readers off from the content, that Maimonides understands the prophets as reaching toward essence while the philosophers remain outside in their dealing with the question of existence, and that, for Maimonides, Aristotle wrote of the knowledge that was fully available to the patriarchs, the prophets, and many of the sages who may never have had any contact with the Greek sources.

For Maimonides, Aristotle is highly qualified with respect to the demonstration of the existence of God. The Aristotelian demonstrations with respect to God arise from considerations of what exists, necessitating the existence of God as a First Cause. However, he makes it very plain that Aristotle is not capable of reaching the question of bringing something into existence that did not exist before. Maimonides presents a succinct statement of the premises of Aristotle in connection with the existence of God, but not of the essence of God. Thus he presents a succinct summary of Aristotle in the form of twenty-five premises: "The premises needed for establishing the existence of the deity, and for the demonstration that He is neither a body nor a force in a body and that He . . . is one are twenty-five" [*Guide*, p. 235]. Maimonides indicates his full assent with respect to these twenty-five premises. But then he indicates that Aristotle has one further premise, "the twenty sixth . . . that time and movement are eternal, perpetual, existing in actu. [This premise] affirms as necessary the eternity of the world. Aristotle deemed it to be correct and the most fitting to be believed" [*Guide*, p. 241].

It is this twenty-sixth premise that effectively separates Aristotle from the question of the creativity of God, in the sense of bringing beings into existence out of nonexistence. It is the twenty-sixth premise that separates the philosophers from the prophets, the latter capable of reaching toward the creativity of God through the exercise of the imagination, and through sexual representation.

> **AND [WE] HAVE EXPLAINED THE RABBINIC SAYING: *THE MAASEH MERKABAH OUGHT NOT TO BE TAUGHT EVEN TO ONE MAN, EXCEPT IF HE BE WISE AND UNDERSTANDING OF HIS OWN KNOWLEDGE* (*Hagigah* 11b) IN WHICH CASE ONLY THE CHAPTER HEADINGS MAY BE TRANSMITTED TO HIM (*Hagigah* 13a). HENCE YOU SHOULD NOT ASK OF ME HERE ANYTHING BEYOND THE CHAPTER HEADINGS. [*Guide*, p. 6]**

Maimonides intends the reader to grasp something concerning the "chapter headings" from the *Mishneh Torah*. There he provides certain patent indications in both content and structure. We can gain some further understanding of how Maimonides appreciates the distinction between the *Maaseh Bereshit* and the *Maaseh Merkabah* by looking again at the four chapters in the *Mishneh Torah*. For there, as we have indicated, he clearly labels the first two chapters as *Maaseh Merkabah* and the next two chapters as *Maaseh Bereshit*, and we can thereby identify the "chapter headings" that belong to each.

Consider first how Maimonides appreciates the fundamental structure of the created world:

> All that God created in the universe is divided into three parts. There are those comprised of body and form and which continuously come into being and decay, such as the bodies of humans and the animals, plants and minerals. There are those of body and form which do not change . . . the heavenly spheres and the stars. . . . And there are those of form but no body. These are the angels, for the angels are without body, but their forms are distinguishable. [*Yesodei Hatorah* II:3]

Maimonides indicates the ground for this in the opening verse of Scripture in *The Guide of the Perplexed*: "Among the things you ought to know is the fact that the Sages have explicitly stated in a number of passages that the word *et* figuring in his words *et hash-shamayim ve-et ha-arez* (the heaven and the earth) has in that verse the meaning *with*" [*Guide*, p. 350].

The word *et* in Hebrew can mean two things. It can mean that the word that follows is the object of the verb, or it can mean "with." In order to get the meaning "In the beginning *Elohim* [God] created the heaven and the earth," one takes the meaning in the first sense. If, however, the word has the meaning of "with," as Maimonides says here, the sentence has the meaning "In the beginning [He] created the *Elohim* with the heaven and with the earth." Now while the word *Elohim* is characteristically taken to mean God, Maimonides clearly indicates that *Elohim* is a word with great latitude of meaning [*Guide*, pp. 23–26].

Maimonides structures the first four chapters of the *Mishneh Torah* in accordance with this understanding of the structure of the universe. The first chapter is on God, while the next three chapters are on the angels or intellects—or the *Elohim*—the heaven and the earth, respectively. Maimonides actually marks the chapters accordingly. The letters of the first four words of the first chapter make *YHWH* as an acronym. The first word of the second chapter is *ha-El*, the *El*. The first word of the third chapter is *ha-galgalim*, the spheres [of the heaven]. And the first words of the fourth chapter are "four bodies," referring to the four elements (fire, air, water, and earth) that comprise the earth.

Now since the third and fourth chapters are explicitly stated as dealing with the *Maaseh Bereshit*, it is clear that this deals with the natural world—that is, the natural world that was the result of creation.

We draw attention to three items in the first chapter of the *Mishneh Torah*, the first of the two chapters on the *Maaseh Merkabah*, and the chapter on God. First, the chapter deals with the existence of God. Second, God is the Creator who brings whatever exists into being. Third, God has an ongoing role in the universe beyond simply having created it: "This Being is the God of the universe, the Lord of all the earth. And he controls the sphere. . . . The sphere always revolves. It is impossible for it to revolve without one revolving it" (*Yesodei Hatorah* I:5).

With God as a continuing presence in history, as it were, Maimonides includes in this chapter a discussion of the apprehension of Moses, the section alluded to in the Mishnaic law, the "front" and the "behind" of Exodus 33:17–23. He tells how Moses made the request "Show me, I pray Thee, thy Glory" (Exodus 33:18), how the request is refused, and how instead God allows "thou shalt see My behind; but My face shall not be seen" (Exodus 33:23) (*Yesodei Hatorah* I:10).

Now, in Maimonides' thought, there are two forms of prophecy, indicated in Scripture:

> And He said: Hear now my words. If there be a prophet among you, I the Lord do make Myself known to him in a vision, I do speak with him in a dream. My servant Moses is not so. He is trusted in all My house. With him do I speak mouth to mouth, even manifestly, and not in dark speeches, and the similitude of the Lord doth he behold. [Numbers 12:6–8]

There is thus the prophecy of Moses, and the prophecy of the other prophets. Since this chapter is the first of the two chapters dealing with the *Maaseh Merkabah*, we should expect to find some indication in this chapter concerning the prophecy of the prophets other than Moses as well. This we find as follows: "And so the sages have said, Above there is no sitting. . . ." (*Yesodei Hatorah* I:11). The key word here, as we will see, is "sitting" as a euphemism for sexual intercourse. This is an allusion to the account in the Talmud of what was apprehended when the four delved into the esoteric topics. It is of the apprehension of Aher:

> He saw that permission was granted to Metatron to sit. . . . Said he: It is taught as a tradition that above there is no sitting. . . . [Therefore] they led Metatron forth and punished him with sixty fiery lashes, saying to him, why did you not rise when you saw Him? [*Hagigah* 15a]

"Sitting" and "laughing" are traditionally taken as euphemisms for sexual conduct. There is the verse in the account of the activities in connection with the Golden Calf:

> And the people *sat* to eat and drink and rose to *laugh*. [Exodus 32:6]

The Midrash comments on this verse that:

> Wherever you find [the word] "sitting" there you
> will also find some failing. [Exodus *Rabbah*
> 41:7]

The Midrash backs this up by indicating that:

> [Scripture says] And Israel sat in Shittim (Numbers 25:1). What was the
> failing there? [Scripture continues with] and the people began to be
> unchaste with the daughters of Moab (Numbers 25:11). [Exodus
> *Rabbah* 41:7]

The word "laugh" is patently a euphemism for sexual intercourse, as in

> And it came to pass . . . that Abimelech . . .
> looked out at a window and saw and behold
> Isaac was laughing his wife Rebekah. [Genesis
> 26:9]

If we allow that Maimonides was certainly aware of this, we must
take note of the very next comment Maimonides makes:

> This being so [that God may be described as though he had a body] the
> expressions in the Pentateuch and the words of the Prophets . . . are all
> metaphorical and rhetorical, as, for example, He that sits in heaven
> laughs (Psalms 2:4). [*Yesodei Hatorah* I:12]

We take this as an intimation that the apprehension of the prophets
is both sexual and metaphorical, quite in the manner indicated and
appropriately dealt with in accordance with the principle of Rabbi
Akiva of both apprehending the imagery as it is and recognizing it
immediately as metaphorical.

We also identify three items in the second chapter of the *Mishneh
Torah*, which is the second chapter on the *Maaseh Merkabah*, and the
topic of which is *Elohim*. The first is that Maimonides presses hard to
convert the commandments with respect to the love and fear of God,
commandments with respect to affect, to commandments with respect
to cognition. Fear turns into apprehension, and love is the consequence of apprehension. This leads Maimonides to discuss the created
world as the way to guide the reader:

. . . I will explain some great generalities concerning the Work of the Sovereign of the worlds, that it might be an entryway for those who understand to love the Name, as the sages have said in connection with love: Observe the universe, and you will recognize Who it was that spoke, that the universe existed. [*Yesodei Hatorah* II:2]

Second, he asserts the existence of angels while stressing that the descriptions of these forces in the created world are metaphorical:

What is meant by the prophets saying that they saw an angel of fire possessed of wings? All the prophetic visions are spoken in the metaphorical mode. It is only to say that they have no bodies and no weight. . . . [*Yesodei Hatorah* II:4]

Third, it is to note the two notions of God, which we interpret him to have intended as the existence and the essence of God. Thus, we find in this chapter the Aristotelian notion of God that

He is the Knower, and he is the Known, and
He is the Knowledge. [*Yesodei Hatorah* II:11]

At the same time in this chapter Maimonides takes great pains to distinguish the Creator (*habore*):

All the beings, except the Creator, from the
first form to the smallest insect . . . , exist by
the power of his Essence. [*Yesodei Hatorah*
II:9]

As we have already indicated, the third and fourth chapters consider the *Maaseh Bereshit*: the third chapter is devoted to a summary of the astronomical knowledge of the day, and the fourth chapter, to the four elements of the earth. From these two chapters on the *Maaseh Bereshit*, we would highlight the following three observations for their significance in helping to understand *The Guide of the Perplexed*, especially with respect to "chapter headings," and Maimonides' presumption that what had been covered in the *Mishneh Torah* was already clear and known to the reader. They are: first, the Earth is the locus of generation and corruption; second, intellection is a universal and objective characteristic of the universe, as well as being the special characteristic of human beings; and third, the human being has a special place in the cosmos as coming directly from God. We will amplify briefly.

First, the earth, existing below the sphere of the moon, is generated out of

> . . . matter which is unlike that of the [other] spheres. . . . Fire . . . Air . . . Water . . . Earth. These four bodies are without souls. . . . Each of them has a governing principle of which it has no knowledge nor apprehension. . . . [They] are the basic elements of all created things [on Earth]. . . . Accordingly . . . all bodies . . . are composed of a substance and form. . . . Everything made up of these four elements ultimately disintegrates. . . . [*Yesodei Hatorah*, III:10,11, IV:1 3]

Second, intellection characterizes the universe, while at the same time it characterizes the human being. Our dualistic use of the word "reason" may be invoked as a way of comprehending what this might mean. Indeed, our dualistic use of the word "reason" is our heritage from the thought along these lines in which Maimonides was involved. Thus, we have the conviction that all events take place because there are "reasons" for them to take place that way. That, we would stress, is *on the one hand*. Then, *on the other hand*, reason is a certain psychological property or capacity or function of human beings. Human beings are said to have—or not to have when they are immature or insane—reason. This is one of the central notions in the Aristotelian view that Maimonides shared, and which, for him, provided the basis for his understanding of the nature of prophecy: "Every star and sphere has a soul and is endowed with knowledge and intelligence" (*Yesodei Hatorah* III:9).

Third, Maimonides, in the fourth chapter of the *Mishneh Torah*, devoted to the Earth, gives some indications concerning the nature of human beings who dwell on that Earth. The human being is something special on the Earth by virtue of its soul, the soul being intellect, and being in the image of God. He states: "The soul (*nephesh*) of all fleshly being is the form given to it by God (*El*). The dearer knowledge that is found in the soul of the human being is [precisely] the form of the mentally normal human being."

This is the meaning of the Torah when it says: "Let us make a man in our image, after our likeness" (Genesis 1:26) (*Yesodei Hatorah* IV:8). And "This [soul] comes [directly] from the Lord [YY] in heaven" (*Yesodei Hatorah* IV:9).

It is the process whereby the souls are so generated that constitutes the content of the prophetic apprehension. That is the ultimate creation out of nothingness which continues to take place in history after the creation of the universe. The work of God in that first creation is the *Maaseh Bereshit*. The apprehension of the ongoing creativeness of God in history is the *Maaseh Merkabah*. Moses had a glimpse of it in a way that we cannot hope to reach. The prophets had a glimpse of it through their dreams and visions in which the creative act is represented in sexual metaphors.

AND EVEN THOSE [CHAPTER HEADINGS] ARE NOT SET DOWN IN ORDER OR ARRANGED IN A COHERENT FASHION IN THIS TREATISE, BUT RATHER ARE SCATTERED AND ENTANGLED WITH OTHER SUBJECTS THAT ARE TO BE CLARIFIED. [Guide, p. 6]

The reader must himself identify and organize the information contained in *The Guide of the Perplexed*. For the chapter headings are not identified by rubrics. They are scattered, and scattered among other subjects. But these "other subjects" are subjects that are "to be clarified." That is, they are there not only for the purpose of concealment, but also because they need to be clarified.

The structure of *The Guide of the Perplexed* can be identified as follows:

The *Maaseh Bereshit* and the *Maaseh Merkabah* designate the two creations, the initial creation of the universe and the subsequent continuing creativity of God in the history of the universe. Maimonides comments on the *Maaseh Bereshit* in Chapter II:30. There is an introduction to the *Maaseh Bereshit* and the *Maaseh Merkabah* that begins in the middle of Chapter II:29. Maimonides comments on the *Maaseh Merkabah* in the Introduction to Part III and the subsequent seven chapters, Chapters III:1–7.

The essential *Guide of the Perplexed* comes to an end with Chapter III:7. Maimonides indicates the completeness of his presentation up to this point: "If you consider all that we have said in the chapters of this Treatise up to this chapter, the greater part or the entirety of the subject in question . . . will become clear to you. Perhaps upon thorough consideration . . . nothing of this will remain hidden" [*Guide*, p. 430]. He makes it clear that from this point to the end of *The Guide of the Perplexed*, he will deal with "other subjects."

> Do not hope that, after this chapter, you will hear from me even a single word about this subject, be it as an explicit statement or in a flashlike allusion. For everything that it is possible to say about this has been said; I have even plunged deep into this with temerity. We shall accordingly start upon other subjects. . . . [*Guide*, p. 430]

Between these two foci of *The Guide of the Perplexed*, Maimonides intersperses two things: First, there is a chapter on the Sabbath, Chapter II:31. That is followed by a discussion of the psychology of prophecy in Chapters II:32–48.

Indeed, we may identify the scattered segments of a "Treatise on Prophecy" within *The Guide of the Perplexed*, the treatise that ends at the end of Chapter III:7, as follows:

1. Chapters I:1–16; 18–30; 37–45 on the terms of prophecy.
2. Chapter I:17 on the sexual allegory.
3. Chapters I:31–36 on the limitations of intellectual apprehension.
4. Chapters I:46–70 on the distinction between existence and essence as the object of apprehension.
5. Chapters I:71 to the middle of Chapter II:29 (p. 346) on the philosophers and their approach to the problem of the existence of God, dealing with the Mutakallimum and the Aristotelians. In the middle of Chapter II:29 he begins a new segment: "As the exposition has finally reached this point, we shall now put in a chapter that shall . . . give several indications as to texts concerned with the *Maaseh Bereshit*. For the first purpose of this Treatise is to explain what can be explained of the *Maaseh Bereshit* and of the *Maaseh Merkabah*" (*Guide*, p. 346).
6. Chapters II:32–48 on the psychology of prophecy.
7. An introduction to the direct explication of the *Maaseh Bereshit*

and the *Maaseh Merkabah* from the middle of Chapter II:29 (p. 346) to the end of that chapter.
8. Chapter II:30 on the *Maaseh Bereshit*.
9. Chapter II:31 on the Sabbath.
10. Introduction to Part III, and Chapters III:1–7 on the *Maaseh Merkabah*.

The main part of *The Guide of the Perplexed* is a three-part unit, *Maaseh Bereshit*–Sabbath–*Maaseh Merkabah*. The Sabbath is the critical divider between the *Maaseh Bereshit* and the *Maaseh Merkabah*. The Sabbath, the first Sabbath, is the divider between the expression of God's creativity in connection with the creation of the universe in the first place, and the expression of creativity of God in the history that follows.

Maimonides shows how this is indicated in Scripture in a discussion that is divided in two scattered chapters, Chapter II:31, the chapter that lies between the *Maaseh Bereshit* and the *Maaseh Merkabah*, and Chapter I:67, a chapter within the section on the distinction between the existence and the essence of God.

The critical verse Maimonides draws attention to is Exodus 31:17, in which Scripture indicates that on the seventh day: "[He] rested (*shabbat*) and ensouled (*vayyinaphash*)" (Exodus 31:17) (*Guide*, p. 162). Maimonides is at pains to indicate that the second word applies to soul, explicitly saying that, ". . . the verb *vayyinaphash* . . . derive[s] from the word *nephesh* (soul)" (*Guide*, p. 162).

Maimonides draws attention to the duality of that predicated of God on the Sabbath by pointing out that two different reasons are given for observing the Sabbath:

> For this commandment [to observe the Sabbath] two different causes are given, corresponding to two different effects. . . . In the first Decalogue . . . *For in six days the Lord made, and so on* (Exodus 20:11). . . . [In the second Decalogue] *And thou shalt remember that thou wast a slave in Egypt* (Deuteronomy 5:15). [*Guide*, p. 359]

The first refers backward from the first Sabbath and the second refers forward from the first Sabbath.

Thus we have the intimation from Maimonides that the Sabbath refers backward to the first creation, the *Maaseh Bereshit,* and forward into the events that take place afterward. Thus it is fitting for Maimonides to place the chapter on the Sabbath precisely between his discussions of the *Maaseh Bereshit* and the *Maaseh Merkabah.* He must also hide it in some way. He does that by sandwiching in the lengthy discussion of the psychology of prophecy after the chapter on the Sabbath and before the material on the *Maaseh Merkabah.*

There is an important tradition relevant to this dualism with respect to the Sabbath in its references to that associated with the *Maaseh Bereshit* in the first place and the *Maaseh Merkabah* in the second. The tradition is that the work God did on the second day of creation was left unfinished. Leaving it unfinished left work for God to do in the days following the first Sabbath. Maimonides cites the tradition explicitly: "Among the things you ought to know . . . is the reason why it is not said regarding the work of the second day that it was good. . . . that was so because the work . . . had not been terminated" [*Guide,* p. 353].

The scriptural foundation of this is the peculiarity of the story of the creation in Genesis in which a declaration by God saying that what was done was good is missing, in contrast to the other five days prior to the Sabbath (Genesis 1:6–8). The source on this states: "Why is 'that it was good' not written in connection with the second day? R. Samuel b. Nahman said: Because the making of the waters was not finished" (*Bereshit Rabbah* IV:6).

The idea that this incompleteness within the *Maaseh Bereshit* provided for the *Maaseh Merkabah* is the subject of Chapter IV of the *Pirke de Rebbe Eliezer,* a work that Maimonides variously cites and discusses in *The Guide of the Perplexed* (pp. 149, 174, 330, 332).

FOR MY PURPOSE IS THAT THE TRUTHS BE GLIMPSED AND THEN AGAIN CONCEALED. [*Guide,* pp. 6–7]

It is to be noted that Maimonides is fully confident in his own understanding of what it is that he takes the prophetic meanings, the internal meanings, to be. The lack of clarity that exists in *The Guide of the Perplexed* is not to be attributed to any uncertainty in the author. If there is lack of clarity in the presentation, it is the result of two things, the deliberate lack of clarity on the author's part and the limitations that exist in the reader. Thus, while Maimonides is in possession of "truths," they will at most be only glimpsed by the reader, even the qualified reader. The prophets and the sages who understood these "truths" before him certainly did not express themselves clearly either. Maimonides, seeking to express himself, is under pressure to speak clearly, but cannot.

Maimonides is here alluding to the implied instruction given in the Talmud, and which he variously alludes to. In the Talmud, the discussion indicates in various ways that the critical word in the account of the vision of Ezekiel is the word *hashmal*, which is found in two places, Ezekiel 1:27 and Ezekiel 8:2 (in the seemingly feminine form of *hashmalah* in the latter). This is said, in the Talmud, to mean: "At times they are silent, at times they speak" (*Hagigah* 13b). He then continues:

SO AS NOT TO OPPOSE THAT DIVINE PURPOSE WHICH ONE CANNOT POSSIBLY OPPOSE. [*Guide*, p. 7]

Alluding to the Mishnaic law's constraint on exposition.

AND WHICH HAS CONCEALED FROM THE VULGAR AMONG THE PEOPLE THOSE TRUTHS ESPECIALLY REQUISITE FOR HIS APPREHENSION. [*Guide* p. 7]

We note here a virtual definition of prophecy.

Let us assume that Maimonides understands vulgarity as lack of education combined with lack of constraint with respect to sexual expression or conduct. The vulgar might not have the capability indicated in the principle of Rabbi Akiva. If they were exposed to the images of divine sexuality that Maimonides believes are apprehended by the prophets, they would remain at the concrete level of those images, not being able to reach beyond and prone to dwell within the images as though they were concrete realities. Therefore Maimonides is particularly concerned not to reveal these "truths" to the vulgar:

AS HE HAS SAID: *THE SECRET OF THE LORD IS WITH THEM THAT FEAR [APPREHEND] HIM* (Psalms 25:14). [*Guide*, p. 7]

What is the meaning of this citation? And what is its connection to that which Maimonides says in the preceding? There are several meanings here by virtue of the fact that the verse may mean either or both: *The secret of the Lord is with them that fear Him*, or *The secret of the Lord is with them that apprehend Him* [or *envision Him*].

Among the meanings possible is one which suggests that fear is a prerequisite for vision—that is, to those who fear Him—and then, the word changing meaning, that they may apprehend him in a vision. One consequence is, perhaps, that the vulgar do not fear, and thus may not envision. Or since the word is one of the commandments, ordinarily translated as the commandment to *fear the Lord*, those who understand will understand the commandment as *apprehend the Lord*. We take it that some order of understanding of this verse is behind the strong distinction Maimonides makes with respect to who is and who is not a proper receiver of that which is written in *The Guide of the Perplexed*. We take it also that Maimonides derives from this some moral obligation toward understanding as the fulfillment of the commandment to fear the Lord. It is an interesting thing that the English word "apprehend" has the two meanings of envision and fear as well.

KNOW THAT WITH REGARD TO NATURAL MATTERS AS WELL, IT IS IMPOSSIBLE TO GIVE A CLEAR EXPOSI-TION WHEN TEACHING SOME OF THEIR PRINCIPLES AS THEY ARE. FOR YOU KNOW THE SAYING ... : THE *MAASEH BERESHIT* OUGHT NOT TO BE TAUGHT IN THE PRESENCE OF TWO. [*Guide*, p. 7]

We take note of how explicit Maimonides' drawing of attention to the Mishnaic law is. It is patent that Maimonides wishes the reader to understand that the Mishnaic law is central to his concerns. The fact of the matter is that much of what Maimonides says in the pages of *The Guide of the Perplexed* refer to the Mishnah and to the Gemara on the Mishnah which is to be found in the Talmud (*Hagigah* 11b–16a). Maimonides is sending his reader to that source.

Maimonides is explicit in indicating his interest in alienating those of his readers he regards as vulgar. We can identify another device in what he is doing here: It is a deflection that has had an extremely important effect over the centuries in keeping the veil over *The Guide of the Perplexed*. Maimonides may have had no idea of how influential the thought of the Greek philosophers would become in the centuries after him, or of how his explications of Greek thought would be the very thing that would draw the attention of many people to *The Guide of the Perplexed*. Indeed, the idea that one like Thomas Aquinas, who would come to be judged as among the greatest of the Catholic theologians, would be studying *The Guide of the Perplexed*, and refer variously to the thought of "Rabbi Moses," would have been unimaginable to him. Yet many turned to Maimonides' book to use it as a guide not to get out of the perplexity caused by reading philosophy and failing to understand the prophetic writings in Scripture, but to learn philosophy from him, as many of the Scholastics did.

The fact is that Maimonides' writing does suggest this, for he leads the reader to believe that philosophy and the esoteric secrets are the same. We suspect that Maimonides does this, at least in part, as a way of misdirecting some of his readers. The great secrets are disguised in the prophetic writings. The prophets were philosophers. One might be led to think that one should thank the prophets for their provisional services and proceed to study the writings of the philosophers directly. Thus, one would have little interest in reading Maimonides' *The Guide of the Perplexed* for any reason other than that of historical curiosity. If we follow through with this misdirection, all we would expect to find after our labors in trying to decipher the prophetic writings is that which is stated so much more clearly in the writings of the philosophers.

As we have indicated above, in the later pages of *The Guide of the Perplexed* we learn of the superiority of the apprehension of the prophets to that of the philosophers, and we learn quite specifically that the philosophers, who are lacking in the necessary imaginative powers, can reach no further than the existence of God, while the prophets can, through the exercise of the imagination, reach toward the essence of God.

That Maimonides would send some of his readers off to read science and philosophy forever is shown in another blatant example of misdirection to be found within the pages of *The Guide of the Perplexed*. It is within his direct exposition of the *Maaseh Bereshit*, in Chapter II:30. We present it here as a kind of microscopic version of what is represented in *The Guide of the Perplexed* more macroscopically. There, in speaking of the meaning of the water apprehended by Rabbi Akiva in the story of the four who entered PaRDeS, and clearly suggesting that water is to be understood as a metaphor and not literally, Maimonides throws in an insertion that we take as intended for those who might have stumbled onto those pages inadvertently. After quoting the passage from the Talmud in connection with the water apprehended, Maimonides says: "Reflect, if you are one of those who reflect. . . ."

He clearly has in mind two classes of readers, those who reflect and those who do not reflect. And this is an injunction to reflect for those who are capable of reflecting: ". . . to what extent he has made clear and revealed the whole matter in this statement. . . ." And again an alert: ". . . provided you consider it well. . . ." This much is patently an instruction to bring to bear the ". . . method of non-literal interpretation . . ." which he mentions almost immediately afterward. However, consider the text as it is written:

> Reflect, if you are one of those who reflect, to what extent he has made clear and revealed the whole matter in this statement [Four entered PRDS, and so on. Rabbi Akiva said to them: When you come to the stones of pure marble, do not say Water, Water, for it is written: He that speaketh falsehood will not be established before My fountains], provided that you consider it well, understand all that has been demonstrated in the "Meteorologica," and examine everything that people have said about every point mentioned in that work. [*Guide*, p. 353]

Let us highlight: ". . . understand all that has been demonstrated in the 'Meteorologica,' and examine everything that people have said about every point mentioned in that work." Anyone who might try to follow this instruction would never return to the topic. The *Meteorologica* is a treatise by Aristotle dealing mainly with the weather. Sending someone off to read it, and to read "everything that people have said about every point mentioned in that work," is to have given any reader who took it literally a lifetime occupation. These words have been inserted by Maimonides as a "red herring" at the point at which he is intimating what "the whole matter" might be: to divert those who have not appreciated the "method of nonliteral interpretation" and the principle of Rabbi Akiva.

**NOW IF SOMEONE EXPLAINED ALL THOSE MATTERS IN
A BOOK, HE IN EFFECT WOULD BE TEACHING THEM TO
THOUSANDS OF MEN.** [*Guide,* p. 7]

Maimonides is deeply ambivalent about whether he should or should not write *The Guide of the Perplexed*. He himself has seen into Scripture. He has discovered a great deal of what he identifies as the internal meaning of the texts representing the apprehension of prophets expressed metaphorically. He is quite persuaded that that which he has thus discovered in the text is objectively there. What is at issue for him is whether or not to reveal his discoveries, and how he should go about saying what he knows.

The Mishnaic law constrains him to address himself to a single student orally—or rather, somehow through oral indications to guide a suitably qualified student. The *Maaseh Bereshit* is to be taught to one person, and the *Maaseh Merkabah* not even to one, unless he has certain qualifications, and then only by providing him with the "chapter headings." In putting this into writing at all, Maimonides does so in the second person, as an address in letters, to a single student whom he identifies in the Epistle Dedicatory with which *The Guide of the Perplexed* opens. In that preface to the book, Maimonides gives the reason for writing it. The tutelage could not continue on a face-to-face basis because the student had to leave: "Then when God decreed our separation these meetings [which we had had] aroused in me a resolution that had slackened." That is, the resolution to write *The Guide of the Perplexed* evidently had other motives in Maimonides. However, this separation provided an immediate stimulus: "Your absence made moved me to compose this Treatise, which I have composed for you and for those like you, however few they are. I have set it down in dispersed chapters. All of them that are written down will reach you where you are, one after another" [*Guide,* p. 4].

In this preface of address to the student, Maimonides is at pains to recite the qualifications of the student as if to show that he was eligible in the terms suggested by the Talmud. The level the student had attained was that of Ben Zoma, which he describes later in the book. In this preface, Maimonides writes:

I saw that your longing for mathematics was great, and hence I let you train yourself in that science, knowing where you would end. When thereupon you read under my guidance texts dealing with the art of logic, my hopes fastened upon you, and I saw that you are one worthy to have the secrets of the prophetic books revealed to you so that you would consider in them that which perfect men ought to consider. [*Guide*, p. 3]

The Ben Zoma level is described by Maimonides as follows:

Know, my son, that as long as you are engaged in studying the mathematical sciences and the art of logic, you are one of those who walk around the house searching for its gate, as [the Sages] . . . have said resorting to a parable: *Ben Zoma is still outside* (*Hagigah* 15a). [*Guide*, p. 619]

The indication Maimonides makes to mathematics should be regarded with reference to the neo-Platonic pedagogy that gave emphasis to mathematics, not only because mathematics exemplified Platonic idealism, but also because of the autogenic nature of mathematics. The idea that mathematics is autogenic was indicated by Socrates in the *Meno*, where he gets a slave boy to produce the Pythagorean theorem simply by asking him questions. This neo-Platonic pedagogy converged with the Mishnaic law that the student of esoteric topics should be capable of understanding his own knowledge.

There are two more stages, the level of the philosopher who knows natural and divine science and then the level of the prophet. Maimonides' aim is to bring the student to appreciate the prophets through the study of that which he offers in *The Guide of the Perplexed*, after being assured he has at least reached the stage of Ben Zoma. Yet the writing of a book is against the Mishnaic law. As we have indicated, Maimonides does find some license to write if he limits himself to the "chapter headings." That is a kind of legalistic license. There is a much more important reason for Maimonides to put his understandings down in a book, and that reason is the loss of these understandings to the Jewish community. Maimonides gives a criticism of the Mishnaic law for the effect that it has had: "Know that the many sciences devoted to establishing the truth regarding these matters that have existed in our religious community have perished. . . ." He offers two reasons why they have perished. The first is: ". . . because of our being dominated by pagan nations," but the second is: "and because . . . it is not permitted to divulge these matters to all people. . . . This was the cause that necessitated the disappearance of these great roots of knowledge from the nation."

Some traces are to be found in the Talmud and the Midrashim, he says: "These are . . . a few grains belonging to the core, which are overlaid by many layers of rind. . . ." And even that has led to negative consequences, because: ". . . people were occupied with these layers of rind and thought that beneath them there was no core whatsoever" [*Guide*, p. 175].

Another negative effect that Maimonides points to is that Jewish thinkers, faced with this vacuum, turned toward the "scanty bit of argument" [*Guide*, p. 176] of the Mutakallimum, the practitioners of the *Kalam*, the speculative Islamic theology, and to the amplifications associated with the Islamic receipt of the Greek sources. Neither of these constitute a fully correct understanding. This damage calls for repair; and the need for such repair is a license for Maimonides' lengthy discussion of both the Mutakallimum and the philosophers in *The Guide of the Perplexed*.

HENCE THESE MATTERS TOO OCCUR IN PARABLES IN THE BOOKS OF PROPHECY. THE SAGES . . . FOLLOWING IN THE TRAIL OF THESE BOOKS, LIKEWISE HAVE SPOKEN OF THEM IN RIDDLES AND PARABLES, FOR THERE IS A CLOSE CONNECTION BETWEEN THESE MATTERS AND THE DIVINE SCIENCE, AND THEY TOO ARE SECRETS OF THAT DIVINE SCIENCE. [*Guide*, p. 7]

There is an internal content which is known to prophets and sages. And Maimonides has a theory of the way in which texts from the prophets and the sages derive. That which prophets apprehend, that which is the referent of the internal content of the texts reporting their accounts, occurs to them in dreams and visions and is reported only in riddles and parables. And the sages have followed somewhat the same path, expressing themselves also in riddles and parables. We take

Maimonides to imply that there is both similarity and difference, by his saying that there is a close connection between that which is apprehended by the prophets and sages and what is to be found in the Aristotelian divine science. It is the difference between the essence of God, toward which the former reach, and the existence of God, to which the latter is limited.

> YOU SHOULD NOT THINK THAT THESE GREAT SE-CRETS ARE FULLY AND COMPLETELY KNOWN TO ANYONE AMONG US. THEY ARE NOT. [*Guide*, p. 7]

Here Maimonides, at the outset of a book which promises to tell certain secrets, qualifies what it is that he, or anyone else, might know. For, for Maimonides the apprehension of Moses was greater than that of all the other prophets, and even the apprehension of Moses had to be restricted to "back" rather than "face." Maimonides then proceeds to outline the range of variation of this as insight, in terms of the metaphor of light:

> BUT SOMETIMES TRUTH FLASHES OUT TO US SO THAT WE THINK IT IS DAY, AND THEN MATTER AND HABIT IN THEIR VARIOUS FORMS CONCEAL IT SO THAT WE FIND OURSELVES AGAIN IN AN OBSCURE NIGHT, AL-MOST AS WE WERE BEFORE. [*Guide*, p. 7]

We take note that that which is designated as interfering with the insight are "matter and habit." Maimonides then gives the degrees of this insight in terms of the light metaphor:

> WE ARE LIKE SOMEONE IN A VERY DARK NIGHT OVER WHOM LIGHTNING FLASHES TIME AND TIME AGAIN. [*Guide*, p. 7]

At the extreme there is Moses:

> AMONG US THERE IS ONE FOR WHOM THE LIGHTNING FLASHES TIME AND TIME AGAIN, SO THAT HE IS AL-WAYS, AS IT WERE, IN UNCEASING LIGHT. THUS NIGHT APPEARS TO HIM AS DAY. THAT IS THE DEGREE OF THE GREAT ONE AMONG THE PROPHETS, TO

WHOM IT WAS SAID: BUT AS FOR THEE, STAND THOU HERE BY ME (Deuteronomy 5:28) AND OF WHOM IT IS SAID: THAT THE SKIN OF HIS FACE SENT FORTH BEAMS, AND SO ON. [*Guide*, p. 7]

Those with one flash:

AMONG THEM THERE IS ONE TO WHOM THE LIGHT-NING FLASHES ONLY ONCE IN THE WHOLE OF HIS NIGHT; THAT IS THE RANK OF THOSE OF WHOM IT IS SAID: THEY PROPHESIED, BUT THEY DID SO NO MORE (Numbers 11:25). [*Guide*, p. 7]

Variation in terms of flash interval:

THERE ARE OTHERS BETWEEN WHOSE LIGHTNING FLASHES THERE ARE GREATER OR SHORTER INTER-VALS. [*Guide*, p. 7]

For some there is illumination by some lesser light than a lightning flash:

THEREAFTER COMES HE WHO DOES NOT ATTAIN A DEGREE IN WHICH HIS DARKNESS IS ILLUMINED BY ANY LIGHTNING FLASH. IT IS ILLUMINED, HOWEVER, BY A POLISHED BODY OR SOMETHING OF THAT KIND, STONES OR SOMETHING ELSE THAT GIVE LIGHT IN THE DARKNESS OF THE NIGHT. [*Guide*, p. 7]

And even such lesser lights than a lightning flash are not steadily available:

AND EVEN THIS SMALL LIGHT THAT SHINES OVER US IS NOT ALWAYS THERE, BUT FLASHES AND IS HIDDEN AGAIN, AS IF IT WERE THE FLAMING SWORD WHICH TURNED EVERY WAY (Genesis 3:24).

IT IS IN ACCORD WITH THESE STATES THAT THE DE-GREES OF THE PERFECT VARY. [*Guide*, p. 7]

He then goes back to the first group, those who never see the light. These are the vulgar.

AS FOR THOSE WHO NEVER ONCE SEE A LIGHT, BUT GROPE ABOUT IN THEIR NIGHT, OF THEM IT IS SAID: THEY KNOW NOT, NEITHER DO THEY UNDERSTAND; THEY GO ABOUT IN DARKNESS (Psalms 82:5). THE TRUTH, IN SPITE OF THE STRENGTH OF ITS MANIFES-TATION, IS ENTIRELY HIDDEN FROM THEM, AS IT IS SAID OF THEM: AND NOW MEN SEE NOT THE LIGHT WHICH IS BRIGHT IN THE SKIES. THEY ARE THE VULGAR AMONG THE PEOPLE. THERE IS THEN NO OCCASION TO MENTION THEM IN THIS TREATISE. [*Guide*, pp. 7–8]

While he says that there is no occasion to speak of the vulgar in *The Guide of the Perplexed*, he does, of course, mention them. For the project is to keep the secrets from the vulgar; and thus they must in some sense command attention all the time.

We take note that Maimonides identifies two reasons as to why things are not presented clearly. One of these is as a matter of injunction, as in compliance with the Mishnah. Another reason is that one may not have a choice by virtue of the limitations of the human being with respect to being able to sustain conscious thought with respect to it. We would highlight the latter at this point, because an important psychological principle is involved: The specific content of that which is apprehended may have a determinative influence on the process of apprehension. We take note of this in that which Maimonides then addresses:

KNOW THAT WHENEVER ONE OF THE PERFECT WISHES TO MENTION, EITHER ORALLY OR IN WRIT-ING, SOMETHING THAT HE UNDERSTANDS OF THESE SECRETS, ACCORDING TO THE DEGREE OF HIS PERFEC-TION, HE IS UNABLE TO EXPLAIN WITH COMPLETE CLARITY AND COHERENCE EVEN THE PORTION THAT HE HAS APPREHENDED, AS HE COULD DO WITH THE OTHER SCIENCES WHOSE TEACHING IS GENERALLY RECOGNIZED. [*Guide*, p. 8]

It is of value in our understanding Maimonides' meaning to consider the notion of the Active Intellect again. The notion of the Active
Intellect arises from a very short passage in Aristotle's *De Anima*. The
notion of the Active Intellect has to be considered from a psychological point of view, as well as from a transcendental point of view. The
latter derives largely from the commentary of Alexander of Aphrodi-
sias in the second century. Aristotle says that:

> . . . since, as in the whole of nature, to something which serves as a
> matter . . . there corresponds something else . . . which . . . makes them
> . . . as art [is to] material, [so must] these differences be found also in the
> soul. . . . To the one intellect [the Passive Intellect] which . . . becomes
> all things corresponds the other [the Active Intellect] [which] makes all
> things, like . . . light. For . . . light . . . converts colors which are
> potential into actual colors. [*De Anima* 3:5, p. 135]

This idea is developed in Al Farabi's *Letter on the Intellect* which is
cited by Maimonides on p. 207 of the *Guide*. The psychological
phenomenon to which Maimonides is referring is the variation in
consciousness with respect to things known unconsciously:

RATHER THERE WILL BEFALL HIM WHEN TEACHING
ANOTHER THAT WHICH HE HAD UNDERGONE WHEN
LEARNING HIMSELF. I MEAN TO SAY THAT THE SUB-
JECT MATTER WILL APPEAR, FLASH, AND THEN BE
HIDDEN AGAIN [*Guide*, p. 8]

We note the importance of pedagogy in Maimonides' considerations. This is consistent with the Mishnaic law's use of the rhetoric of
injunction with respect to teaching while at the same time giving many
indications concerning the content involved.

We note that in the very act of teaching, that critical psychological
phenomenon entailing knowledge held unconsciously and then becoming conscious characterizes not only the prophets and sages, as he
has already indicated, but the teacher as well. It is the critical feature
of the learning process. For the learning process, as the Mishnaic law
indicates, is to be directed toward him who has the ability to come to
understand the knowledge he already has. Here what Maimonides

indicates is that even when one has, at some time, come to understand one's own knowledge, come to have in consciousness what one has had unconsciously, it happens that the content returns to unconsciousness.

AS THOUGH THIS WERE THE NATURE OF THIS SUB-JECT MATTER, BE THERE MUCH OR LITTLE OF IT. [*Guide*, p. 8]

Maimonides clearly has a notion of the content that is apprehended. He clearly attributes the appearance and disappearance of this content in consciousness to the character of that content. The special character of that content, which is thus subject to repression, is Oedipal. The Mishnaic law suggests that the content is Oedipal, for it issues the warning precisely with respect to him who would not be forbearing with respect to the honor of his maker.

The appreciation that Maimonides understands the content to be Oedipal helps us to understand the contradiction he openly places in *The Guide of the Perplexed* at this point. For that which he has thus far taken as an involuntary process is now to be taken as a voluntary process. That is, not only is there a natural force that keeps the Oedipal apprehension unconscious, so that it flashes into consciousness only occasionally, and only for some, but the covering of the knowledge of the sexuality of one's maker should be concealed. Thus, he says:

FOR THIS REASON [*Guide*, p. 8]

And we are compelled to ask, For what reason?

... ALL THE SAGES POSSESSING KNOWLEDGE OF GOD THE LORD, KNOWERS OF THE TRUTH, WHEN THEY AIMED AT TEACHING SOMETHING OF THIS SUBJECT, SPOKE OF IT ONLY IN PARABLES AND RIDDLES. [*Guide*, p. 8]

That the hidden content is of a sexual and Oedipal nature may well have been in Maimonides' mind even as far back as his composition of his *Commentary on the Mishnah*, which he had composed even before he had written the *Mishneh Torah*. There he discusses how the sages expressed their ideas with seeming absurdity deliberately such that ". . . the mind of a fool would reject them. . . ." He states that: ". . . the subjects do not contain what should be openly taught and demonstrated in the Yeshivas."

He offers three categories of reasons. First, to sharpen the minds of some. Second, to deceive fools who would thereby not detect the meanings. And third, because of the appropriateness of using parables in the education of the intellectually unprepared and immature, and the obligation of giving them provisional instruction until their intellects were developed (Introduction to *Seder Zeraim*, Chapter 8). We then understand the "reason" mentioned to be the natural repression that goes with sexuality in the human being in the first place, and the social obligation to conceal sexuality from public display in the second. The first is displayed in the variation in insight in the teacher, the second in the use of parables, even those appearing absurd, by the sages.

Maimonides provides indications concerning the different ways that the hypothetical internal content is changed in the process prior to entering into the text as external content. This may be considered to be Maimonides' presentation of the "encoding" process, which can equally be regarded as instruction with respect to the "decoding" process. He provides an enumeration:

THEY ... MULTIPLIED THE PARABLES AND MADE THEM DIFFERENT IN SPECIES AND EVEN IN GENUS.

IN MOST CASES THE SUBJECT TO BE EXPLAINED WAS PLACED IN THE BEGINNING OR IN THE MIDDLE OR AT THE END OF THE PARABLE; THIS HAPPENED WHERE A PARABLE FOR THE INTENDED SUBJECT FROM START TO FINISH COULD NOT BE FOUND.

SOMETIMES THE SUBJECT INTENDED TO BE TAUGHT ... WAS DIVIDED – ALTHOUGH IT WAS ONE AND THE SAME SUBJECT – AMONG MANY PARABLES REMOTE FROM ONE ANOTHER.

EVEN MORE OBSCURE IS THE CASE OF ONE AND THE SAME PARABLE CORRESPONDING TO SEVERAL SUB-JECTS, ITS BEGINNING FITTING ONE SUBJECT AND ITS ENDING ANOTHER.

SOMETIMES THE WHOLE IS A PARABLE REFERRING TO TWO COGNATE SUBJECTS WITHIN THE PARTICULAR SPECIES OF SCIENCE IN QUESTION. [*Guide*, p. 8]

The foregoing is as though it were from a manual on cryptography. It is, however, actually from the great treatise by Maimonides on how to interpret the dreams and visions of the prophets, and the interpre-tations of those dreams and visions by the sages:

THE SITUATION IS SUCH THAT THE EXPOSITION OF ONE WHO WISHES TO TEACH WITHOUT RECOURSE TO PARABLES AND RIDDLES IS SO OBSCURE AND BRIEF AS TO MAKE OBSCURITY AND BREVITY SERVE IN PLACE OF PARABLES AND RIDDLES. [*Guide*, p. 8]

Here Maimonides is beginning to talk in a way that refers more to himself directly in connection with the composition of the book at hand. In it he indicates one alternative that is available to him, should he not want to take the path of the sages:

THE MEN OF KNOWLEDGE AND THE SAGES ARE DRAWN, AS IT WERE, TOWARD THIS PURPOSE BY THE DIVINE WILL JUST AS THEY ARE DRAWN BY THEIR NATURAL CIRCUMSTANCES. [*Guide*, p. 8]

We take this to be a "flash" on the part of Maimonides, as well as an example for the reader of the method he has been outlining. The issue is a major theoretical issue that greatly preoccupies the author. It is the question of the relationship between "the divine will" and that which happens "by their natural circumstances." It is the question that he deals with extensively in the book, in the third part, where he attempts to probe the nature of providence and evil, with respect to how they are related to the "the divine will." It is also a parable. For it appears as part of a story about how the sages expressed themselves obscurely, with Maimonides imparting "secrets" whereby we might be equipped to decode the reported words of the sages.

We also note that Maimonides says "the men of knowledge and the sages." Now, we must understand that, for Maimonides, there can be men of knowledge who are not the sages; the sages for Maimonides are already men of knowledge. Indeed, this is a flash ahead already, as we shall presently note.

DO YOU NOT SEE THE FOLLOWING FACT? GOD ... WISHED US TO BE PERFECTED AND THE STATE OF OUR SOCIETIES TO BE IMPROVED BY HIS LAWS REGARDING ACTIONS. NOW THIS CAN COME ABOUT ONLY AFTER THE ADOPTION OF INTELLECTUAL BELIEFS, THE FIRST OF WHICH BEING HIS APPREHENSION ... ACCORDING TO OUR CAPACITY. [Guide, pp. 8-9]

We take note of the distinction Maimonides makes between beliefs and actions. For Maimonides the first commandments, those on the existence and unity of God, are belief commandments. All Jews believe in the existence and unity of God as law, independent of capacity. The prophetic stage, however, depends on capacity. It also depends on having reached divine science, the rational demonstration of the existence and unity of God.

THIS, IN ITS TURN [Guide, p. 9]

We take Maimonides to be referring to prophecy.

CANNOT COME ABOUT EXCEPT THROUGH DIVINE SCIENCE, AND THIS DIVINE SCIENCE CANNOT BECOME ACTUAL EXCEPT AFTER STUDY OF NATURAL SCIENCE. [Guide, p. 9]

The prophets have studied natural science, the nature of the created world. And divine science, the demonstration of the existence and unity of God, has become actual in them. As we have indicated, Maimonides was in the ancient tradition of Jewish writers which held that the content of the Greek writers had been available to the Jewish prophets long before the Greeks arrived on the intellectual scene. Maimonides then proceeds with some comments on the relationship between natural science and divine science:

THIS IS SO SINCE NATURAL SCIENCE BORDERS ON DI-
VINE SCIENCE, AND ITS STUDY PRECEDES THAT OF
DIVINE SCIENCE IN TIME AS HAS BEEN MADE CLEAR
TO WHOEVER HAS ENGAGED IN SPECULATION ON
THESE MATTERS. HENCE GOD ... CAUSED HIS BOOK
TO OPEN WITH THE *MAASEH BERESHIT,* WHICH ... IS
NATURAL SCIENCE. [*Guide,* p. 9]

We note the pedagogical point with natural science being, as it
were, a prerequisite for divine science. The relationship between the
two is like that between, say, algebra and analytical geometry. It is
essential to know algebra before proceeding to the study of analytical
geometry. The knowledge of the world that one obtains in studying
natural science is essential for the demonstration of the existence of
God.

AND BECAUSE OF THE GREATNESS AND IMPORTANCE
OF THE SUBJECT AND BECAUSE OUR CAPACITY FALLS
SHORT OF APPREHENDING THE GREATEST OF SUB-
JECTS AS IT REALLY IS, WE ARE TOLD ABOUT THESE
PROFOUND MATTERS—WHICH DIVINE WISDOM HAS
DEEMED NECESSARY TO CONVEY TO US—IN PARABLES
AND RIDDLES AND IN VERY OBSCURE WORDS. [*Guide,* p.
9]

What Maimonides alludes to here may be called the universal
philosophical experience—that is, the experience of existence as such
arising out of many particular experiences. It is that primordial
experience by which, say, a person is brought to wonder "What is this
all about, anyhow?", to have identified a general "this" so as to ask this
ultimate existential question. The question is asked very early in the
life of a child, sometime around the very opening of consciousness.
For the consciousness of the particular characteristically engages the
consciousness of the whole in the first place, even as learning and
maturation consist in part in isolating the particulars from the consciousness of the whole. One particularization is that of a self. At some
stage there is the recognition of the existence of the self. And the
questions: Who am I? What am I? Where did I come from? And in this
there is a sense that certain experiences, which we later come to

designate as sexual, are critically involved in this existence. We learn the awesome fact that it is the sexual act of our parents that is the cause of our existence. That, for a variety of reasons, must be covered. It must be covered in conversation. It must be covered in consciousness. It must be covered within us in order that the rest of our day-to-day activities should not be overwhelmed by this that is ultimate. It must be covered because of the danger associated with sexuality.

We take it that something like what we have said is that which is concealed, and is the great and important subject Maimonides refers to. And this is the subject with respect to which "our capacity falls short." The obstacles are twofold. The human mind cannot reach to answer the existential question definitively, because the answer is simply outside the reach of human beings. For Maimonides, there is a limit that a human being may reach in the "behind" of God, but not the "face." This was reached by Moses, and by no one else. The prophets can reach some lesser level than that through their visions and dreams. This reaches to essence, but not as far as Moses could reach. The philosophers can reach only to the existence, but never the essence of God.

AS [THE SAGES] ... HAVE SAID: IT IS IMPOSSIBLE TO TELL MORTALS OF THE POWER OF THE *MAASEH BE-RESHIT*. FOR THIS REASON SCRIPTURE TELLS YOU OB-SCURELY: IN THE BEGINNING GOD CREATED, AND SO ON. THEY THUS HAVE DRAWN YOUR ATTENTION TO THE FACT THAT THE ABOVE-MENTIONED SUBJECTS ARE OBSCURE. YOU LIKEWISE KNOW SOLOMON'S SAY-ING: THAT WHICH IS FAR OFF AND EXCEEDINGLY DEEP. WHO CAN FIND IT OUT? (Ecclesiastes 7:24) [*Guide*, p. 9]

Maimonides here mentions only the *Maaseh Bereshit*. However, it is clear enough. For if this be the case with respect to the *Maaseh Bereshit*, it is so much more the case with respect to the *Maaseh Merkabah*, applying the classical hermeneutic principle. Furthermore, the *Maaseh Bereshit* is genuinely secured against penetration. That is, it is very remote. For the human mind cannot reach the universe prior to the creation of the universe. The *Maaseh Merkabah*, however, has a touchstone in the sexual emotions and experience. Reaching that touchstone alone, and not being able to transcend it to the more general, would itself be damaging to the person.

THAT WHICH IS SAID ABOUT ALL THIS IS IN EQUIV-OCAL TERMS SO THAT THE MULTITUDE MIGHT COM-PREHEND THEM IN ACCORD WITH THE CAPACITY OF THEIR UNDERSTANDING AND THE WEAKNESS OF THEIR REPRESENTATION [Guide, p. 9]

There are two positive ideas in Maimonides to highlight. The first is that albeit the multitude might not appreciate the internal sense at all, there is value in the external sense of the text. The second is that in some way the internal meaning is communicated, albeit not through conscious processes. On the negative side, there is the danger that the texts will be read literally, in such a way as to be misunderstood entirely.

WHEREAS THE PERFECT MAN, WHO IS ALREADY IN-FORMED, WILL COMPREHEND THEM OTHERWISE. [Guide, p. 9]

Maimonides provides a detailed example of the way in which being informed plays a role in apprehension in the *Commentary on the Mishnah*.

. . . there are some things which seem to be the epitome of truth and clarity . . . while someone else considers them far-fetched and even impossible. . . . Imagine a man who is a scholar . . . but who is nevertheless intellectually void as far as geometric and astronomical sciences are concerned. Suppose we would inform him of, and ask his opinion of, a man who claims that the form of the sun . . . is really a sphere, and that the size of that sphere is $166\frac{3}{8}$ times the size of the earth; that the earth's sphere . . . is a globe with a perimeter of 24,000 miles [according to Ptolemy]; and through this method the number of miles in the sun's perimeter can be determined. There is no doubt that our [scholar] will be incapable of tolerating such a belief. All this, in his eyes, is far-fetched and incomprehensible. Immediately his mind will tell him that even a claim to any knowledge of such a thing is absurd.

How could it be possible, he will challenge, for a mortal who occupies but one span of the earth's surface, to know the dimensions of the solar sphere, its perimeter and area, to the extent that his mind could comprehend it as it comprehends the proportions of a piece of land? He will demand, "How is such a thing possible? The solar sphere is in the heaven at the furthest distance; it is impossible for us to even suitably discern the sun's composition—we can only perceive its glow; how then can a mortal reach on high to measure it and be precise to ⅜ths of exactitude? This is unheard of nonsense!" There will be no doubt in his mind as to the absurdity and impossibility of such a claim.

Yet, if he would acquaint himself with the study of geometry texts and understand the mathematical computations of relations which are determined by the known properties of spherical and other types of forms, and then proceed to study the texts written for this purpose . . . then the meaning of the claim would become clear to him. . . . His mind will become most accustomed to accepting that which he had originally considered to be most far-fetched nonsense. . . . We are not establishing our example of a man . . . who is ignorant. . . . How much more would our point be true with one who has no wisdom at all. When such a person will be asked pertaining to [what is] hidden beneath the surface of the drashos [of the Sages] they will undoubtedly seem as far-fetched . . . and his eyes will be powerless to understand a word of them. [*Maimonides' Introduction to the Talmud*, pp. 152–153]

WE HAD PROMISED IN THE COMMENTARY ON THE MISHNAH THAT WE WOULD EXPLAIN STRANGE SUBJECTS IN THE "BOOK OF PROPHECY" AND IN THE "BOOK OF CORRESPONDENCE"–THE LATTER BEING A BOOK IN WHICH WE PROMISED TO EXPLAIN ALL THE DIFFICULT PASSAGES IN THE MIDRASHIM WHERE THE EXTERNAL SENSE MANIFESTLY CONTRADICTS THE TRUTH AND DEPARTS FROM THE INTELLIGIBLE. THEY ARE ALL PARABLES. [*Guide*, p. 9]

Maimonides here identifies two characteristics of the external text that provide difficulty: seeming untruth and unintelligibility.

Maimonides then begins to explain the problem he faced when he began to attempt to identify such internal meanings in Scripture:

HOWEVER, WHEN, MANY YEARS AGO, WE BEGAN THESE BOOKS AND COMPOSED A PART OF THEM, OUR

BEGINNING TO EXPLAIN MATTERS IN THIS WAY DID NOT COMMEND ITSELF TO US. [*Guide*, p. 9]

For he too, it would seem, embarked upon the presentation of his ideas in the form of parables:

FOR WE SAW THAT IF WE SHOULD ADHERE TO PARABLES AND CONCEALMENT OF WHAT OUGHT TO BE CONCEALED, WE WOULD NOT BE DEVIATING FROM THE PRIMARY PURPOSE. [*Guide*, p. 9]

We take it that he understands "primary purpose" here to be the purpose to conceal.

We should note the confidence that Maimonides has that he has himself penetrated to the internal meanings of the texts:

WE WOULD, AS IT WERE, HAVE REPLACED ONE INDIVIDUAL BY ANOTHER OF THE SAME SPECIES. [*Guide*, p. 9]

That is, one form of concealment for another.

IF, ON THE OTHER HAND, WE EXPLAINED WHAT OUGHT TO BE EXPLAINED [*Guide*, p. 9]

We take that to mean the internal meanings being made explicit.

IT WOULD BE UNSUITABLE FOR THE VULGAR AMONG THE PEOPLE. [*Guide*, p. 9]

Up to this point we would have thought that Maimonides had little interest in communicating at all with the vulgar. Yet he says:

NOW IT WAS TO THE VULGAR THAT WE WANTED TO EXPLAIN THE IMPORT OF THE MIDRASHIM AND THE EXTERNAL MEANINGS OF PROPHECY. [*Guide*, pp. 9–10]

Maimonides, in his emphasis in *The Guide of the Perplexed* on the internal meanings, does not lose any sense of the value of the external

meanings for the people. However, he has great fear of the possibility
of extravagant, imaginative, and irrational enthusiasms from ignorant
religious leaders:

> WE ALSO SAW THAT IF AN IGNORAMUS AMONG THE
> MULTITUDE OF RABBANITES SHOULD ENGAGE IN
> SPECULATION ON THESE MIDRASHIM, HE WOULD
> FIND NOTHING DIFFICULT IN THEM, INASMUCH AS A
> RASH FOOL, DEVOID OF ANY KNOWLEDGE OF THE NA-
> TURE OF BEING [Guide, p. 10]

"The nature of being" including its creation is the ultimate subject
matter under discussion.

> DOES NOT FIND IMPOSSIBILITIES HARD TO ACCEPT.
> [Guide, p. 10]

He now considers how it would be if his targeted reader should
receive his explanations in the form of parables as he intended to write
them in the first place. Such a reader of such a work could react to it
in one of two ways:

> IF, HOWEVER, A PERFECT MAN OF VIRTUE SHOULD
> ENGAGE IN SPECULATION ON THEM, HE CANNOT ES-
> CAPE ONE OF TWO COURSES. [Guide, p. 10]

The first:

> EITHER HE CAN TAKE THE SPEECHES IN QUESTION [OF
> MAIMONIDES] IN THEIR EXTERNAL SENSE AND, IN SO
> DOING, THINK ILL OF THEIR AUTHOR AND REGARD
> HIM AS AN IGNORAMUS – IN THIS THERE IS NOTHING
> THAT WOULD UPSET THE FOUNDATIONS OF BELIEF
> [Guide, p. 10]

The second reaction such a reader might have:

> OR HE CAN ATTRIBUTE TO THEM AN INNER MEAN-
> ING, THEREBY EXTRICATING HIMSELF FROM HIS PRE-

DICAMENT AND BEING ABLE TO THINK WELL OF THE AUTHOR [*Guide*, p. 10]

Except that this might have a negative consequence of failing to teach what was to be taught:

WHETHER OR NOT THE INNER MEANING OF THE SAYING IS CLEAR TO HIM. [*Guide*, p. 10]

These negative outcomes with respect to three groups of persons, the vulgar, the ignorant teachers, and the targeted "perfect," indicate that another method is needed.

WITH REGARD TO THE MEANING OF PROPHECY, THE EXPOSITION OF ITS VARIOUS DEGREES, AND THE ELU-CIDATION OF THE PARABLES OCCURRING IN THE PRO-PHETIC BOOKS, ANOTHER MANNER OF EXPLANATION IS USED IN THIS TREATISE. [*Guide*, p. 10]

He abandoned his first plan:

IN VIEW OF THESE CONSIDERATIONS, WE HAVE GIVEN UP COMPOSING THESE TWO BOOKS IN THE WAY IN WHICH THEY WERE BEGUN. [*Guide*, p. 10]

He describes the essence of the plan for composing *The Guide of the Perplexed*:

WE HAVE CONFINED OURSELVES TO MENTIONING BRIEFLY THE FOUNDATIONS OF BELIEF [*Guide*, p. 10]

Which we take to mean that which comes under the rubrics of the *Maaseh Bereshit* and the *Maaseh Merkabah*.

AND GENERAL TRUTHS [*Guide*, p. 10]

Which we take to mean the natural and divine sciences of Aristotle.

... WHILE DROPPING HINTS THAT APPROACH A
CLEAR EXPOSITION, JUST AS WE HAVE SET THEM
FORTH IN THE GREAT LEGAL COMPOSITION, *MISH-
NEH TORAH.* [*Guide*, p. 10]

Which we take to be a citation to the first four chapters of the *Mishneh
Torah* in which Maimonides does just that, providing a clear exposition, which is at the same time a set of hints.

In an extraordinary way, Maimonides' *The Guide of the Perplexed* is
a work that states precisely what the author means, and yet at the
same time only hints at the full meaning. That is, the book is one of
wonderfully clear exposition. At the same time, the major thought is
hidden.

It is this that lies at the heart of a good deal of the literary history of
this work in the hundreds of years since its composition. Its eminent
clarity makes the book very attractive. The discussions of any number
of topics, at least in minuscule, cannot help but edify the reader.
Maimonides, with the minor exception of the story of the king in the
city, which we have already mentioned, does not himself use parable.
And where he uses metaphor of any kind, he characteristically makes
it clear that he does.

He continues with further indications concerning his writing of *The
Guide of the Perplexed.* He summarizes the characteristics of his addressee in terms of three characteristics: a grounding in philosophy, a
belief in Jewish law, and perplexity.

MY SPEECH IN THE PRESENT TREATISE IS DIRECTED,
AS I HAVE MENTIONED, TO ONE WHO HAS PHILOSO-
PHIZED AND HAS KNOWLEDGE OF THE TRUE SCIENCES
BUT BELIEVES AT THE SAME TIME IN THE MATTERS
PERTAINING TO THE LAW AND IS PERPLEXED AS TO
THEIR MEANING [*Guide*, p. 10]

And then provides a basic distinction between two categories of
obscurities in Scripture, terms and parables:

BECAUSE OF THE UNCERTAIN TERMS AND PARABLES.
[*Guide*, p. 10]

This is an important distinction, for it indicates two ways in which content may be encoded, and thus two approaches to decoding. These may be considered to be two hermeneutic tools for identifying internal content.

In connection with terms, Scripture may use terms that suggest a number of meanings. While one of the meanings fits into the context externally, another of the meanings is intended internally.

In connection with parable, we consider that a narrative may be analyzed into its characters, its setting, and its theme. Thus, for example, in the classical story of the fox and the grapes, where the fox cannot reach the grapes and thus declares them to be sour, we can identify the three things into which the story may be analyzed. Fox is the character. The setting is a vineyard through which the fox is passing. Now the story is not truly a story of a fox, nor of a vineyard. The story is rather of how human beings encountering what they cannot have may find those things undesirable. While a parable also involves a division being imposed in order to extract the meaning, it has to be considered as a whole in order to be able to identify the theme. In the case of terms, the division is the separation of the word from the thematic context. In the case of the parable, the division is the separation of the theme from the characters and setting.

As Freud pointed out in the early pages of *The Interpretation of Dreams*, these two hermeneutic tools are classical with respect to dream interpretation. Freud states that the

> . . . world has from the earliest times concerned itself with "interpret-ing" dreams and in its attempts to do so it has made use of two essentially different methods.
>
> The first of these procedures considers the content of the dream as a whole and seeks to replace it by another content which is intelligible and in certain respects analogous to the original one. This is "symbolic" dream-interpreting. . . . An example of this procedure is to be seen in the explanation of Pharaoh's dream propounded by Joseph in the Bible. The seven fat kine followed by seven lean kine that ate up the fat kine — all this was a symbolic substitute for a prophecy of seven years of famine in the land of Egypt which should consume all that was brought forth in the seven years of plenty. . . .
>
> The second of the two popular methods of interpreting dreams . . . might be described as the "decoding" method, since it treats of dreams as

a kind of cryptography in which each sign can be translated into another sign having a known meaning. . . . The essence of the decoding procedure . . . lies in the fact that the work of interpretation is not brought to bear on the dream as a whole but on each portion of the dream's content independently. [Freud, pp. 97–99]

These clearly correspond to the "parables" and the "uncertain terms" of Maimonides.

Maimonides provides another indication concerning his order of presentation:

WE SHALL INCLUDE IN THIS TREATISE SOME CHAP-TERS IN WHICH THERE WILL BE NO MENTION OF AN EQUIVOCAL TERM. SUCH A CHAPTER WILL BE PREPA-RATORY FOR ANOTHER, OR IT WILL HINT AT ONE OF THE MEANINGS OF AN EQUIVOCAL TERM THAT I MIGHT NOT WISH TO MENTION EXPLICITLY IN THAT PLACE, OR IT WILL EXPLAIN ONE OF THE PARABLES OR HINT AT THE FACT THAT A CERTAIN STORY IS A PARABLE. SUCH A CHAPTER MAY CONTAIN STRANGE MATTERS REGARDING WHICH THE CONTRARY OF THE TRUTH IS SOMETIMES BELIEVED, EITHER BE-CAUSE OF THE EQUIVOCALITY OF THE TERMS OR BE-CAUSE A PARABLE IS TAKEN FOR THE THING BEING REPRESENTED OR VICE VERSA. [*Guide*, p. 10]

Chapter I:17 is a clear example of such a chapter. Chapters I:1–16 are patently lexicographical. Chapter I:17 does not have a mention of an equivocal term. It is, however, of extraordinary importance. In it, Maimonides presents the Platonic idea of sexuality as the metaphor for generativity at large. He cites—or more accurately mis-cites in an interesting way which we will point out presently—a passage from Plato's *Timaeus*.

It might be appropriate at this point to make some parenthetical comments about Maimonides' use of Plato. It is fashionable in current philosophical thought to note the differences between Plato and Aristotle. If the question is forced as to whether to regard Maimonides as a Platonist or an Aristotelian, one would incline to classify him as an Aristotelian. At least one would come to this conclusion on the basis of the extensive treatment of Aristotle by Maimonides, the various favorable mentions with respect to him, and the variety of ways in which Maimonides' thought is patently influenced by Aristotle. Toward the confirmation of such a view of identifying Maimonides as an Aristotelian there is a letter from Maimonides cited by Pines in which Maimonides explicitly says:

> The writings [literally: words] of Aristotle's teacher Plato are in parables and hard to understand. One can dispense with them, for the writings of Aristotle suffice, and we need not occupy [our attention] with the writings of earlier [philosophers]. Aristotle's intellect [represents] the extreme of human intellect, if we except those who have received divine inspiration. [*Guide*, p. lix]

Yet these words should be looked upon carefully. For there are two indications in them which might, at least for the purpose of understanding *The Guide of the Perplexed*, claim our attention. The first is that Maimonides makes special reference to Plato in connection with parables. The second is that he makes special reference as well to "those who have received divine inspiration," which, we can presume, at least indicates the prophets. Prophets are, for Maimonides, accomplished in the knowledge associated with Aristotle. They are, however, beyond them in their apprehensions in dreams and visions.

We note that within the pages of *The Guide of the Perplexed* Maimonides clearly distinguishes between the positions of Aristotle and Plato with respect to belief in eternity: ". . . the belief in eternity the way Aristotle sees it . . . destroys the Law . . . If, however, one believed in eternity according to . . . the opinion of Plato . . . this opinion would not destroy the foundations of the Law. . . ." [*Guide*, p. 328]. A reason that he gives for Plato's position being the better one is because Plato's opinion makes it ". . . possible to interpret [the texts] figuratively . . ." [*Guide*, p. 328].

Let us consider that it is that which is suggested in the immediately preceding chapter, Chapter I:16, which has impelled Maimonides to write what he writes about Plato in Chapter I:17. That is, let us allow that it is the content of Chapter I:16 that is the chapter that Chapter I:17 is connected with. Let us allow that Chapter I:17 is the chapter which is "preparatory for another" (p. 10) and that the other is

Chapter I:16. Chapter I:16 makes reference to some very pruriently suggestive lines in the book of Isaiah. They are as follows: "Look unto the rock whence ye were hewn, And to the hole of the pit whence ye were digged. Look unto Abraham your father, And unto Sarah that bore you" (Isaiah 51:1–2). By the principle of parallelism, Abraham is rock and Sarah is hole.

What Maimonides would then make of this is that the sexual which is brought to mind is only an allegory of a greater principle of some kind, in accordance with the principle of Rabbi Akiva. What Maimonides then seeks to do is to raise it to being a matter of the relationship between form and matter, with Abraham contributing the form, and Sarah contributing the matter.

Chapter I:16 is manifestly a chapter that explains the various meanings of the word rock (*zur*). After indicating that the word has the meanings of "mountain" and of "hard stone," Maimonides opens a discussion of the use of the term in the verses indicated above from Isaiah.

Now, in order to appreciate what Maimonides is seeking to intimate in Chapters I:16–17, it is important to take note of the fact that the word used to mean "rock" in Scripture also has the meaning of "form." Thus, we find the word used several times in that sense in Ezekiel 43:11:

> And if they be ashamed of all that they have done, make known unto them the form (*zurat*) of the house, and the fashion thereof, and the goings out thereof, and the comings in thereof, and all the forms (*zuratai*) thereof, and all the ordinances thereof, and all the forms (*zurotav*) thereof, and all the laws thereof and write it in their sight; that they may keep the whole form (*zurato*) thereof, and all the ordinances thereof, and do them.

The term is also used for "form," in the sense of the soul in the afterlife, as in Psalms 49:15–16:

> Like sheep they are appointed for the
>   nether-world;
> Death shall be their shepherd;
> And the upright shall have dominion over them
>   in the morning;

And their form (*ziram*) shall be for the
   nether-world to wear away,
That there be no habitation for it.
But God will redeem my soul from the power of
   the nether-world;
For He shall receive me.

The term *zur* also occurs as the verb *yazar*, meaning "to form," as one of the three verbs used in Scripture with respect to God's fashioning of human beings, as in Isaiah: "And whom I have created (*berativ*) for My glory, if have formed (*yezartiv*) him, yea, I have made (*asa*) him (*asitiv*) (Isaiah 43:7). Maimonides covers the prurient part of the citation from Isaiah by merely identifying the passage with an "and so on": "It is on this account that after saying: *Look unto the rock whence you were hewn*, Scripture continues: *Look unto Abraham your father, and so on . . .*" [*Guide*, p. 42]. At the same time he makes plain the idea that the human being derives from the "rock"—which we must now translate rather as "form"—of the father: ". . . giving, as it were, an interpretation according to which *the rock (form) whence ye were hewn* is *Abraham your father*" [*Guide*, p. 42].

Maimonides thus leads the reader equally to the identification of Sarah with the word for hole, in parallel to the identification of Abraham with the word for rock. Maimonides carries the prurient suggestion even further. He does this by indicating that the reader is at the "entryway." "This is the entryway through which you shall come to Him . . ." [*Guide*, p. 42]. This extraordinary notion, of a reentry into the womb, received renewed expression hundreds of years later by Sigmund Freud.

Maimonides gives us a further indication of his thought of the relevance of this extraordinary notion in connection with Moses by citing a verse from the account of Moses' apprehension of the Glory. What he says is: "This is the entryway through which you shall come to Him, as we have made clear when speaking of His saying [to Moses]: *Behold, there is a place by Me*" (Exodus 33:21) [*Guide*, p. 42]. The idea of Moses having had sexual intercourse with the Shekhinah is made explicit by Moses de Leon in his composition of the *Zohar* (I:22a). We may speculate that Moses de Leon derived this from Maimonides.

One further lexicographical notion that this chapter then suggests is that the Hebrew word for place, *maqom*, is understood by Maimonides as meaning the female genitalia. Maimonides has a special chapter on the word *maqom*, Chapter I:8. In that chapter he indicates two meanings for the word, one "the meaning of particular and general place," and the other "a term denoting an individual's rank and situation."

He then, in that chapter, goes on to indicate that there is another meaning he is not mentioning, but that it is associated with the same words from the account of Moses' apprehension, *Behold there is a place by Me*:

> Know with regard to every term whose equivocality we shall explain to you in this Treatise that our purpose in such an explanation is not only to draw your attention to what we mention in that particular chapter. Rather do we open a gate and draw your attention to such meanings of that particular term as are useful for our purpose, not for the various purposes of whoever may speak the language of this or that people. [*Guide*, pp. 33–34]

Thus the word *maqom* may have some other meaning, and that other meaning may be one that is not found in ordinary usage of the language. It is a meaning, however, that is useful for the purposes of understanding prophecy. He continues:

> As for you, you should consider the books of prophecy and other works composed by men of knowledge, reflect on all the terms used therein, and take every equivocal term in that one from among its various senses that is suitable in that particular passage. These our words are the key to this Treatise and to others; a case in point being the explanation we have given here of the meaning of the term *maqom* in the dictum: *Blessed be the glory of the Lord from His maqom* (Ezekiel 3:12). [*Guide*, p. 34]

Thus assigning the *maqom* to the Lord. He continues: "For you should know that this very meaning is that of the term *maqom* in its dictum: *Behold, there is a maqom by Me*" (Exodus 33:21) [*Guide*, p. 34]. And then quickly to indicate that it is allegorical, quite in accord with the principle of Rabbi Akiva, he follows this up with: "In this verse the term signifies a rank in theoretical speculation and the contemplation of the intellect. . . ." [*Guide*, p. 34].

What we would observe about Chapter I:16 further, considering it as the reference for the nonlexicographical chapter that follows, is that it begins with *zur* (form) and ends with *maqom* (female genitalia). It would appear essential that Maimonides should make as clear as he can that if the reader has understood what he is intimating, he also understand that that which is understood is allegorical. This is provided by the immediately succeeding chapter, Chapter I:17, which we consider now.

The question of male-female, form-matter, is discussable as both *Maaseh Merkabah* and *Maaseh Bereshit*. In the figurative form of male-female with respect to the divine, it is *Maaseh Merkabah*. However, insofar as it also represents the Greek physical theory concerning the relationship between form and matter, it is *Maaseh Bereshit*, the nature of the world as it is, as it was created by God.

Maimonides seems to have this on his mind in the first sentence of Chapter I:17: "Do not think that only the divine science should be withheld from the multitude" [*Guide*, p. 42]. We take this as a reference to that which he writes immediately above, the allusion to the pudendum of the Glory of God. For this is precisely that which is to be "withheld from the multitude."

It also holds for the *Maaseh Bereshit*, which he has identified with natural science: "This holds for the greater part of natural science." To make this point, he says: "For they concealed what they said about first principles and presented it in riddles. Thus Plato and his predecessors designated Matter as the female and Form as the male" [*Guide*, p. 43].

There are several observations that need to be made about this. First, that with this device Maimonides has managed to at least degrade that which he has revealed from the *Maaseh Merkabah* to the *Maaseh Bereshit*, a lesser degree of secrecy. That is, if he could divert his reader from thinking about the *Maaseh Merkabah* to the *Maaseh Bereshit* at this point, he would be in greater compliance with the Mishnaic law.

The second point is to highlight his attraction to Plato in this connection. The citation is to the account of creation provided in the *Timaeus*, which, as we have already observed, is a work cited explicitly by name in *The Guide of the Perplexed*. What Maimonides is referring to is the section in which generation out of matter is explained in which it is claimed that there is

> . . . the universal nature which receives all bodies . . . while receiving all things, she never departs at all from her own nature, and never . . . assumes a form like that of any of the things which enter into her. . . . But the forms which enter into and go out of her are the likenesses of real existences modelled after their patterns in a wonderful and inexplicable manner. . . . For the present we have only to conceive of three natures: first, that which is in the process of generation; secondly, that in which the generation takes place; and thirdly, that of which the thing generated is the resemblance. And we may liken the receiving principle to a mother, and the source or spring to a father, and the intermediate nature to a child. . . . [Jowett, vol. 2, pp. 30–31]

However, Maimonides does not do justice to Plato on two counts, which are related to each other, and constitute misconstructions on his part which serve to help us understand better what he has in his mind. First, Maimonides is in error. Plato refers to mother and father, rather than to male and female. The point is not a minor one. For if we might distinguish in sex the two things, generation and copulation, mother and father refer to generation, while female and male refer to copulation. Thus, Maimonides' error in his citation of Plato is to give to Plato an interpretation that is more rather than less prurient. The second is that in Plato's *Timaeus* there is little to support Maimonides' statement that the sexual metaphor is designed to conceal the deeper meanings. Quite the contrary, the metaphor for Plato is there to facilitate the communication, to provide an image for the mind, while the matter is explained more precisely. Thus, for example, in continuing the discussion, we find that image supplemented by another image. After the image of the mother and the father, Plato presents other images, of perfume and of molding material, to add to the clarification.

> Wherefore, that which is to receive all forms should have no form; as in making perfumes they first contrive that the liquid substance which is to receive the scent be as inodorous as possible; or as those who wish to

impress figures on soft substances do not allow any previous impression
to remain. . . . [Jowett, vol. 2, p. 31]

Maimonides is making his own case concerning the nature of
prurience, which is suggested in some of the prophetic writings in
Scripture, and ascribing it to Plato. Actually, by making his view
explicit with respect to Plato, albeit hardly accurately, he indicates his
view with respect to prophecy for the reader who knows Plato, and
would then know how to discount that which is not exactly as he says
for what remains. What remains is Maimonides' theory that the
prophets apprehend in dreams and visions that have a prurient
external content.

This brings us to the third observation. Sexual generation has a
characteristic that may not be associated with other forms of generation, the characteristic of desire. Now, in the generalization of the
generative process in the passage from Plato's *Timaeus* in which the
mother is made to correspond to matter and the father to correspond
to form, the quality of desire is not touched upon. However, Maimonides requires a prurient element for his theory of prophecy. He finds
a way to inject it at this point. For he follows up his comment about
Plato and his predecessors with the following:

> Now you know that the principles of the existents subject to generation
> and corruption are three: Matter, Form and Particularised Privation,
> which is always conjoined with Matter. For, were it not for this
> conjunction with Privation, Matter would not receive Form. It is in this
> sense that Privation is to be considered as one of the principles. [*Guide*,
> p. 43]

Maimonides then ends this chapter "in which there will be no mention
of an equivocal term" [*Guide*, p. 10] by using Plato in the form of a
classical hermeneutical argument:

> Now as even those upon whom the charge of corruption would not be
> laid in the event of clear exposition used terms figuratively and resorted
> to teaching in similes, how much all the more is it incumbent on us, the
> community of those adhering to the Law, not to state explicitly a
> matter that is either remote from the understanding of the multitude or

the truth of which as it appears to the imagination of these people is different from what is intended by us. Know this also. [*Guide*, p. 43]

AS I HAVE MENTIONED PARABLES, WE SHALL MAKE THE FOLLOWING INTRODUCTORY REMARKS: KNOW THAT THE KEY TO THE UNDERSTANDING OF ALL THAT THE PROPHETS ... HAVE SAID, AND TO THE KNOWLEDGE OF ITS TRUTH [*Guide*, p. 10]

We note the distinction between what the prophets have said, and the knowledge of the truth that they have. The point of Maimonides' discussion is that there is a great difference between them in that their apprehension is of truth in a way that their expression of it in Scripture may not be.

IS AN UNDERSTANDING OF PARABLES, AND THEIR IM-PORT, AND OF THE MEANINGS OF THE WORDS OCCUR-RING IN THEM. [*Guide*, pp. 10–11]

This is the distinction he has already made between the two purposes of *The Guide of the Perplexed*, the first purpose in reference to terms and the second purpose the explanation of very obscure parables.

Maimonides then proceeds to provide some textual foundation for his taking Scripture as the object of such an enterprise:

YOU KNOW WHAT GOD ... HAS SAID: *AND TO THE MINISTRY OF THE PROPHETS HAVE I USED SIMILI-TUDES* (Hosea 12:11). [*Guide*, p. 11]

The whole verse is

> I have also spoken unto the prophets,
> And I have multiplied visions;
> And to the ministry of the prophets have I used
> similitudes. [Hosea 12:11]

Both ground and license for Maimonides' enterprise is clearly to be found here. He provides further texts to ground and to license his enterprise:

AND YOU KNOW THAT HE HAS SAID: *PUT FORTH A RIDDLE AND SPEAK A PARABLE* (Ezekiel 17:2). [*Guide*, p. 11]

Allowing this as an instruction to Ezekiel, the reader of Ezekiel is prepared to find riddles and parables; even, as we have already pointed out, Maimonides interprets the numbers at the beginning of the book of Ezekiel as letters that make the word *ledah*, meaning "beget" and the place as an anagram of *cherub*, which he takes to mean "child," solving the riddle as meaning "the begetting of a child."

YOU KNOW TOO THAT BECAUSE OF THE FREQUENT USE PROPHETS MAKE OF PARABLES [*Guide*, p. 11]

We note here that Maimonides says of parables that they are frequent, informing us that they are not rare. This becomes all the more important when Maimonides would consider the narratives with respect to the Patriarchs as prophetic parables, as in the case of the binding of Isaac.

THE PROPHET HAS SAID: *THEY SAY OF ME: IS HE NOT A MAKER OF PARABLES?* (Ezekiel 21:5). [*Guide*, p. 11]

These two citations from Ezekiel highlight the fact that it is precisely the account of the vision of Ezekiel that is the ultimate expression of the *Maaseh Merkabah*:

YOU KNOW HOW SOLOMON BEGAN HIS BOOK: *TO UN-DERSTAND A PROVERB, AND A FIGURE: THE WORDS OF THE WISE AND THEIR DARK SAYINGS* (Proverbs 1:6). [*Guide*, p. 11]

There is a design among these four citations which may be more than fortuitous. There is first a citation from Hosea, then two citations from Ezekiel, and then one from Proverbs. Both Hosea and Proverbs may be distinguished because of their use of the sexual allegory. Hosea beings with his account of his "wife of harlotry and children of harlotry" (Hosea 1:2). And as we will presently note, Maimonides uses an extraordinarily prurient passage from Proverbs (Proverbs 7:6–21) to exemplify the use of sexual content as allegorical (pp. 13–14). Maimonides has thus sandwiched in the two citations from Ezekiel with citations that are most indicative of the sexual allegory. This may be an intimation to the reader that he might be alert to find the same in Ezekiel.

Maimonides then presents us with what we may consider a parable concerning parables, a hermeneutical parable.

AND IT IS SAID IN THE MIDRASH: TO WHAT WERE THE WORDS OF THE TORAH TO BE COMPARED BEFORE THE ADVENT OF SOLOMON? TO A WELL OF WATERS OF WHICH ARE AT A GREAT DEPTH AND COOL, YET NO MAN COULD DRINK OF THEM. NOW WHAT DID ONE CLEVER MAN DO? HE JOINED CORD WITH CORD AND ROPE WITH ROPE AND DREW THEM UP AND DRANK. THUS DID SOLOMON SAY ONE PARABLE AFTER ANOTHER AND SPEAK ONE WORD AFTER ANOTHER UNTIL HE UNDERSTOOD THE MEANING OF THE WORDS OF THE TORAH. [Guide, p. 11]

In the composition of The Guide of the Perplexed Maimonides in effect divides the cords and ropes and scatters them among the pages, and he challenges the reader to be as Solomon and join cord with cord and rope with rope. Just as the content is disguised in the Torah, so does he disguise the content in his book. And indeed Maimonides himself had to so join cord with cord and rope with rope from the Torah in order to be able to apprehend that which he would then seek to explicate in his book.

And in doing that Maimonides found that he had to make a definite distinction between the legalistic regulation of conduct of the Jewish tradition and prophecy. For he follows up his comment about cords and ropes by making that distinction:

THAT IS LITERALLY WHAT THEY SAY. I DO NOT THINK THAT ANYONE POSSESSING AN UNIMPAIRED CA-

PACITY IMAGINES THAT THE *WORDS OF THE TORAH*, REFERRED TO HERE, THAT ONE CONTRIVES TO UN-DERSTAND THROUGH UNDERSTANDING THE MEANING OF PARABLES, ARE ORDINANCES CON-CERNING THE BUILDING OF *TABERNACLES*, THE *LU-LAB*, AND THE *LAW OF THE FOUR TRUSTEES*. RATHER WHAT THIS TEXT HAS IN VIEW HERE IS, WITHOUT ANY DOUBT, THE UNDERSTANDING OF OB-SCURE MATTERS. [*Guide*, p. 11]

This is analogous to the way in which Rabbi Akiva is scolded in the Talmud:

So Ben Azariah said to Rabbi Akiva [after Rabbi Akiva had interpreted the meaning of the two thrones mentioned in the Book of Daniel sexually and allegorically]: Akiva! What business do you have with Aggadah? Confine your words to [the laws respecting] signs of leprosy and tents. [*Hagigah* 14a]

Maimonides keeps the distinction but seems to scold Ben Azariah and his like for their literal legalism.

Maimonides then presents a second hermeneutical parable con-cerning parables.

ABOUT THIS IT HAS BEEN SAID: *OUR RABBIS SAY: A MAN WHO LOSES A SELA OR A PEARL IN HIS HOUSE CAN FIND THE PEARL BY LIGHTING A TAPER WORTH AN ISSAR. IN THE SAME WAY THIS PARABLE IS WORTH NOTHING, BUT BY MEANS OF IT YOU CAN UNDERSTAND THE WORDS OF THE TORAH*. [*Guide*, p. 11]

He then provides an interpretation of this parable:

THIS TOO IS LITERALLY WHAT THEY SAY. NOW CON-SIDER THE EXPLICIT AFFIRMATION OF [THE SAGES] ... THAT THE INTERNAL MEANING OF *THE WORDS OF THE TORAH* IS A *PEARL* WHEREAS THE EXTERNAL MEANING OF ALL PARABLES IS WORTH *NOTHING* [*Guide*, p. 11]

The value of the external meaning of the parables is greater than nothing for Maimonides, for he regards the external meaning as having value, especially for the vulgar. But in this context the "nothing" may, for Maimonides, be hyperbolic:

AND THEIR COMPARISON OF THE CONCEALMENT OF THE SUBJECT BY ITS PARABLE'S EXTERNAL MEANING TO A MAN WHO LET A PEARL DROP IN HIS HOUSE, WHICH WAS DARK AND FULL OF FURNITURE. NOW THE PEARL IS THERE [Guide, p. 11]

We draw attention again to Maimonides' view of the objective reality of hidden meaning in Scripture.

BUT HE DOES NOT SEE IT AND DOES NOT KNOW WHERE IT IS. IT IS AS THOUGH IT WERE NO LONGER IN HIS POSSESSION, AS IT IS IMPOSSIBLE FOR HIM TO DE-RIVE ANY BENEFIT FROM IT UNTIL, AS HAS BEEN MEN-TIONED, HE LIGHTS A LAMP – AN ACT TO WHICH AN UNDERSTANDING OF THE MEANING OF THE PARABLE CORRESPONDS. [Guide, p. 11]

Maimonides continues with a third parable, one that gives an indication of the interpretation of parables:

THE SAGE HAS SAID: A WORD FITLY SPOKEN IS LIKE APPLES OF GOLD IN SETTINGS [MASKIYYOT] OF SILVER (Proverbs 25:11). [Guide, p. 11]

And he explains it now by elaborating not on the meaning of the image, but by providing the concrete meanings associated with the external meaning of the the parable. That is, he provides here not only the internal meaning of the parable, but details that are not stated explicitly in the words themselves.

This, as we shall see, is an extremely important feature of Maimonides' statement. For the sexual details may be of such a limited nature in Scripture and may be insufficient even to be recognized as such. Many readers will be like those who do not know what "apples of gold in settings of silver" are, even prior to knowing what they may be allegories of. Maimonides sets forth to explain what "apples of gold in settings of silver" are:

HEAR NOW AN ELUCIDATION OF THE THOUGHT THAT HE HAS SET FORTH. THE TERM *MASKIYYOT* DENOTES FILIGREE TRACERIES; I MEAN TO SAY TRAC-ERIES IN WHICH THERE ARE APERTURES WITH VERY SMALL EYELETS, LIKE THE HANDIWORK OF SILVER-SMITHS. THEY ARE SO-CALLED BECAUSE A GLANCE PENETRATES THROUGH THEM; FOR IN THE [ARA-MAIC] *TRANSLATION* OF THE BIBLE THE HEBREW TERM *VA-YASHQEPH*–MEANING, HE GLANCED–IS TRANSLATED *VA-ISTEKHE* [FROM THE SAME ROOT AS *MASKIYYOT*]. [*Guide,* pp. 11–12]

Having provided this elaboration of such details unmentioned in the text, Maimonides continues:

THE SAGE ACCORDINGLY SAID THAT A SAYING UT-TERED WITH A VIEW TO TWO MEANINGS IS LIKE AN APPLE OF GOLD OVERLAID WITH SILVER FILIGREE–WORK HAVING VERY SMALL HOLES. NOW SEE HOW MARVELOUSLY THIS DICTUM DESCRIBES A WELL-CON-STRUCTED PARABLE. FOR HE SAYS THAT IN A SAYING THAT HAS TWO MEANINGS–HE MEANS AN EX-TERNAL AND AN INTERNAL ONE–THE EXTERNAL MEANING OUGHT TO BE MORE BEAUTIFUL, THE FORMER BEING IN COMPARISON TO THE LATTER AS GOLD IS TO SILVER. [*Guide,* p.12]

We note here a withdrawal from the idea that the external meaning has no value. Here, in this parable, the external meaning has a lesser value, albeit considerable in itself. Indeed, he carries this point even further to specify two values associated with the external meaning. The first is as an indication concerning the internal meaning:

ITS EXTERNAL MEANING ALSO OUGHT TO CONTAIN IN IT SOMETHING THAT INDICATES TO SOMEONE CONSIDERING IT WHAT IS TO BE FOUND IN ITS IN-TERNAL MEANING, AS HAPPENS IN THE CASE OF AN

APPLE OVERLAID WITH SILVER FILIGREE-WORK
HAVING VERY SMALL HOLES. WHEN LOOKED AT FROM
A DISTANCE OR WITH IMPERFECT ATTENTION, IT IS
DEEMED TO BE AN APPLE OF SILVER; BUT WHEN A
KEEN-SIGHTED OBSERVER LOOKS AT IT WITH FULL
ATTENTION, ITS INTERIOR BECOMES CLEAR TO HIM.
[*Guide*, p. 12]

The second pertains to the consequences to social welfare of the
external meaning:

THE PARABLES OF THE PROPHETS ... ARE SIMILAR.
THEIR EXTERNAL MEANING CONTAINS WISDOM
THAT IS USEFUL IN MANY RESPECTS, AMONG WHICH
IS THE WELFARE OF HUMAN SOCIETIES, AS IS SHOWN
BY THE EXTERNAL MEANING OF *PROVERBS* AND OF
SIMILAR SAYINGS. [*Guide*, p. 12]

His understanding of this value is exemplified in the seduction story
from Proverbs that he is about to cite.

And then, again alluding to the distinction between beliefs and
actions, the former associated with prophecy, the latter with law, he
says:

THEIR INTERNAL MEANING, ON THE OTHER HAND,
CONTAINS WISDOM THAT IS USEFUL FOR BELIEFS CON-
CERNED WITH THE TRUTH AS IT IS. [*Guide*, p. 12]

We note that he says beliefs, and does not say actions.

We note also that for, Maimonides, the "truth as it is" is associated
with the internal meaning of Scripture and not with the external
meaning. This patently indicates Maimonides' belief that there is an
access to "truth as it is" in dreams and visions. Such access is available
to prophets, and not available to philosophers.

Maimonides then returns to elaborate on the notion that

THE PROPHETIC PARABLES ARE OF TWO KINDS. [*Guide*,
p. 12]

In the first kind,

EACH WORD HAS MEANING [*Guide,* p. 12]

In the second kind,

THE PARABLE AS A WHOLE INDICATES THE WHOLE OF THE INTENDED MEANING. [*Guide,* p. 12]

We are cautioned against assuming that the words in the second kind are to be interpreted in the way in which words are interpreted in the first kind.

IN SUCH A PARABLE VERY MANY WORDS ARE TO BE FOUND, NOT EVERY ONE OF WHICH ADDS SOMETHING TO THE INTENDED MEANING. [*Guide,* p. 12]

This, we might say, means that we should not make much of the word "fox" as containing any important meaning in the story of the fox and the grapes:

THEY SERVE RATHER TO EMBELLISH THE PARABLE AND TO RENDER IT MORE COHERENT OR TO CONCEAL FURTHER THE INTENDED MEANING; HENCE THE SPEECH PROCEEDS IN SUCH A WAY AS TO ACCORD WITH EVERYTHING REQUIRED BY THE PARABLE'S EX- TERNAL MEANING. UNDERSTAND THIS WELL. [*Guide,* p. 12]

Maimonides then proceeds to exemplify how one might go about analyzing a parable of the first kind. He uses the account of a dream that Jacob is reported to have had given in Scripture. The scriptural account is as follows:

And Jacob went out from Beer-sheba, and went toward Haran. And he lighted upon the place, and tarried there all night, because the sun had set; and he took one of the stones of the place, and put it under his head, and lay down in that place to sleep. And he dreamed, and behold a ladder set up on the earth, and the top of it reached to heaven; and behold the angels of God ascending and descending on it. And, behold, the Lord stood beside him, and said. . . . [Genesis 28:10–13]

Maimonides' analysis of this proceeds as follows:

AN EXAMPLE OF THE FIRST KIND OF PROPHETIC PAR-
ABLE IS THE FOLLOWING TEXT: *AND BEHOLD A
LADDER SET UP ON THE EARTH, AND SO ON.* IN THIS
TEXT, THE WORD *LADDER* INDICATES ONE SUBJECT;
THE WORDS *SET UP ON THE EARTH* INDICATE A
SECOND SUBJECT; THE WORDS *AND THE TOP OF IT
REACHED TO HEAVEN* INDICATE A THIRD SUBJECT;
THE WORDS *AND BEHOLD THE ANGELS OF GOD* INDI-
CATE A FOURTH SUBJECT; THE WORD *ASCENDING*
INDICATES A FIFTH SUBJECT; THE WORDS *AND DE-
SCENDING* INDICATE A SIXTH SUBJECT; AND THE
WORDS *AND BEHOLD THE LORD STOOD ABOVE IT*
INDICATE A SEVENTH SUBJECT. [*Guide*, p. 12]

He states:

THUS EVERY WORD OCCURRING IN THIS PARABLE
REFERS TO AN ADDITIONAL SUBJECT IN THE COM-
PLEX OF SUBJECTS REPRESENTED BY THE PARABLE AS
A WHOLE. [*Guide*, p. 12]

This idea, that a dream can represent a set of different idea-com-
plexes all superficially united into a narrative in a dream, which we
find here in Maimonides, is taken as fundamental to theory and
practice in dream interpretation by Freud in his *The Interpretation of
Dreams*. Freud states this as follows:

Our first step in the employment [in dream interpretation] of this
procedure teaches us that what we must take as the object of our
attention is not the dream as a whole but the separate portions of its
content. If I say to a patient who is still a novice: "What occurs to you
in connection with this dream?", as a rule his mental horizon becomes
blank. If, however, I put the dream before him cut into pieces, he will
give me a series of associations to each piece, which might be described
as the "background thoughts" of that particular part of the dream. Thus
the method of dream-interpretation which I practice . . . approximates
to the . . . "decoding method." Like the [decoding method] it employs
interpretation *en detail* and not *en masse*; like the latter, it regards

dreams from the very first as being of a composite character, as being conglomerates of psychical formation. [Freud, pp. 103–104]

[We] disregard the apparent coherence between the dream's constituents as an unessential illusion, and . . . trace back the origin of each of its elements on its own account. A dream is a conglomerate which, for purposes of investigation, must be broken up once more into fragments. . . . [A] psychical force is at work in dreams which creates this apparent connectedness. [Freud, p. 449]

In Maimonides' account of the way in which the dream is created he identifies that "psychical force," which "creates this apparent connectedness" which Freud speaks of here, as the imaginative faculty [*Guide*, p. 369].

AN EXAMPLE OF THE SECOND KIND OF PROPHETIC PARABLE IS THE FOLLOWING TEXT [*Guide*, p. 13]

Maimonides takes what is certainly among the most prurient sections of Scripture to exemplify the second kind of prophetic parable. It is the story of the seduction of a young man by a woman whose husband has gone on a long journey. Maimonides recites the story with a number of "and so ons," the latter including some of the more prurient lines. The scriptural text is as follows, the brackets indicating that which Maimonides indicates with "and so on":

> For at the window of my house
> I looked forth through my lattice;
> And I beheld among the thoughtless ones,
> I discerned among the youths,
> A young man void of understanding,
> Passing through the street near her house;
> In the twilight, in the evening of the day,
> In the blackness of night and the darkness.
> And, behold there met him a woman
> With the attire of a harlot, and wily of heart.
> She is riotous and rebellious,
> [Her feet abide not in her house;]

Now she is in the streets, now in the broad
    places,
[And lieth in wait at every corner.]
So she caught him
[and kissed him,
And with an impudent face she said unto
    him:]
Sacrifices of peace-offerings were due from
    me;
[This day have I paid my vows.]
Therefore came I forth to meet thee,
[To seek thy, face, and I have found thee.]
I have decked [my couch] with coverlets,
[With striped cloths of the yarn of Egypt.]
I have perfumed my bed
[With myrrh, aloes, and cinnamon.]
Come, let us take our fill of love
[until the morning;
Let us solace ourselves with loves.]
For my husband is not at home,
[He is gone a long journey;
He hath taken with him]
the bag of money;
[He will come home at the full moon.]
With her much fair speech she causeth him
    to yield,
With the blandishments of her lips she
    enticeth him away. (Proverbs 7:6–21) [*Guide*, p. 13]

We take the fact that Maimonides chooses a prurient passage to
exemplify the parables of the second kind as an indication by him of
the prurient character of the dreams and visions of the prophets.

As has already been indicated, for Maimonides the vision of Ezekiel
as described in Scripture is the ultimate instance of the *Maaseh
Merkabah*. We have also indicated that Maimonides would lead the
reader to understand the sexual content entailed in the vision of
Ezekiel. Thus he leads the reader to interpret the time and place
indications given at the beginning of Ezekiel's account to mean the
begetting of the cherubim, as we have seen. As we have also indicated,
the hermeneutic path ascribed to Rabbi Akiva in the Talmud is

two-stage, one of first apprehending the prurient, and then inter-preting the prurient as allegorical.

There are three distinct levels of interpretation for Maimonides. There is first the level of the external. According to Maimonides, however, the external has itself a value with respect to human welfare. In moving toward the internal meaning, there are the two levels associated with Rabbi Akiva. The first of these two is to note the prurient imagery in the text. And the second is identifying the "truth as it is" which is metaphorically represented by the sexual imagery.

THE OUTCOME OF ALL THIS IS A WARNING AGAINST THE PURSUIT OF BODILY PLEASURES AND DESIRES. [*Guide,* **p. 13**]

This much is clear from the external. Indeed, the scriptural text is quite plain on this, having described the youth as "thoughtless" and "devoid of understanding." And it is clear that the youth places himself in great danger by associating with this woman. For it contin-ues:

> He goeth after her straightway,
> As an ox that goeth to the slaughter,
> Or as one in fetters to the correction of the fool;
> Till an arrow strike through his liver;
> As a bird hasteneth to the snare—
> And knoweth not that it is at the cost of his life.
> [Proverbs 7:21-23]

The message is quite clear that if one associates with such women, one is likely to get into a great deal of trouble.

ACCORDINGLY HE [SOLOMON] LIKENS MATTER ... TO A *HARLOT* WHO IS ALSO A *MARRIED WOMAN*. IN FACT HIS WHOLE BOOK IS BASED ON THIS ALLEGORY. [*Guide,* p. 13]

The sexual is plain in connection with the example from Proverbs. Here he gives an indication that the sexual is not to be understood in the limited sense, but that the sexual is allegorical. Now, in connection with the vision of Ezekiel, the existence of the sexual imagery is obscure. The intimational project involves bringing the reader to recognize that, and then quickly moving on to appreciate the sexual imagery as allegorical.

The female in the narrative is to be understood as an allegory for matter, quite in the way in which Maimonides indicates this in Plato in Chapter I:17.

Maimonides explains how *harlot* and *married woman* are allegorical more clearly in Chapter III:8 than in this introduction:

> Corruption attains the form only by accident, I mean because of [form's] being joined to matter. The nature and the true reality of matter are such that it never ceases to be joined to privation; hence no form remains constantly in it, for it perpetually puts off one form and puts on another. How extraordinary is what *Solomon* said in his wisdom when likening matter *to a married harlot*, for matter is in no way found without form and is consequently always *like a married woman* who is never separated from a man and is never free. However, notwith-standing her being a married woman, she never ceases to seek for another man to substitute for her husband, and she deceives and draws him on in every way until he obtains from her what her husband used to obtain. This is the state of matter. For whatever form is found in it, does but prepare to receive another form. And it does not cease to move with a view to putting off that form that actually is in it and to obtaining another form; and the selfsame state obtains after that other form has been obtained in actu. It has then become clear that all passing-away and corruption or deficiency are due solely to matter. [*Guide*, p. 431]

AND WE SHALL EXPLAIN IN VARIOUS CHAPTERS OF THIS TREATISE HIS WISDOM IN LIKENING MATTER TO A MARRIED HARLOT, AND WE SHALL EXPLAIN HOW HE CONCLUDED THIS BOOK OF HIS WITH A EULOGY OF THE WOMAN WHO IS NOT A HARLOT BUT CONFINES HERSELF TO ATTENDING TO THE WELFARE OF HER HOUSEHOLD AND HUSBAND. [*Guide,* p. 13]

The basic path of Maimonides in *The Guide of the Perplexed* is to note that the text has two levels of meanings, external and internal.

The external is immediately relevant to human welfare. The internal is given in sexual imagery, and is to be interpreted allegorically. But there is yet another part to Maimonides' enterprise; it is to bring that which is comprehended in the allegory, that "truth as it is," to bear on human welfare as well.

Now, with respect to the sexual, Maimonides has a problem. For sexuality unregulated is destructive with respect to human welfare. In this way, matter, which is essential to human existence, also becomes the representative of sexuality in the corrupting sense. In the course of this problem Maimonides is involved in a psychological theory of the relationship of matter to human conduct. Having presented the image of the married harlot, Maimonides seeks to contrast that with the "eulogy of the *woman* who is not a *harlot* but confines herself to attending to the welfare of her household and husband." The allusion is to the celebration of the woman of valor in Proverbs:

> A woman of valor who can find?
> For her price is far above rubies.
>
> The heart of her husband doth safely trust in
>   her,
> And he has no lack of gain.
>
> She doeth him good and not evil
> All the days of her life.
>
> She seeketh wool and flax,
> And worketh willingly with her hands.
>
> She is like the merchant-ships;
> She bringeth food from afar.
>
> She riseth also while it is yet night,
> And giveth food to her household,
> And a portion to her maidens.
>
> She considereth a field, and buyeth it;
> With the fruit of her hands she planteth a
>   vineyard.

She girdeth her loins with strength,
And maketh strong her arms.

She perceiveth that her merchandise is good;
Her lamp goeth not out by night.

She layeth her hands to the distaff,
And her hands hold the spindle.

She stretcheth out her hand to the poor;
Yea, she reacheth forth her hands to the needy.

She is not afraid of the snow for her household;
For all her household are clothed with scarlet.

She maketh for herself coverlets;
Her clothing is fine linen and purple.

Her husband is known in the gates,
When he sitteth among the elders of the land.

She maketh linen garments and selleth them;
And delivereth girdles unto the merchants.

Strength and dignity are her clothing;
And she laugheth at the time to come.

She openeth her mouth with wisdom;
And the law of kindness is on her tongue.

She looketh well to the ways of her household,
And eateth not the bread of idleness.

Her children rise up, and call her blessed;
Her husband also, and he praiseth her:

"Many daughters have done valiantly,
But thou excellest them all."

Grace is deceitful, and beauty is vain;
But a woman that feareth the Lord, she shall be
  praised.

Give her of the fruit of her hands;
And let her works praise her in the gates.
                              [Proverbs 31:10–31]

The story of the married harlot is used by Maimonides to indicate an internal meaning behind the manifestly prurient. The reader should not take that story in Scripture as a model for conduct. In the later story, the model is rather of the woman of valor, if one attends only to the external meaning.

FOR ALL THE HINDRANCES KEEPING MAN FROM HIS ULTIMATE PERFECTION, EVERY DEFICIENCY AF-FECTING HIM AND EVERY DISOBEDIENCE, COME FROM HIS MATTER ALONE, AS WE SHALL EXPLAIN IN THIS TREATISE. [*Guide*, p. 13]

The story of the married harlot is a summary of the theory of the role of matter as causative with respect to human physical, psychological, and social ills.

THIS IS THE PROPOSITION THAT CAN BE UNDER-STOOD FROM THIS PARABLE AS A WHOLE. [*Guide*, pp. 13–14]

Referring to the external meaning:

I MEAN THAT MAN SHOULD NOT FOLLOW HIS BESTIAL NATURE; I MEAN HIS MATTER, FOR THE PROXIMATE MATTER OF MAN IS IDENTICAL WITH THE PROXI-MATE MATTER OF THE OTHER LIVING BEINGS. [*Guide*, p. 14]

He then says:

AND AS I HAVE EXPLAINED THIS TO YOU AND DIS-CLOSED THE SECRET OF THIS PARABLE [*Guide*, p. 14]

That the sexual in it is allegorical, referring to matter.

> YOU SHOULD NOT HOPE [TO FIND SOME SIGNIFICA-
> TION CORRESPONDING TO EVERY SUBJECT OCCUR-
> RING IN THE PARABLE] [*Guide*, p. 14]

That is, this is not a parable of the first kind.

> ... SO THAT YOU COULD SAY: WHAT CAN BE SUB-
> MITTED FOR THE WORDS, *SACRIFICES OF PEACE-OF-
> FERINGS WERE DUE FROM ME: THIS DAY HAVE I PAID
> MY VOWS?* [*Guide*, p. 14]

"This day have I paid my vows" was under an "and so on" in his citation above.

> WHAT SUBJECT IS INDICATED BY THE WORDS, *I HAVE
> DECKED MY COUCH WITH COVERLETS?* [*Guide*, p. 14]

"My couch" was under an "and so on" in his citation above.

> AND WHAT SUBJECT IS ADDED TO THIS GENERAL
> PROPOSITION BY THE WORDS, "FOR MY HUSBAND IS
> NOT AT HOME"? THE SAME HOLDS TRUE FOR THE
> OTHER DETAILS IN THIS CHAPTER. FOR ALL OF THEM
> FIGURE IN THE CONSISTENT DEVELOPMENT OF THE
> PARABLE'S EXTERNAL MEANING [*Guide*, p. 14]

In this parable, which is a parable of the second kind, the sexuality referred to is in the external meaning. In the vision of Ezekiel, the text is less open with respect to sexuality in the external meaning. Thus, while attention to the sexual is to be drawn at this early point in *The Guide of the Perplexed* toward the end of making the reader have some sense of the significance of sexuality with respect to understanding prophecy, this prurient passage is not thereby representative of the imagery to be found in the dreams and visions of the prophets, in which that imagery serves to represent the creativity of God in the ongoing world after the first Sabbath.

THE CIRCUMSTANCES BEING DESCRIBED IN IT BEING
OF A KIND TYPICAL FOR ADULTERERS. ALSO THE
SPOKEN WORDS AND OTHER SUCH DETAILS ARE OF A
KIND TYPICAL OF WORDS SPOKEN AMONG ADULTER-
ERS. [*Guide*, p. 14]

And then, a special drawing of the reader's attention to the
significance of sexuality in connection with the appreciation of prophecy:

UNDERSTAND THIS WELL FROM WHAT I HAVE SAID
FOR IT IS A GREAT AND IMPORTANT PRINCIPLE WITH
REGARD TO MATTERS THAT I WISH TO EXPLAIN.
[*Guide*, p. 14]

Maimonides then provides some warning. He is very aware of the
variety of ways in which what he says can lead a reader astray, albeit
he is certain that if the student truly follows the way he has in mind,
he will be led to the most glorious of human conditions.

One of the ways in which one can go astray is to make the mistake
of taking a parable of the second kind—let us call it the parable-in-
whole—as a parable of the first kind—let us call that a parable-conglomerate.

Now, for Maimonides, the parable-conglomerate is rare. He is
aware that assuming that a parable is a parable-conglomerate can lead
to serious error. Thus, while it was necessary for him to identify and
suggest the method of interpretation associated with the parable-conglomerate, as in Jacob's dream of the ladder, he ends this section as
though to wave it aside:

WHEN, THEREFORE, YOU FIND THAT IN SOME
CHAPTER OF THIS TREATISE I HAVE EXPLAINED THE
MEANING OF A PARABLE AND HAVE DRAWN YOUR
ATTENTION TO THE GENERAL PROPOSITION SIGNI-
FIED BY IT, YOU SHOULD NOT INQUIRE INTO ALL THE
DETAILS OCCURRING IN THE PARABLE, NOR SHOULD
YOU WISH TO FIND SIGNIFICATIONS CORRESPONDING
TO THEM. [*Guide*, p. 14]

This would result in the kind of thing that happened after the introduction of psychoanalysis by Freud, the rise of "wild psychoanalysis." In doing this the person would lose the right way, and go the wrong way:

FOR DOING SO WOULD LEAD YOU INTO ONE OF TWO WAYS: EITHER INTO TURNING ASIDE FROM THE PARABLE'S INTENDED SUBJECT, OR INTO ASSUMING AN OBLIGATION TO INTERPRET THINGS NOT SUSCEPTIBLE OF INTERPRETATION AND THAT HAVE NOT BEEN INSERTED WITH A VIEW TO INTERPRETATION. [Guide, p. 14]

The wrong way is exemplified by the sects of the world:

THE ASSUMPTION OF SUCH AN OBLIGATION WOULD RESULT IN EXTRAVAGANT FANTASIES SUCH AS ARE ENTERTAINED AND WRITTEN ABOUT IN OUR TIME BY MOST OF THE SECTS OF THE WORLD, SINCE EACH OF THESE SECTS DESIRES TO FIND CERTAIN SIGNIFICATIONS FOR WORDS WHOSE AUTHOR IN NO WISE HAD IN MIND THE SIGNIFICATIONS WISHED BY THEM. [Guide, p. 14]

We note that Maimonides has two standards against which the validity of interpretation is to be measured. The first is "truth as it is." The second is mentioned here, that the interpretation must correspond to the intentions of the author in some fashion. The direction is given:

YOUR PURPOSE, RATHER, SHOULD ALWAYS BE TO KNOW, REGARDING MOST PARABLES, THE WHOLE THAT WAS INTENDED TO BE KNOWN. [Guide, p. 14]

We note that this states clearly "in most parables." That is, Maimonides is indicating that most parables are of the second kind rather than the first. And the following is to be understood with respect to the second kind of parable:

IN SOME MATTERS IT WILL SUFFICE YOU TO GATHER FROM MY REMARKS THAT A GIVEN STORY IS A PARA-BLE, EVEN IF WE EXPLAIN NOTHING MORE; FOR ONCE YOU KNOW IT IS A PARABLE, IT WILL IMMEDIATELY BECOME CLEAR TO YOU WHAT IT IS A PARABLE OF. [Guide, p. 14]

That is, what it is an allegory of. Not, as in the case of the parable of the first kind, in which a word is given its meaning in violation of the context.

MY REMARKING THAT IT IS A PARABLE WILL BE LIKE SOMEONE'S REMOVING A SCREEN FROM BETWEEN THE EYE AND A VISIBLE THING. [Guide, p. 14]

That is, the interpretation will be relatively easy, and require little in the way of additional aid. This contrasts with the parables of the first kind. For there, Maimonides is at pains to write chapter after chapter dealing with terms, and showing a variety of alternative meanings the particular terms may have. The long lexicographical section with which *The Guide of the Perplexed* begins must pertain to the parables of the first kind, although they are fewer in number than the parables of the second kind.

Having, as it were, engaged in this misdirection—of opening the way to appreciate prophecy of the first kind, the prophecy expressed in terms, the prophecy corresponding to "the first purpose of this Treatise" [Guide, p. 5], Maimonides has used his discussion of the prophecy of allegorical parables, the prophecy corresponding to the second purpose [of the Treatise] to confound what he has said about the prophecy of the first kind—Maimonides proceeds to give us a section with a variety of indications and intimations concerning misdirection itself. He thus opens the new section entitled

INSTRUCTION WITH RESPECT TO THIS TREATISE. [Guide, p. 15]

It will be helpful if we give some notion of what it is that Maimonides is so concerned with both revealing and concealing. Let us consider at least one of the reasons for any reader believing that what is concealed is sexual. Let us highlight the account of the child who died as a result of apprehending the meaning of *hashmal* in the book of

Ezekiel, which is cited in the Talmud. We place ourselves in the position of Maimonides reading this, and we speculate what his idea of it could have been. We will be able to understand Maimonides' concealment process the better if we have some notion of what it is that he thinks is being concealed.

The matter of the child is mentioned twice in the Talmud. We cite them both.

> But may one expound [the mysteries of] *hashmal?* For behold there was once a child who expounded [the mysteries of] *hashmal*, and a fire went forth and consumed him. [*Hagigah* 13a]

And then again:

> The Rabbis taught: There was once a child who was reading in his teacher's house the Book of Ezekiel, and he apprehended what *hashmal* was, whereupon a fire went forth from *hashmal* and consumed him. [*Hagigah* 13a]

Let us look at the three places in which the word *hashmal* appears. If we allow the word *ein* to mean a well—or a fountain or a spring—as Maimonides leads us to in Chapter I:4, the three instances are as follows:

> And I looked, and behold . . . a great cloud . . . and out of the midst thereof as a fountain of *hashmal*. . . . [Ezekiel 1:4]

> And I saw, as a fountain of *hashmal* . . . from the appearance of his loins and upward, and from the appearance of his loins and downward. . . . [Ezekiel 1:27]

> And I saw . . . from the appearance of his loins and downward . . . and from his loins upward . . . as the appearance . . . as a fountain of *hashmalah*. [Ezekiel 8:2]

It could not be otherwise but that these verses have been taken as intimating sexuality to some readers. And if we seek to find an explanation as to why a story might exist that a child apprehended the meaning of *hashmal* and was destroyed, it is that the child took these verses in the sexual sense. The story itself, as presented in the Talmud, is then an indication of the sexual sense. Nor can we imagine that any scholar of stature, let alone of Maimonides' stature, could read this in the Talmud and not have it occur to him that the child apprehended the words from the account by Ezekiel in the sexual sense.

The task that Maimonides has in *The Guide of the Perplexed* is to write eventually of the full meaning of the vision of Ezekiel, taking it to the sexual, and then going from the sexual to the more general meaning that the sexual is a representation of, and *not revealing the sexual to any reader who has not apprehended it on his own.*

IF YOU WISH TO GRASP THE TOTALITY OF WHAT THIS TREATISE CONTAINS [*Guide*, p. 15]

There is a totality, a unity to the whole of it.

SO THAT NOTHING OF IT WILL ESCAPE YOU, THEN YOU MUST CONNECT ITS CHAPTERS TO ONE AN-OTHER; [*Guide*, p. 15]

We recall that Maimonides has "scattered" what he has to say. The wholeness of that which he has to say and the wholeness of the literary components coincide.

AND WHEN READING A GIVEN CHAPTER, YOUR IN-TENTION MUST BE NOT ONLY TO UNDERSTAND THE TOTALITY OF THE SUBJECT OF THAT CHAPTER, BUT ALSO TO GRASP EACH WORD THAT OCCURS IN IT IN THE COURSE OF THE SPEECH, EVEN IF THAT WORD DOES NOT BELONG TO THE INTENTION OF THE CHAP-TER. [*Guide*, p. 15]

We note that in the same way as Maimonides has led the reader to read with a sense of the necessity of violating context with respect to Scripture, he is to read *The Guide of the Perplexed* in the same manner. Maimonides tells the reader he should expect little or nothing in *The Guide of the Perplexed* to be accidental in the sense of being outside the conscious intention of its author.

FOR THE DICTION OF THIS TREATISE HAS NOT BEEN CHOSEN AT HAPHAZARD, BUT WITH EXACTNESS AND EXCEEDING PRECISION [*Guide*, p. 15]

It is also complete with respect to the relevant points.

AND WITH CARE TO AVOID FAILING TO EXPLAIN ANY OBSCURE POINT. [*Guide*, p. 15]

Maimonides makes it clear that there is a totally organized text of *The Guide of the Perplexed* in his mind. What he says suggests that he had a clearer, less scattered pre-manuscript or outline of *The Guide of the Perplexed*, which was not for publication.

AND NOTHING HAS BEEN MENTIONED OUT OF ITS PLACE, SAVE WITH A VIEW TO EXPLAINING SOME MATTER IN ITS PROPER PLACE. [*Guide*, p. 15]

Maimonides then turns to some specific instructions to the reader as to how to deal with a work that has been so composed. He has two instructions. The first is constraint:

YOU THEREFORE SHOULD NOT LET YOUR FANTASIES ELABORATE ON WHAT IS SAID HERE, FOR THAT WOULD HURT ME AND BE OF NO USE TO YOURSELF. [*Guide*, p. 15]

The constraint is with respect to the use of the imagination. The point is to be highlighted. For we have noted that Maimonides has a significant place for the role of the imagination in connection with prophecy. But it is that the imagination works on material that is apprehended by a cultivated, rational intellect in the first place. Imagination that operates in a void of contribution from the rational faculty is something to be avoided. It is indeed the psychological basis of idolatry for Maimonides.

The next instruction is great diligence in studying *The Guide of the Perplexed*.

YOU OUGHT RATHER TO LEARN EVERYTHING THAT
OUGHT TO BE LEARNED AND CONSTANTLY STUDY
THIS TREATISE. [*Guide*, p. 15]

Following these two rules will produce the result intended by
Maimonides:

FOR IT THEN WILL ELUCIDATE FOR YOU MOST OF THE
OBSCURITIES OF THE LAW THAT APPEAR AS DIFFI-
CULT TO EVERY INTELLIGENT MAN. [*Guide*, p. 15]

The word "law" here, Torah, is to be taken in the largest sense of the
word as meaning "the teaching." It is not in the sense of the commandments with respect to conduct; it is with respect to belief and opinion,
for the project is the explanation of prophecy.

Maimonides then makes some requests with respect to communication to others by the reader. These instructions have played a
significant role in the literary history of *The Guide of the Perplexed* from
the time of its composition. They have imposed a kind of silence with
respect to exposition, for many who read it felt constrained to obey
Maimonides as they understood him and to withhold their understandings from others. This instruction must, however, be read carefully, for it is not an instruction to be silent. It is an instruction not to
deviate from that which Maimonides takes to be that which is truly
indicated, the nature of prophecy as this was understood by the sages.
Maimonides says:

I ADJURE ... EVERY READER OF THIS TREATISE NOT
TO COMMENT UPON A SINGLE WORD OF IT AND NOT
TO EXPLAIN TO ANOTHER ANYTHING IN IT [*Guide*, p.
15]

But it does not end there. Rather, it continues with:

SAVE THAT WHICH HAS BEEN EXPLAINED AND COM-
MENTED UPON IN THE WORDS OF THE FAMOUS SAGES
OF OUR LAW WHO PRECEDED ME. [*Guide*, p. 15]

Maimonides is against independent exposition without reference to the sages. Indeed, the whole of *The Guide of the Perplexed* is not, from the point of view of Maimonides, an original work. Quite the contrary. His only claim with respect to his own understanding is that he has understood that which the sages understood in the material on the prophets to be found in Scripture.

As a teacher, it is Maimonides' aim to direct the attention of the reader to the same sources he draws from:

BUT WHATEVER HE UNDERSTANDS FROM THIS TREATISE OF THOSE THINGS THAT HAVE NOT BEEN SAID BY ANY OF THE FAMOUS SAGES OTHER THAN MYSELF SHOULD NOT BE EXPLAINED TO ANOTHER [*Guide*, p. 15]

And certainly the reader should not make the mistake of misattributing things to Maimonides:

NOR SHOULD HE HASTEN TO REFUTE ME, FOR THAT WHICH HE UNDERSTOOD ME TO SAY MIGHT BE CONTRARY TO MY INTENTION. HE THUS WOULD HARM ME IN RETURN FOR MY HAVING WANTED TO BENEFIT HIM AND WOULD *REPAY EVIL FOR GOOD* (Psalm 38:21). [*Guide*, p. 15]

It is clear that Maimonides does not constrain the communication of these materials; he would constrain only the communication of that which is not close to his text and the texts of the sages. The communication of what is in *The Guide of the Perplexed* should not be made without consideration of the sources from which the understanding of the author derives. It is likely to be misleading, likely to be the product of the ill-informed imagination of a reader. There is, unfortunately, much commentary on *The Guide of the Perplexed* that is not conscientious in going to the sources, especially the Talmudic sources, that he indicates.

He speaks of three possible kinds of readings. There might be a reader who is helped with one point, and that would be good.

ALL INTO WHOSE HANDS IT FALLS SHOULD CONSIDER
IT WELL; AND IF IT SLAKES HIS THIRST, THOUGH IT BE
ON ONLY ONE POINT FROM AMONG THE MANY THAT
ARE OBSCURE, HE SHOULD THANK GOD AND BE CON-
TENT WITH WHAT HE HAS UNDERSTOOD. [*Guide*, p. 15]

Or one who is not helped even on one point.

IF, ON THE OTHER HAND, HE FINDS NOTHING IN THIS
TREATISE THAT MIGHT BE OF USE TO HIM IN ANY
RESPECT, HE SHOULD THINK OF IT AS NOT HAVING
BEEN COMPOSED AT ALL. [*Guide*, p. 15]

And there may even be readers who may think that what he reads is
harmful. He begs them to give him the benefit of the doubt.

IF ANYTHING IN IT, ACCORDING TO HIS WAY OF
THINKING [*Guide*, p. 15]

which, of course, Maimonides knows to be in error.

APPEARS TO BE IN SOME WAY HARMFUL, HE SHOULD
INTERPRET IT, EVEN IF IN A FAR-FETCHED WAY, IN
ORDER TO *PASS A FAVORABLE JUDGMENT* [*Guide*,
p. 15]

So, says Maimonides, just as one gives the vulgar the benefit of the
doubt, so do with respect to him.

FOR AS WE ARE ENJOINED TO ACT IN THIS WAY TO-
WARD OUR VULGAR ONES, ALL THE MORE SHOULD
THIS BE WITH RESPECT TO OUR ERUDITE ONES AND
SAGES OF OUR LAW WHO ARE TRYING TO HELP US TO
THE TRUTH AS THEY APPREHEND IT. [*Guide*, pp. 15-16]

Just as Maimonides is concerned with a reader who fails to appreciate the work of the sages in connection with making the meanings of
the prophetic writings in Scripture meaningful, so is he concerned
with a reader who fails to have an adequate background in philosophy. We must recall that Maimonides is in the tradition that regarded

Abraham and Moses as the originators of philosophical thought, and that the knowledge contained in the works of Aristotle was already known to the prophets before Aristotle. And we must recall that the prophets both possessed that knowledge and came to knowledge not accessible to those who are only philosophers.

However, for a reader to be able truly to appreciate the indications of prophecy in Scripture, knowledge of philosophy is a prerequisite. That is, while the history is one in which Abraham and Moses were prior to Aristotle, and while the prophets were presumed to be fully knowledgeable in regard to philosophy prior to their prophecy, yet pedagogically Maimonides understood a progression from the study of the commandments, to the study of philosophy, to the appreciation of prophecy.

I KNOW THAT, AMONG MEN GENERALLY, EVERY BE-GINNER WILL DERIVE BENEFIT FROM SOME OF THE CHAPTERS OF THIS TREATISE, THOUGH HE LACKS EVEN AN INKLING OF WHAT IS INVOLVED IN SPECULA-TION. [*Guide*, p. 16]

It is an interesting fact that Maimonides' *The Guide of the Perplexed* played the role of textbook in philosophy for many in the centuries that followed Maimonides' lifetime. As, for example, Aristotelianism became an integral part of Christianity, many Christians acquired knowledge of Aristotle through the succinct summary of Aristotelian thought contained within the pages of *The Guide of the Perplexed*. But this is a kind of historical accident, in that it is clearly beyond Maimonides' intention. Rather, he presumes that the reader of his book knows philosophy already.

A PERFECT MAN, ON THE OTHER HAND, DEVOTED TO LAW AND, AS I HAVE MENTIONED, PERPLEXED, WILL BENEFIT FROM ALL ITS CHAPTERS. HOW GREATLY WILL HE REJOICE IN THEM AND HOW PLEASANT WILL IT BE TO HEAR THEM! [*Guide*, p. 16]

Such a person, well versed in Jewish law, open to the content of philosophy, perplexed by statements in Scripture that appear impossible by virtue of what he may have learned in his study of philosophy, is prepared to enter into the kind of intellectual enterprise that *The Guide of the Perplexed* is supposed to be a guide for. He will learn to become sensitive to the fact that Scripture gives accounts of the dreams and visions of prophets, the internal content expressed unclearly; and that clarity was reserved for the prophecy of Moses, as in the clearly formulated commandments.

He will find within the pages of Maimonides' book, for example, that the account of creation given in Scripture coincides precisely with what he knows about the world from the study of philosophy—as, for example, the theory of the four elements of matter: "... the four elements [earth, water, air and fire] are ... mentioned [in the Scriptural account of creation]. ... [*Guide*, p. 351]. This, he will learn, is one of the great mysteries of the Torah. And he will appreciate that there is no discrepancy between what he knows to be the case and what he reads in Scripture.

But with those who do not know what is the case in the universe that God created, especially those who have accepted views about the nature of the universe that are false, as the Mutakallimum, it is different:

BUT THOSE WHO ARE CONFUSED AND WHOSE BRAINS HAVE BEEN POLLUTED BY FALSE OPINIONS AND MISLEADING WAYS DEEMED BY THEM TO BE TRUE SCIENCES, AND WHO HOLD THEMSELVES TO BE MEN OF SPECULATION WITHOUT HAVING ANY KNOWLEDGE OF ANYTHING THAT CAN TRULY BE CALLED SCIENCE, THOSE WILL FLEE FROM MANY OF ITS CHAPTERS. INDEED, THESE CHAPTERS WILL BE VERY DIFFICULT FOR THEM TO BEAR BECAUSE THEY CANNOT APPREHEND THEIR MEANING AND ALSO BECAUSE THEY WOULD BE LED TO RECOGNIZE THE FALSENESS OF THE COUNTERFEIT MONEY IN THEIR HANDS—THEIR TREASURE AND FORTUNE HELD READY FOR FURTHER CALAMITIES.
[*Guide*, p. 16]

Their misunderstanding with respect to philosophy constitutes a barrier. For the prophets understood the natural world properly, in the way that Aristotle—later—understood the natural world. Thus the task for the author of *The Guide of the Perplexed* is also to disabuse the reader of inappropriate philosophical notions. In the Epistle Dedicatory, the introductory letter to the single student to whom *The Guide of the Perplexed* is presumably addressed, Maimonides cites how this path into inappropriate philosophy was part of the instigation to his own pedagogy with respect to this student:

> . . . you demanded of me additional knowledge and asked me . . . to inform you of the intentions of the Mutakallimum. . . . As . . . you had already acquired some smattering of this subject. . . . you were perplexed, as stupefaction had come over you. . . . [*Guide*, pp. 3–4]

Maimonides then deals with the question of his own writing down in a book the information about the *Maaseh Bereshit* and the *Maaseh Merkabah* when the Mishnaic law would seem to forbid it:

> GOD . . . KNOWS THAT I HAVE NEVER CEASED TO BE EXCEEDINGLY APPREHENSIVE ABOUT SETTING DOWN THOSE THINGS THAT I WISH TO SET DOWN IN THIS TREATISE. FOR THEY ARE CONCEALED THINGS; NONE OF THEM HAS BEEN SET DOWN IN ANY BOOK – WRITTEN IN THE RELIGIOUS COMMUNITY IN THESE TIMES OF *EXILE* – THE BOOKS COMPOSED IN THESE TIMES BEING IN OUR HANDS. [*Guide*, p. 16]

In spite of these misgivings Maimonides does, of course, publish a book on the *Maaseh Bereshit* and the *Maaseh Merkabah*. Here he provides license to himself based on "two premises," bespeaking a sense of obligation to publish such a book:

> HOW THEN CAN I NOW INNOVATE AND SET THEM DOWN? HOWEVER, I HAVE RELIED ON TWO PREMISES, THE ONE BEING [THE SAGES'] SAYING IN A SIMILAR CASE, *IT IS TIME TO DO SOMETHING FOR THE LORD, AND SO ON*; THE SECOND BEING THEIR SAYING, *LET ALL THY ACTS BE FOR THE SAKE OF HEAVEN*. UPON THESE TWO PREMISES HAVE I RELIED WHEN SETTING DOWN WHAT I HAVE COMPOSED IN SOME OF THE CHAPTERS OF THIS TREATISE. [*Guide*, p. 16]

The "and so on" is "for they have infringed thy law" (Psalms 119:126). The thought is, even as Maimonides had explained earlier, that "Let all thy acts be for the sake of heaven" includes what might in some sense be transgression (Gorfinkle, pp. 73–74).

We have already identified Chapter II:30 on the *Maaseh Bereshit* and Chapters III:1–7 on the *Maaseh Merkabah*.

Maimonides indicates, in the introduction which he places immediately prior to his exposition of the *Maaseh Merkabah*, that the Mishnaic law has had a negative effect of making the knowledge associated with the *Maaseh Bereshit* and the *Maaseh Merkabah* nonexisting. He manifestly has some sorrow concerning this:

> This is the reason why the knowledge of this matter has ceased to exist in the entire religious community, so that nothing great or small remains of it. And it had to happen like this, for this knowledge was only transmitted from one chief to another and has never been set down in writing. [*Guide*, p. 415]

He indicates his dilemma. If he were to continue in this path, having been convinced that he had come to understand that which was concealed, ". . . as indubitably clear, manifest, and evident. . . ." [*Guide*, p. 415]. Maimonides expresses the writing of *The Guide of the Perplexed* as an obligation:

> . . . if I had omitted setting down something of that which has appeared to me as clear, so that the knowledge would perish when I perish, as is inevitable, I should have considered that conduct as extremely cowardly with regard to you and everyone who is perplexed. It would have been, as it were, robbing one who deserves the truth of the truth, or begrudging an heir his inheritance. And both of these traits are blameworthy. [*Guide*, pp. 415–416]

He states that this seems to be contrary to the Mishnaic law, ". . . as has been stated before, an explicit exposition of this knowledge is denied by a legal prohibition . . ." and even contrary to good judgment, ". . . in addition to that which is imposed by judgment" [*Guide*, p. 416]. For the Mishnaic law is not arbitrary. It, like all Jewish law, is aimed at the welfare of human beings. The Talmud indicates the view that premature exposure of children to matters associated with sexuality can be damaging. There are also the dangers of dualism and idolatry if people are exposed to these contents when they are not sufficiently mature and prepared. However, Maimonides finds two loopholes that derive from the fact that ". . . with regard to these matters, [he] followed conjecture and supposition . . ." [Guide, p. 416]. The first loophole is: ". . . no divine revelation [came to him] to teach [him] . . ." [Guide, p. 416]. The second loophole is that he, like Rabbi Akiva, ". . . did not receive . . . in these matters from a teacher" [Guide, p. 416].

The first excludes it from prophecy. That is, what he himself knows is not under the rubric of prophecy and therefore not under the ban in any way. The second excludes it from Kabbalah, the essence of which is that it is received orally from one teacher to another.

There are two further grounds for license to write his book in the face of the Mishnaic law that Maimonides invokes. One of these is that the book is written in the second person singular to an excellent person in seeming deference to the Mishnaic law that exposition is to be with respect to a single person for the Maaseh Bereshit, and not even to one person, unless he has certain characteristics, for the Maaseh Merkabah.

Maimonides indicates the pressure he was under:

TO SUM UP: I AM THE MAN WHO WHEN THE CONCERN PRESSED HIM [Guide, p. 16]

That is, the concern to teach these things.

AND HIS WAY WAS STRAITENED AND HE COULD FIND NO OTHER DEVICE BY WHICH TO TEACH A DEMON-STRATED TRUTH OTHER THAN BY GIVING SATISFAC-TION TO A SINGLE VIRTUOUS MAN WHILE DIS-PLEASING TEN THOUSAND IGNORAMUSES–I AM HE WHO PREFERS TO ADDRESS THAT SINGLE MAN BY HIMSELF, AND I DO NOT HEED THE BLAME OF THOSE MANY CREATURES. [Guide, p. 16]

But there is yet another ground Maimonides now alludes to. We recall that the Talmud has it that being "anxious of heart" is a necessary qualification—or the only qualification—for being the recipient of these esoteric teachings. We have seen how Maimonides identifies perplexity with heartache, how he would address in this book that person who ". . . would not cease to suffer from heartache and great perplexity" [Guide, p. 6].

The claim is that appropriately engaging in the exercise which The Guide of the Perplexed is, indeed, a guide to, is therapeutic:

FOR I CLAIM TO LIBERATE THAT VIRTUOUS ONE FROM THAT INTO WHICH HE HAS SUNK, AND I SHALL GUIDE HIM IN HIS PERPLEXITY UNTIL HE BECOMES PERFECT AND HE FINDS REST. [Guide, pp. 16-17]

It is to be pointed out that according to Jewish law, all Jewish law, with the exceptions of idolatry, sexual offenses, and murder, may be suspended for therapy if life is in danger, even as Maimonides states that in the Mishneh Torah, almost directly after his exposition of the Maaseh Merkabah and the Maaseh Bereshit, there in the first four chapters: "Except for the worship of strange gods, the uncovering of nakedness, and the spilling of blood, anything forbidden in the Torah may be used as a cure in the case of mortal illness" (Yesodei Hatorah V:6). We recall that Ben Azzai died, and Ben Zoma went mad, for taking a journey into these places without proper guidance.

COMMENTARY ON MAIMONIDES' STATEMENT ON CONTRADICTIONS [PAGES 17–20]

Maimonides closes this introductory chapter of The Guide of the Perplexed with a statement concerning contradictory or contrary statements to be found in literary works.

ONE OF SEVEN CAUSES SHOULD ACCOUNT FOR THE CONTRADICTORY OR CONTRARY STATEMENTS TO BE FOUND IN ANY BOOK OR COMPILATION. [Guide, p. 17]

Maimonides thus enumerates the two kinds of divergences, the contradictory, in which one member is bound to be true and the other false; and the contrary, in which two propositions cannot both be true but can both be false. The word "contradiction," used in a loose sense, often applies to both.

It will help us to understand Maimonides' intentions with respect to these seven types of contradictions by classifying them. We will modify the order in which Maimonides presents them.

True Contradiction

We indicate what may be called *true* contradiction. It is the sixth in Maimonides' enumeration.

THE SIXTH CAUSE. THE CONTRADICTION IS CON-CEALED AND BECOMES EVIDENT ONLY AFTER MANY PREMISES. THE GREATER THE NUMBER OF PREMISES NEEDED TO MAKE THE CONTRADICTION EVIDENT, THE MORE CONCEALED IT IS. IT THUS MAY ESCAPE THE AUTHOR, WHO THINKS THERE IS NO CONTRA-DICTION BETWEEN HIS TWO ORIGINAL PROPOSI-TIONS. BUT IF EACH PROPOSITION IS CONSIDERED SEP-ARATELY – A TRUE PREMISE BEING JOINED TO IT AND THE NECESSARY CONCLUSION DRAWN – AND THIS IS DONE TO EVERY CONCLUSION – A TRUE PREMISE BEING JOINED TO IT AND THE NECESSARY CONCLU-SION DRAWN – AFTER MANY SYLLOGISMS THE OUT-COME OF THE MATTER WILL BE THAT THE TWO FINAL CONCLUSIONS ARE CONTRADICTORY OR CONTRARY TO EACH OTHER. THAT IS THE KIND OF THING THAT ESCAPES THE ATTENTION OF SCHOLARS WHO WRITE BOOKS. IF, HOWEVER, THE TWO ORIGINAL PROPOSI-TIONS ARE EVIDENTLY CONTRADICTORY, BUT THE AUTHOR HAS SIMPLY FORGOTTEN THE FIRST WHEN WRITING DOWN THE SECOND IN ANOTHER PART OF HIS COMPILATION, THIS IS A VERY GREAT WEAKNESS, AND THAT MAN SHOULD NOT BE RECKONED AMONG THOSE WHOSE SPEECHES DESERVE CONSIDERATION.
[*Guide,* p. 17]

Historical Contradictions

Under the heading of *historical* contradictions, contradictions arising out of the history of the composition of the works, we include that which Maimonides designates as the first and second causes.

> THE FIRST CAUSE. THE AUTHOR HAS COLLECTED THE REMARKS OF VARIOUS PEOPLE WITH DIFFERING OPIN- IONS, BUT HAS OMITTED CITING HIS AUTHORITIES AND HAS NOT ATTRIBUTED EACH REMARK TO THE ONE WHO SAID IT. CONTRADICTORY OR CONTRARY STATEMENTS CAN BE FOUND IN SUCH COMPILATIONS BECAUSE ONE OF THE TWO PROPOSITIONS IS THE OPINION OF ONE INDIVIDUAL WHILE THE OTHER PROPOSITION IS THE OPINION OF ANOTHER INDIVID- UAL.

> THE SECOND CAUSE. THE AUTHOR OF A PARTICULAR BOOK HAS ADOPTED A CERTAIN OPINION THAT HE LATER REJECTS; BOTH HIS ORIGINAL AND LATER STATEMENTS ARE RETAINED IN THE BOOK. [*Guide*, p. 17]

Prophetic Contradictions

The *prophetic* contradictions, which are the third and the fourth in Maimonides' enumeration, are designated as such by Maimonides. Indeed, he indicates that it is precisely in connection with these prophetic contradictions that the whole of the introduction was written: "That some passages in every prophetic book, when taken in their external sense, appear to contradict or to be contrary to one another is due to the third cause and to the fourth. It was with this in view that this entire introduction was written" [*Guide*, p. 19].

The first of these two types of prophetic contradiction, which is third in Maimonides' enumeration, arises out of the difference be- tween the external and the internal meaning. There can be contradic- tion between the external and internal meanings, and there can be contradictions among the various external meanings.

THE THIRD CAUSE. NOT ALL THE STATEMENTS IN QUESTION ARE TO BE TAKEN IN THEIR EXTERNAL SENSE; SOME ARE TO BE TAKEN IN THEIR EXTERNAL SENSE, WHILE SOME OTHERS ARE PARABLES AND HENCE HAVE AN INNER CONTENT. ALTERNATIVELY, TWO APPARENTLY CONTRADICTORY PROPOSITIONS MAY BOTH BE PARABLES AND WHEN TAKEN IN THEIR EXTERNAL SENSE MAY CONTRADICT, OR BE CONTRARY TO, ONE ANOTHER. [*Guide*, p. 17]

The second of these two types of prophetic contradiction, which is Maimonides' fourth, is due to the lack of specification of some proviso or explanation in its place.

THE FOURTH CAUSE. THERE IS A PROVISO THAT, BECAUSE OF A CERTAIN NECESSITY, HAS NOT BEEN EXPLICITLY STATED IN ITS PROPER PLACE; OR THE TWO SUBJECTS MAY DIFFER, BUT ONE OF THEM HAS NOT BEEN EXPLAINED IN ITS PROPER PLACE, SO THAT A CONTRADICTION APPEARS TO HAVE BEEN SAID, WHEREAS THERE IS NO CONTRADICTION. [*Guide*, p. 17]

Pedagogical Contradictions

Maimonides then indicates two categories of *pedagogical* contradiction. These are the fifth and the seventh in his enumeration. His fifth deals with sequence of presentation:

THE FIFTH CAUSE ARISES FROM THE NECESSITY OF TEACHING AND MAKING SOMEONE UNDERSTAND. FOR THERE MAY BE A CERTAIN OBSCURE MATTER THAT IS DIFFICULT TO CONCEIVE. ONE HAS TO MENTION IT OR TO TAKE IT AS A PREMISE IN EXPLAINING SOMETHING THAT IS EASY TO CONCEIVE AND THAT BY RIGHTS OUGHT TO BE TAUGHT BEFORE THE FORMER, SINCE ONE ALWAYS BEGINS WITH WHAT IS EASIER. THE TEACHER, ACCORDINGLY, WILL HAVE TO BE LAX AND, USING ANY MEANS THAT OCCUR TO HIM OR GROSS SPECULATION, WILL TRY TO MAKE THAT FIRST MATTER SOMEHOW UNDERSTOOD. HE WILL

NOT UNDERTAKE TO STATE THE MATTER AS IT TRULY IS IN EXACT TERMS, BUT RATHER WILL LEAVE IT SO IN ACCORD WITH THE LISTENER'S IMAGINATION THAT THE LATTER WILL UNDERSTAND ONLY WHAT HE NOW WANTS HIM TO UNDERSTAND. AFTERWARDS, IN THE APPROPRIATE PLACE, THAT OBSCURE MATTER IS STATED IN EXACT TERMS AND EXPLAINED AS IT TRULY IS. [*Guide*, pp. 17–18]

His seventh deals with the content of what is concealed, and of what is disclosed.

THE SEVENTH CAUSE. IN SPEAKING ABOUT VERY OB-SCURE MATTERS IT IS NECESSARY TO CONCEAL SOME PARTS AND TO DISCLOSE OTHERS. SOMETIMES IN THE CASE OF CERTAIN DICTA THIS NECESSITY REQUIRES THAT THE DISCUSSION PROCEED ON THE BASIS OF A CERTAIN PREMISE, WHEREAS IN ANOTHER PLACE NE-CESSITY REQUIRES THAT THE DISCUSSION PROCEED ON THE BASIS OF ANOTHER PREMISE, CONTRA-DICTING THE FIRST ONE. IN SUCH CASES THE VULGAR MUST IN NO WAY BE AWARE OF THE CONTRADIC-TION; THE AUTHOR ACCORDINGLY USES SOME DE-VICE TO CONCEAL IT BY ALL MEANS. [*Guide*, p. 18]

Maimonides observes that he, in *The Guide of the Perplexed*, makes use of the *pedagogical* contradictions: "Divergences that are to be found in this Treatise are due to the fifth cause and the seventh. Know this, grasp its true meaning, and remember it very well so as not to become perplexed by some of its chapters" [*Guide*, p. 20]. We expect no true, historical, or prophetic contradictions; only the pedagogical ones.

Maimonides then brings his Introduction to the First Part to a close:

AND AFTER THESE INTRODUCTORY REMARKS, I SHALL BEGIN TO MENTION THE TERMS. [*Guide*, p. 20]

These are the terms that occur in the prophetic writings, and that have internal meanings.

WHOSE TRUE MEANING, AS INTENDED IN EVERY PAS-
SAGE ACCORDING TO ITS CONTEXT, MUST BE INDI-
CATED. [*Guide*, p. 20]

This refers to the lexicographical section that he is about to begin.
Here he enumerates various meanings that the words he selects may
have in a variety of contexts. We take him to mean that by taking
some distant meaning associated with a word in another context the
meaning in a prophetic passage will be revealed. And if we do this we
will have the extraordinary reward of being as in the Garden of Eden.

THIS, THEN, WILL BE A KEY PERMITTING ONE TO
ENTER PLACES THE GATES TO WHICH WERE LOCKED.
AND WHEN THESE GATES ARE OPENED AND THESE
PLACES ARE ENTERED INTO, THE SOULS WILL FIND
REST THEREIN, THE EYES WILL BE DELIGHTED, AND
THE BODIES EASED OF THEIR TOIL AND LABOR. [*Guide*,
p. 20]

II

A Commentary on Chapter II:30, on the Maaseh Bereshit

$\mathbf{M}$aimonides' explicit commentary on the *Maaseh Bereshit* is made in Chapter II:30, pp. 348–359. We will, however, begin our commentary at a point somewhat earlier, where Maimonides opens a new introduction in Chapter II:29 with

AS THE EXPOSITION HAS FINALLY REACHED THIS POINT [*Guide*, p. 346]

Maimonides is about to embark on the critical portion of the book, which comprises these sections:

1. The explication of the *Maaseh Bereshit*, Chapter II:30, dealing with the scriptural account of creation.
2. The chapter on the Sabbath, Chapter II:31, alluding to the creative role of God both before and after the first Sabbath.
3. The explication of the *Maaseh Merkabah*, the Introduction to Part III, and Chapters III:1–7, dealing with the scriptural account of God's ongoing acts of creation in history following the first Sabbath.

"The exposition has finally reached this point" refers to Maimonides' treatment of Aristotle. The difference with Aristotle is critical in that Aristotle's view leaves no place for God as creator—not the creation of the universe in the first place, and not a creative role for God in history subsequently.

> The matter has now become clear to you and the doctrine epitomized. Namely, we agree with Aristotle with regard to one half of his opinion . . . that what exists . . . will last forever. . . . However [we differ with Aristotle in that we believe that] that which exists has had a beginning. . . . His wisdom required that He should bring creation into existence. . . . This is our opinion and the basis of our Law. [*Guide*, p. 346]

Thus although Aristotle gives a cogent demonstration of the existence of God, at this point in the discussion, entering upon the essence of God, which is the bringing of being into being out of nothingness, Aristotle has to be dismissed:

WE SHALL NOW PUT IN A CHAPTER THAT SHALL LIKE-WISE GIVE SEVERAL INDICATIONS AS TO TEXTS CONCERNED WITH THE MAASEH BERESHIT. [*Guide*, p. 346]

This refers to Chapter II:30:

FOR THE FIRST PURPOSE OF THIS TREATISE IS TO EXPLAIN WHAT CAN BE EXPLAINED OF THE MAASEH BERESHIT AND THE MAASEH MERKABAH. [*Guide*, p. 346]

We need to juxtapose this with the statements about the first purpose being of terms, and the second purpose being of parables, which Maimonides indicated in the Introduction. Here he states the purposes as the explication of the *Maaseh Bereshit* and the *Maaseh Merkabah*. The two statements of sets of purposes converge on the topic of prophecy. While the identification of the *Maaseh Merkabah* with prophecy is not controversial, Maimonides' identification of the *Maaseh Bereshit*, with the account of creation at the beginning of Genesis, with prophecy rather than history, needs to be mentioned.

WE SHALL PUT IN THIS CHAPTER AFTER WE HAVE
FIRST SET FORTH TWO PREAMBLES OF GENERAL IM-
PORT. [*Guide*, p. 346]

As we will note, the first of the two preambles refers to the *Maaseh
Bereshit*, and the second refers to the *Maaseh Merkabah*.

ONE OF THESE IS AS FOLLOWS: NOT EVERYTHING MEN-
TIONED IN THE TORAH CONCERNING THE *MAASEH
BERESHIT* IS TO BE TAKEN IN ITS EXTERNAL SENSE AS
THE VULGAR IMAGINE. [*Guide*, p. 346]

We take note of the sharpness with which Maimonides divides the
Maaseh Bereshit from the *Maaseh Merkabah*. We take note of his
drawing attention again to the distinction between the external and
internal meanings of the texts of Scripture. We note his identification
of the taking of the external meaning as exhaustive as that which
characterizes the vulgar. And we note especially that his major point
that prophecy has both internal and external meanings applies to the
text of Genesis.

FOR IF THE MATTER WERE SUCH, THE MEN OF KNOWL-
EDGE WOULD NOT HAVE BEEN CHARY OF DIVULGING
KNOWLEDGE WITH REGARD TO IT, AND THE SAGES
WOULD NOT HAVE EXPATIATED ON ITS BEING KEPT
SECRET AND ON PREVENTING THE TALK ABOUT IT IN
THE PRESENCE OF THE VULGAR. [*Guide*, pp. 346–347]

Here he is alluding to the Mishnah and the Gemara on it. For
Maimonides, the external sense is problematic. He is persuaded that
there is some value in it, especially for the immature and the uneducated. On the other hand, the acceptance of the external as literally
true can be damaging in the sense of leading to idolatry.

FOR THE EXTERNAL SENSE OF THESE TEXTS LEADS
EITHER TO A GRAVE CORRUPTION OF THE IMAGINA-
TION [*Guide*, p. 347]

This is not the use of the imagination in the sense of prophecy in which the imaginative faculty receives from the the rational faculty.

> AND TO GIVING VENT TO EVIL OPINIONS WITH RE-
> GARD TO THE DEITY [Guide, p. 347]

Or, with respect to those who are somewhat more sophisticated,

> OR TO AN ABSOLUTE DENIAL OF THE ACTION OF THE
> DEITY AND TO DISBELIEF IN THE FOUNDATIONS OF
> THE LAW. [Guide, p. 347]

With respect to the first case, that is, with respect to those who are immature and uneducated:

> THE CORRECT THING TO DO IS TO REFRAIN, IF ONE
> LACKS ALL KNOWLEDGE OF THE SCIENCES, FROM CON-
> SIDERING THESE TEXTS MERELY WITH THE IMAGINA-
> TION. ONE SHOULD NOT ACT LIKE THE WRETCHED
> PREACHERS AND COMMENTATORS WHO THINK THAT
> A KNOWLEDGE OF THE INTERPRETATION OF WORDS IS
> SCIENCE AND IN WHOSE OPINION WORDINESS AND
> LENGTH OF SPEECH ADD TO PERFECTION. [Guide, p. 347]

The ideal path is indicated:

> ON THE OTHER HAND IT IS OBLIGATORY TO CON-
> SIDER THEM WITH WHAT IS TRULY THE INTELLECT
> AFTER ONE HAS ACQUIRED PERFECTION IN THE DE-
> MONSTRATIVE SCIENCES AND KNOWLEDGE OF THE
> SECRETS OF THE PROPHETS. [Guide, p. 347]

Again, Maimonides must allude to the Mishnaic law constraining exposition.

> HOWEVER, AS I HAVE EXPLAINED SEVERAL TIMES IN
> OUR COMMENTARY ON THE MISHNAH, NONE OF
> THOSE WHO KNOW SOMETHING OF IT SHOULD DI-
> VULGE IT. [Guide, p. 347]

At this point Maimonides throws out a hint with respect to what it is that is not to be divulged:

**AND THEY SAY EXPLICITLY: *AS FROM THE BEGIN-
NING OF THE BOOK UP TO HERE, THE GLORY OF GOD
[REQUIRES] TO CONCEAL THE THING.* THEY SAY IT AT
THE END OF WHAT IS SAID CONCERNING THE *SIXTH
DAY* [OF THE BEGINNING]. THUS WHAT WE HAVE SAID
HAS BECOME CLEAR. [*Guide,* p. 347]**

This is an allusion to the Mishnaic law, which warns against exposing the glory of one's maker. We are aware that the degree of secrecy rises from the *Maaseh Bereshit* to the *Maaseh Merkabah.* The termination of the *Maaseh Bereshit* is with the creation of man. Then comes the Sabbath, and then the *Maaseh Merkabah.* And we are led from the creation of man as a species, which took place prior to the end of the sixth day, to the creation of individual human beings, to the creation of the souls of individual human beings, after that first Sabbath. Or perhaps, even as the Jewish tradition indicates, with Friday night being favored for sexual intercourse, the creation of human souls begins with the onset of the Sabbath itself.

Immediately after having provided this hint, Maimonides tells the reader how it is his design to present such hints. In this way we are told that what has just been given is a hint.

**HOWEVER, INASMUCH AS THE DIVINE COMMAND-
MENT NECESSARILY OBLIGES EVERYONE WHO HAS OB-
TAINED A CERTAIN PERFECTION TO LET IT OVERFLOW
TOWARDS OTHERS [*Guide,* p. 347]**

We note here that Maimonides speaks not only of a license to violate the Mishnaic law, but an obligation:

**AS WE SHALL MAKE CLEAR IN THE CHAPTERS ON
PROPHECY THAT FOLLOW [*Guide,* p. 347]**

Chapter II:30 on the *Maaseh Bereshit,* Chapter II:31, the chapter on the Sabbath, the unit on the psychology of prophecy, Chapters

II:32–48, the Introduction to the Third Part, and Chapters III:1–7 on the *Maaseh Merkabah*. We take note here of how Maimonides helps the reader to identify the structure of his presentation.

Referring to himself:

EVERY MAN ENDOWED WITH KNOWLEDGE WHO HAS COME TO POSSESS AN UNDERSTANDING OF SOMETHING PERTAINING TO THESE SECRETS, EITHER THROUGH HIS OWN SPECULATION [*Guide,* p. 347]

Referring to others:

OR THROUGH BEING CONDUCTED TOWARD THIS BY A GUIDE, [*Guide,* p. 347]

including those who might read his book

MUST INDUBITABLY SAY SOMETHING. [*Guide,* p. 347]

Maimonides here even licenses commentators on his book.

It is revelatory of his state of mind that he should have moved so far in deviating from the patent sense of the Mishnaic law. Here he has generalized it to an obligation. He has even invoked some "divine commandment." The extension of this obligation to those who might just read this book, being guided by this particular "guide," *The Guide of the Perplexed* and its author who is also a guide, allows the classical reasoning: If the reader is obliged, is not the author?

Maimonides indicates his method of using hints or "flashes":

IT IS, HOWEVER, FORBIDDEN TO BE EXPLICIT ABOUT IT. HE MUST ACCORDINGLY MAKE THE SECRET APPEAR IN FLASHES. [*Guide,* p. 347]

And he defends his use of this method by indicating that such was also the practice of the sages, with the implicit argument: If the sages use the method of flashes, may this author not?

MANY SUCH FLASHES, INDICATIONS, AND POINTERS OCCUR IN THE SAYINGS OF SOME OF THE SAGES [*Guide*, p. 347]

And the sages use the method of "scattering" to which he refers in the Introduction.

BUT THESE SAYINGS ARE MIXED UP WITH THE SAY-INGS OF OTHERS AND WITH SAYINGS OF ANOTHER KIND. [*Guide*, p. 347]

Maimonides ends this explanation, after providing a critical flash in this preamble, which is presented as the first of two preambles, prior to the critical sections of the book, on *Maaseh Bereshit*, Sabbath, and *Maaseh Merkabah*, with the clear statement:

FOR THIS REASON YOU WILL FIND THAT WITH RE-GARD TO THESE MYSTERIES [*Guide*, p. 347]

The mysteries of the *Maaseh Bereshit*, and the *Maaseh Merkabah*

I ALWAYS MENTION THE SINGLE SAYING ON WHICH THE MATTER IS BASED, WHILE I LEAVE THE REST TO THOSE WHOM IT BEFITS THAT THIS SHOULD BE LEFT TO THEM. [*Guide*, p. 347]

Maimonides proceeds to the second of the two preambles:

THE SECOND PREAMBLE [*Guide*, p. 347]

We note that the two preambles correspond to the two purposes Maimonides indicated in the Introduction, with respect to words and parables. The first preamble alludes to parables, and this second preamble corresponds to words.

AS WE HAVE SAID, THE PROPHETS USE IN THEIR SPEECHES EQUIVOCAL WORDS AND WORDS THAT ARE NOT INTENDED TO MEAN WHAT THEY INDICATE AC-CORDING TO THEIR FIRST SIGNIFICATION [*Guide*, p. 347]

"First signification" being the external meaning, and the meaning dictated by the manifest context.

THE WORD BEING MENTIONED BECAUSE OF ITS DERI-VATION. [*Guide*, p. 347]

Two categories are indicated here. *Equivocal* refers to the class of homonyms designated by the letters and sounds. These are noted in the chapters of the beginning lexicographical section, with words selected, and citations to various parts of Scripture. The second category is the category of the *derivative*. There is a chapter devoted to the way in which such derivation may exist, Chapter II:43. Maimonides mentions here the example of *maqqel shaqed* [a rod of an almond tree] from Jeremiah 1:11-12, which he explains in detail in that chapter [*Guide*, p. 392].

FOR INSTANCE, THE WORDS *MAQQEL SHAQED* (A ROD OF AN ALMOND TREE) (Jeremiah 1:11) ARE USED BE-CAUSE FROM THIS INDICATION ONE MAY GO ON TO THE WORDS THAT FOLLOW: *SHOQED ANI*, AND SO ON (I WATCH OVER) (Jeremiah 1:12), AS WE SHALL EXPLAIN IN THE CHAPTERS ON PROPHECY. [*Guide*, pp. 347-348]

Maimonides then goes on to provide a list of words that are to be interpreted in accordance with the principles indicated here with respect to the *Maaseh Merkabah*.

We take note of the indication of the structure of the presentation given here by Maimonides. Placing two preambles before his explication of the *Maaseh Bereshit*, the second of the two preambles referring specifically to the *Maaseh Merkabah*, indicates that the section made up of two preambles is an introduction to both, the *Maaseh Bereshit* and then the *Maaseh Merkabah*. It is left to the reader to assess the significance of what then appears as interruption by the chapter on the Sabbath, Chapter II:31, and then the lengthy treatise on the psychology of prophecy, Chapters II:32-48, referred to above as "the chapters on prophecy" [*Guide*, p. 348].

WITH REGARD TO THE SAME PRINCIPLE, IN REFER-ENCE TO THE *MERKABAH* THERE OCCURS THE WORD

HASHMAL (Ezekiel 1:4, 27; 8:2), AS THEY HAVE EXPLAIN-
ED, AND ALSO REGEL EGEL (THE FOOT OF A CALF)
(Ezekiel 1:7) AND NEHOSHET QALAL (BURNISHED
BRASS) (Ezekiel 1:7). THE SAME APPLIES TO OTHER
WORDS. [Guide, p. 348]

The reader has to be cautioned that the translations of these terms
given in brackets are of the external meanings; the very point being
made is that the words represent something else.

Maimonides gives a hint that whatever nehoshet means in Ezekiel, it
has the same meaning when it is used by Zechariah.

IN A SIMILAR WAY, ZECHARIAH SAYS: AND THE MOUN-
TAINS WERE MOUNTAINS OF NEHOSHET (BRASS) (Zechariah 6:1). [Guide, p. 348]

A fuller explication of this hint is given by Maimonides in Chapter
II:10 [Guide, pp. 272-273].

As we will presently indicate, there are signs that Maimonides
intimates that these words refer to the existence of sexuality with
respect to the living creatures of the vision of Ezekiel, regel egel to the
male principle and nehoshet qalal to the female principle, in his direct
commentary III:2 [Guide, p. 418]; and hashmal refers to the generative
figure of Ezekiel's vision, in his direct commentary in Chapter II:7
[Guide, pp. 429-430]. The details of the argument as to how these are
intimated by Maimonides are given in chapter IV.

We mention this at this point in our discussion without argument
to indicate that, in Maimonides' reference in this introduction within
Chapter II:29, referring forward to the Maaseh Merkabah, he singles
out these words as if to indicate that that which is represented by them
is the main thing about the Maaseh Merkabah. We need to appreciate
that it is the sexuality associated with the generation of the living
creatures as well as the sexuality of the living creatures themselves that
he would draw our attention to. There is a repetition of this enumeration of words at the end of Chapter II:43, in which Maimonides has
explained the nature of derivation in connection with words:
"Through this method [of derivation] very strange things appear,
which are likewise secrets, as in its dictum with regard to the Merka-

bah: nehoshet and qalal and regel and egel (Ezekiel 1:7) and barak (bazak; Ezekiel 1:14), and in other passages."

We note that there is a change, with the word barak substituted for the word hashmal. The word barak is discussed by Maimonides within his discussion of the vision of Ezekiel [Guide, p. 419], with respect to living creatures. Maimonides is here making a point of the parallel between human beings and the divine, the discussion of which is to be found below.

Maimonides concludes Chapter II:29 by announcing:

AFTER THESE TWO PREAMBLES I SHALL GIVE THE CHAPTER THAT WE HAVE PROMISED. [*Guide,* **p. 348**]

That is, the chapter on the Maaseh Bereshit, Chapter II:30 [Guide, pp. 348–359].

KNOW [*Guide,* p. 348]

Maimonides appears to punctuate eighteen items in connection with the Maaseh Bereshit in Chapter II:30. He uses "know" in sixteen instances and "reflect" in two instances as punctuation indicators. It is convenient that we number them.

1. *Know* that there is a difference between "the first" and "the principle" [Guide, p. 348].
2. Among the things you ought to *know* is the fact that the sages have explicitly stated . . . that the word eth figuring in his words et hash-shamayim ve-et ha-aretz (the heaven and the earth) has in that verse the meaning: with [Guide, p. 350].
3. Among the things you ought to *know* is that earth is an equivocal term used in a general and in a particular sense [Guide, p. 350].
4. Among the things you ought to *know* is that the four elements are the first to be mentioned after the heaven [Guide, p. 351].
5. Among the things you ought to *know* is that the words, And He divided between the waters, and so on, do not refer merely to a division in place in which one part is located above and one below, while both have the same nature [Guide, p. 352].

6. Among the things you ought to *know* . . . is the reason why it is not said regarding the work of the second day *that it was good* [*Guide*, p. 353].

7. Among the things you ought to *know* is that the *Sages* have made it clear that God only made grass and trees grown from the earth after He had caused rain to fall upon them . . . [*Guide*, p. 354].

8. You . . . *know* that . . . the first of the causes producing generation and passing-away are light and darkness . . . [*Guide*, p. 354].

9. Among the things you ought to *know* is their saying: *All the works of the Beginning were created according to their [perfect] stature, [perfect] reason, and [perfect] beauty (le-sibyonam)* [*Guide*, pp. 354–355].

10. Among the things on which you ought to *reflect* . . . is the fact that it mentions the creation of *man* in the *six days of the Beginning* and says: *Male and female created He them* [*Guide*, p. 355].

11. Among the things you ought to *know* is . . . that *Sammael* is *Satan* [*Guide*, p. 356].

12. Among the things you ought to *know* . . . is the fact that the *Serpent* had in no respect direct relations with Adam. . . . Among the amazing dicta . . . is their statement [that] *the Serpent . . . cast pollution into* [*Eve*] [*Guide*, pp. 356–357].

13. Among the things you ought to *know* is their dictum: [*The size of*] *the tree of life [corresponds] to a walk of five hundred years, and all the waters of the Beginning spring up from beneath it* [*Guide*, p. 357].

14. Among the things you ought also to *know* is their dictum: *As for the tree of knowledge, the Holy One, blessed be He, has never revealed that tree to man and will never reveal it* [*Guide*, p. 357].

15. Among the things you ought to *know* is their dictum: *And the Lord God took the man* — [*that is,*] *raised him* — *and put him into the garden of Eden* — [*that is,*] *He gave Him rest* [*Guide*, p. 357].

16. Among the things you ought also to *know* . . . [are the facts concerning Cain, Abel and Seth] [*Guide*, p. 357].

17. Among the things you ought to *know* . . . is the dictum: *And the man gave names, and so on* [*Guide*, p. 357].

18. Among the things you ought to *reflect* upon are the four words that occur with reference to the relation between heaven and God [*Guide*, p. 358].

The word "reflect" occurs in the tenth and the eighteenth items. The first "reflect" is at the beginning of the items dealing with things associated with the creation of man prior to the first Sabbath. The second "reflect" is in the item that draws the reader's attention to the word *yezirah*, the word for God's creation of human being with the meaning of "form" and alluding to the creation of human beings after the first Sabbath, as we will note. Thus, the second "reflect" is the transition from the discussion of the *Maaseh Bereshit* to the discussion of the *Maaseh Merkabah*.

THAT THERE IS A DIFFERENCE BETWEEN "THE FIRST" AND "THE PRINCIPLE." [*Guide*, p. 348]

As a preliminary to the appreciation of this first item, some comments are in order concerning the view of time that Maimonides has and the relationship between time and creation.

For Maimonides, time exists before the creation only as a manner of speaking. For time itself came into existence with the creation of the universe.

. . . according to us, time is a created and generated thing as are the other accidents and the substances serving as the substrata to these accidents. Hence God's bringing the world into existence does not have a temporal beginning, for time is one of the created things. [*Guide*, p. 282]

. . . God has brought the world into being out of nothing without there having been a temporal beginning. For time is created, being consequent upon the motion of the sphere. . . . [*Guide*, pp. 349–350]

. . . if you affirm as true the existence of time prior to the world, you are necessarily bound to believe in the eternity [of the world, as Aristotle did]. . . . For time is an accident which necessarily must have a substratum. Accordingly it follows necessarily that there existed some thing prior to the existence of this world existing now. But this notion must be avoided. [*Guide*, p. 282]

Maimonides' view converges with a view of time indicated in Plato's *Timaeus* as well. This is the view that time, as part of creation, is merely a copy of eternity:

> . . . the father and creator . . . resolved to have a moving image of eternity, and when he set in order the heaven, he made this image eternal but moving according to number, while eternity itself rests on unity; and this image we call time. For there were no days and nights and months and years before the heaven was created, but when he constructed the heaven he created them also. They are all the parts of time, and the past and future are created species of time, which we unconsciously but wrongly transfer to the eternal essence; for we say that he "was," he "is," he "will be," but the truth is that "is" alone is properly attributed to him, and that "was" and "will be" are only to be spoken of becoming in time, for they are motions, but that which is immovably the same cannot become older or younger by time, nor ever did or has become, or hereafter will be, older or younger, nor is subject at all to any of those states which affect moving and sensible things and of which generation is the cause. These are the forms of time, which imitates eternity and revolves according to the law of number. Moreover, when we say that what has become *is* become and what becomes *is* becoming, and that what will become *is* about to become and that the non-existent *is* non-existent, – all these are inaccurate modes of expression. [Jowett, vol. 2, p. 19]

It is then desirable to make the distinction between two kinds of priority – priority in terms of time, and then priority in some other sense. This is the purpose of Maimonides' first item in connection with the *Maaseh Bereshit*. He first explains a timeless "principle":

NAMELY, A PRINCIPLE EXISTS IN THE THING WHOSE PRINCIPLE IT IS OR SIMULTANEOUSLY WITH IT, EVEN IF IT DOES NOT PRECEDE IT IN TIME. THUS IT IS SAID THAT THE HEART IS THE PRINCIPLE OF THE LIVING BEING, AND THE ELEMENT THE PRINCIPLE OF THAT OF WHICH IT IS THE ELEMENT. [*Guide*, p. 348]

Maimonides then indicates that the language is sometimes confounded, and does not fully honor the distinction.

"FIRST" IS ALSO SOMETIMES USED IN THIS SENSE.
[*Guide*, p. 348]

Maimonides explains firstness with respect to time:

SOMETIMES, HOWEVER, "THE FIRST" IS APPLIED SOLE-
LY TO WHAT IS PRIOR IN TIME [*Guide*, p. 348]

He then indicates that there can be two kinds of firstness, noncausative and causative.

EVEN WHEN THAT WHICH IS PRIOR IN TIME IS NOT
THE CAUSE OF THAT WHICH IS POSTERIOR TO IT.
[*Guide*, p. 348]

He exemplifies noncausative firstness.

THUS IT MAY BE SAID THAT THE FIRST ONE WHO
LIVED IN THAT HOUSE WAS SO AND SO AND AFTER
HIM SO AND SO. [*Guide*, p. 348]

In this case there is no principle involved, as might be the case if there
were a causative relationship.

IT MAY NOT, HOWEVER, BE SAID [IN A CASE LIKE THIS]
THAT SO AND SO IS THE PRINCIPLE OF SO AND SO.
[*Guide*, p. 348]

The purpose of this discussion is to make a place, as it were, for a
sense of priority in connection with the first word of Scripture. And
we get a distinction between *tehillah* and *reshit*, the latter being in the
first word of Scripture *be-reshit*, characteristically translated as "In the
beginning."

THE WORD INDICATIVE OF "THE FIRST" IN OUR LAN-
GUAGE IS *TEHILLAH* (BEGINNING). THUS: THE BEGIN-

NING OF (*TEHILLAT*) THE WORD OF THE LORD TO HO-
SEA. THAT INDICATIVE OF "THE PRINCIPLE" IS
RESHIT. FOR IT DERIVES FROM *ROSH* (HEAD). WHICH
IN VIEW OF ITS POSITION IS THE PRINCIPLE OF THE
LIVING BEINGS. [*Guide*, p. 348]

Maimonides then makes clear his understanding of the opening
words of Scripture that time itself began with the creation.

NOW THE WORLD HAS NOT BEEN CREATED IN A TEM-
PORAL BEGINNING, AS WE HAVE EXPLAINED, FOR
TIME BELONGS TO THE CREATED THINGS. FOR THIS
REASON IT SAYS: IN THE BEGINNING [*BERESHIT*]. FOR
THE *BE* HAS THE MEANING OF "IN." THE TRUE TRANS-
LATION OF THIS VERSE IS: IN THE ORIGIN GOD CRE-
ATED WHAT IS HIGH AND WHAT IS LOW. THIS IS THE
TRANSLATION THAT FITS IN WITH CREATION IN
TIME. [*Guide*, p. 349]

However, Maimonides faces a problem in that views have been
expressed which allow that time existed prior to the creation. It is
necessary for him to clearly dissociate himself from these views, which
he does as follows:

ON THE OTHER HAND THE STATEMENT, WHICH YOU
FIND FORMULATED BY SOME OF THE SAGES, THAT
AFFIRMS THAT TIME EXISTED BEFORE THE CREATION
OF THE WORLD IS VERY DIFFICULT. FOR THAT IS THE
OPINION OF ARISTOTLE, WHICH I HAVE EXPLAINED
TO YOU: HE HOLDS THAT TIME CANNOT BE CON-
CEIVED TO HAVE A BEGINNING, WHICH IS INCONGRU-
OUS. [*Guide*, p. 349]

It is to be pointed out that in this instance there is a difference in the
views of Plato and Aristotle, with Maimonides opting for the view of
Plato.

Maimonides proceeds to indicate how it was that the sages were led
into a view that he regards as erroneous:

THOSE WHO MADE THIS STATEMENT WERE CON-
DUCTED TO IT BY THEIR FINDING IN SCRIPTURE THE
TERMS: *ONE DAY, A SECOND DAY.* [*Guide*, p. 349]

The error is to take Scripture in its external rather than internal
sense. The error consists in not understanding that time is an accident
of motion:

HE WHO MADE THIS STATEMENT UNDERSTOOOD
THESE TERMS ACCORDING TO THEIR EXTERNAL
SENSE AS FOLLOWS: INASMUCH AS A ROTATING
SPHERE AND A SUN DID NOT EXIST, WHEREBY WAS
THE FIRST DAY MEASURED? [*Guide*, p. 349]

Maimonides identifies two sources of error in this connection, one
from the Midrash, and the other from *Pirke de Rabbi Eliezer*. With
respect to the Midrash, Maimonides says:

THEY EXPRESS THEIR OPINION IN THE FOLLOWING
TEXT: *THE FIRST DAY – RABBI JUDAH, SON OF RABBI
SIMON, SAID: HENCE [WE LEARN] THAT THERE EX-
ISTED BEFORE THAT AN ORDER OF TIME. RABBI
ABAHU SAID: HENCE [WE LEARN] THAT THE HOLY
ONE, MAY HIS NAME BE BLESSED, USED TO CREATE
WORLDS AND TO DESTROY THEM [AGAIN]. THIS
SECOND OPINION IS EVEN MORE INCONGRUOUS
THAN THE FIRST.* [*Guide*, p. 349]

He explains their difficulty:

CONSIDER WHAT WAS THE DIFFICULTY FOR THESE
TWO [SAGES]. IT WAS THE NOTION THAT TIME EX-
ISTED PRIOR TO THE EXISTENCE OF THIS SUN. [*Guide*,
p. 349]

That is, they failed to understand how it is that time is an accident of
motion, and thus that until the creation of the world and its motion,
there could be no time. Maimonides has difficulty allowing that these
sages really meant what was said.

THE SOLUTION OF WHAT SEEMED OBSCURE TO BOTH
OF THEM WILL SOON BECOME CLEAR TO YOU; UN-
LESS – BY GOD! – THOSE TWO MEANT TO SAY THAT
*THE ORDER OF TIME NECESSARILY EXISTS A PARTE
ANTE.* THAT, HOWEVER, IS THE BELIEF IN THE ETER-
NITY A PARTE ANTE OF THE WORLD, AND ALL WHO
ADHERE TO THE LAW SHOULD REJECT IT. [*Guide,* p. 349]

After mentioning this source from the Midrash, he goes on to cite
Pirke de Rabbi Eliezer; which is troublesome on this point.

THIS PASSAGE IS TO MY MIND ONLY THE COUNTER-
PART OF THE PASSAGE IN WHICH RABBI ELIEZER SAYS,
WHEREFROM WERE THE HEAVENS CREATED? [*Guide,*
p. 349]

Maimonides deals with this problem from *Pirke de Rabbi Eliezer* in
greater detail in Chapter II:26. In that chapter Maimonides struggles
with the seeming suggestion that Rabbi Eliezer might believe as
Aristotle did: "Did [Rabbi Eliezer] believe that it is impossible that
something should come into being out of nothing and that there must
necessarily be matter out of which that which is generated is produced?" [*Guide,* p. 330] And thus reject the first verse of Scripture that
God created the universe, out of nothing, as Maimonides understands
it? In that chapter Maimonides struggles to find another way to
interpret the words of Rabbi Eliezer: ". . . that there are two matters,
a high and an inferior one . . ." [*Guide,* p. 331]. The distinction is an
important one, as we shall presently note, for Maimonides and his
appreciation of the vision of Ezekiel. The fact that there are two
matters ". . . is a great mystery. . . . one of the mysteries of being and
a mystery among the mysteries of the Torah" [*Guide,* p. 31]. That
would be the high matter to be noted in the vision of Ezekiel out of
which the soul is generated within the context of the created world
following the first Sabbath. But that matter is not existing matter in
the same sense as all the other matter of the universe exists. For it is
truly *de novo* within the time after the first Sabbath, in the same sense
as the world was *de novo* at the creation.

The reference to *Pirke de Rabbi Eliezer* within this discussion of the first of the items of the *Maaseh Bereshit* has another significance. For the *Pirke de Rabbi Eliezer* is a major source for Maimonides for his understanding of the *Maaseh Bereshit* and the *Maaseh Merkabah*. Maimonides ends his indications with respect to the first of the items by reaffirming the meaning of the first verse of Scripture as meaning that the creation of the universe was a creation out of nothing, which was nothing even with respect to time.

TO SUM UP: YOU SHOULD NOT, IN CONSIDERING THESE POINTS, TAKE INTO ACCOUNT THE STATE-MENTS MADE BY THIS ONE OR THAT ONE. [*Guide*, p. 349]

That is, do not pay attention to the fact that some of the sages appear to have a view of the existence of time prior to the creation.

I HAVE ALREADY MADE IT KNOWN TO YOU THAT THE FOUNDATION OF THE WHOLE LAW IS THE VIEW THAT GOD HAS BROUGHT THE WORLD INTO BEING OUT OF NOTHING WITHOUT THERE HAVING BEEN A TEM-PORAL BEGINNING. FOR TIME IS CREATED, BEING CONSEQUENT UPON THE MOTION OF THE SPHERE, WHICH IS CREATED. [*Guide*, pp. 349–350]

The second item among the items of the *Maaseh Bereshit* is as follows:

AMONG THE THINGS YOU OUGHT TO KNOW [*Guide*, p. 350]

Announcing it as one of the numerable items.

IS THE FACT THAT THE SAGES HAVE EXPLICITLY STATED IN A NUMBER OF PASSAGES THAT THE WORD *ET* FIGURING IN HIS WORDS, *ET HASH-SHAMAYIM VE-ET HA-ARETZ* (THE HEAVEN AND THE EARTH), HAS IN THAT VERSE THE MEANING: WITH. [*Guide*, p. 349]

This refers to the fact that the word *et* has two meanings in Hebrew. It is a grammatical indicator placed between a verb and a noun to indicate that the verb is transitive and that the noun following is the object of the verb. This is the meaning characteristically given in translations of the order, "In the beginning God [Elohim] created the heaven and the earth" (Genesis 1:1). That is, the translations characteristically take Elohim as the subject of the verb for create, and heaven and earth as the objects of the verb. The word *et* appears before the Hebrew word for heaven and before the Hebrew word for earth, making it seem that only heaven and earth were the objects of the verb.

The great secret of this second item is that this interpretation is to be rejected in favor of the meaning indicated by understanding the word *et* in its other sense as meaning "with." If one takes *et* as meaning "with," what emerges is the tripartite universe to which Maimonides variously alludes in his writings, a universe consisting of Elohim, heaven, and earth. With this interpretation it is not necessary even to name the Creator. Following Maimonides indication, the appropriate translation would be

> In the beginning [He] created the Elohim *with*
> the heaven and *with* the earth. [Genesis 1:1]

Elohim is, for Maimonides, an equivocal word: "Every Hebrew knew that the term Elohim is equivocal, designating the deity, the angels and the rulers governing the cities" [*Guide*, p. 23].

Angels for Maimonides comprise all the regulatory forces in existence. They are apprehensible by the mind but not by the senses. They may, however, be represented imaginatively, personified, and believed to have such a personified existence. For Maimonides, the word ". . . Elohim . . . is applied [only] figuratively to the angels and to the deity" [*Guide*, p. 261].

The angels, Maimonides says, ". . . are intellects separate from matter . . . they are the objects of an act, and God has created them. . . . outside the mind they have no fixed corporeal shape . . ." [*Guide*, pp. 108–109]. And ". . . all forces are angels" [*Guide*, p. 263].

Maimonides explains his notion of angels by speaking scornfully of

> . . . one of those who deem themselves the Sages of Israel [who believes]
> that the deity sends an angel, who enters the womb of a woman and

forms the fetus there. . . . But if you tell him that God has placed in the sperm a formative force . . . and that this force is an angel, or that all forms derive from the act of the Active Intellect . . . the man would shrink from this opinion. For he does not understand the notion of the true greatness and power that consists in the bringing into existence of forces active in a thing, forces that cannot be apprehended by any sense. [*Guide*, pp. 263–264]

By identifying angels with forces there is nothing in Scripture that is at variance with Aristotle: "There is . . . nothing in what Aristotle . . . has said about [the separate intellects] that is not in agreement with the Law" [*Guide*, p. 263].

THEY MEAN BY THIS THAT HE CREATED TOGETHER WITH THE HEAVENS ALL THAT IS IN HEAVEN AND TOGETHER WITH THE EARTH ALL THAT IS IN THE EARTH. [*Guide*, p. 350]

It is then clear that what Maimonides wants the reader to understand is that God created the Elohim—the angels, the variety of regulatory forces, the separate intellects of Aristotle—"with the heavens . . ." and, similarly, "with the earth."
Following this, Maimonides says:

YOU ALREADY KNOW THAT THEY MAKE IT CLEAR THAT THE HEAVEN AND THE EARTH WERE CREATED TOGETHER [*Guide*, p. 350]

This follows from Elohim with the heaven, and Elohim with the earth; and then heaven with earth together. That is, all three, Elohim, heaven, and earth, were created together. Thus:

BECAUSE HE SAYS: *I CALL UNTO THEM, THEY STAND UP TOGETHER* (Isaiah 48:13). ACCORDINGLY EVERYTHING WAS CREATED SIMULTANEOUSLY. [*Guide*, p. 350]

Bara applies to this first creation out of nothingness. *Asa* applies to what took place within the days of creation after that first instant. We

will note presently how Maimonides indicates that the third, *yazar*, is
to be taken with respect to the role of God in history from the time of
the first Sabbath.

> THEN GRADUALLY ALL THINGS BECOME DIFFERENTI-
> ATED. THEY HAVE COMPARED THIS TO WHAT HAP-
> PENS WHEN AN AGRICULTURAL LABORER SOWS VAR-
> IOUS KINDS OF GRAIN IN THE SOIL AT THE SAME
> MOMENT. SOME OF THEM SPROUT WITHIN A DAY,
> OTHERS WITHIN TWO DAYS, OTHERS AGAIN WITHIN
> THREE DAYS, THOUGH EVERYTHING WAS SOWED AT
> THE SAME HOUR. [*Guide*, p. 350]

We take note of Maimonides' appreciation of making in terms of an
unfolding of potentiality in a biological or organismic sense. Indeed,
the biological organism is, for Maimonides, the fundamental model
for the universe as a whole, as he develops the point in Chapter I:72:

> Know that the whole of being is one individual and nothing else . . .
> having in respect of individuality the rank of Zayd and Umar . . . just
> as Zayd . . . is one individual and is at the same time composed of
> various parts of the body . . . the sphere . . . as a whole is composed of
> the heavens, the four elements, and what is compounded of the latter.
> [*Guide*, p. 184]

Maimonides sees the very creation within the first days after the
creation out of nothingness in terms of such biological and organismic
unfolding.

> IT IS ACCORDING TO THIS OPINION, WHICH IS INDUBI-
> TABLY CORRECT, THAT THE DOUBT THAT IMPELLED
> *RABBI JUDAH, SON OF RABBI SIMON,* TO SAY WHAT
> HE SAID, MAY BE RESOLVED. [*Guide*, p. 350]

This refers back to the opinion concerning the existence of time
prior to the creation referred to in the discussion of the first item
above.

IT WAS DIFFICULT FOR HIM TO UNDERSTAND
WHEREBY *THE FIRST DAY AND THE SECOND DAY
AND THE THIRD DAY* WERE MEASURED. THERE IS AN
EXPLICIT STATEMENT ON THIS POINT MADE BY THE
SAGES . . . IN *BERESHIT RABBAH*. [*Guide*, p. 350]

The issue here is to be understood in terms of the two forms of
motion associated with the generation of temporality. There is the
motion of the heavenly bodies, the changes associated with the sun,
moon, and stars. And there is the motion associated with the biological, organic development of the created universe. Maimonides here
suggests the sages having an idea of time based primarily on the latter.
This would allow a first day and a second day, and so on, even though
the heavenly bodies were not yet in place.

WITH REFERENCE TO THE *LIGHT* SAID IN THE *TORAH
TO HAVE BEEN CREATED ON THE FIRST DAY*, THEY
MAKE LITERALLY THE FOLLOWING STATEMENT:
*THOSE ARE THE LUMINARIES THAT HAVE BEEN CRE-
ATED ON THE FIRST DAY, BUT THAT HE DID NOT
SUSPEND UNTIL THE FOURTH DAY.* THUS A CLEAR
EXPLANATION AS TO THIS POINT HAS BEEN MADE.
[*Guide*, p. 350]

In the third item Maimonides seeks to make two points. First, he
distinguishes between the use of the term "earth" as meaning all four
elements, and earth as one of the four elements. Second, he makes the
point that earth, as meaning all of the elements, is lowly. There are
two senses:

AMONG THE THINGS YOU OUGHT TO KNOW IS THAT
EARTH IS AN EQUIVOCAL TERM USED IN A GENERAL
AND A PARTICULAR SENSE. [*Guide*, p. 350]

In the general sense:

IN A GENERAL SENSE IT IS APPLIED TO ALL THAT IS
BENEATH THE SPHERE OF THE MOON, I MEAN THE
FOUR ELEMENTS. [*Guide*, p. 350]

In the particular sense:

IN A PARTICULAR SENSE IT IS APPLIED TO ONE ELE-
MENT, THE LAST AMONG THEM, NAMELY, EARTH.
[*Guide*, p. 350]

The scriptural examples:

A PROOF OF THIS IS HIS SAYING: *AND THE EARTH WAS
UNFORMED AND VOID, AND THE DARKNESS WAS
UPON THE FACE OF THE DEEP: AND THE SPIRIT OF
GOD, AND SO ON* (Genesis 1:2). THUS SOMETIMES ALL
THE ELEMENTS ARE CALLED *EARTH.* AFTERWARDS HE
SAYS: *AND GOD CALLED THE DRY LAND EARTH.* (Gen-
esis 1:10). [*Guide*, pp. 350-351]

Scripture shows the distinction by designating the particular:

THAT ALSO IS A GREAT SECRET; NAMELY, WHEREVER
YOU FIND HIM SAYING, *GOD NAMED SOMETHING
THUS,* HE DOES THIS IN ORDER TO DIFFERENTIATE
BETWEEN THE PARTICULAR NOTION ENVISAGED
AND THE OTHER NOTION EQUALLY SIGNIFIED BY THE
TERM. [*Guide*, p. 351]

This allows Maimonides to make his substantive point about the
lowliness of the material world, the latter understood as earth and as
including all four elements.

FOR THIS REASON I HAVE INTERPRETED TO YOU THE
VERSE [in item 1 above] AS FOLLOWS: IN THE ORIGIN GOD
CREATED WHAT IS HIGH AND WHAT IS LOW. HENCE
THE EARTH MENTIONED IN THE FIRST PLACE IS WHAT
IS LOW–I MEAN TO SAY THE FOUR ELEMENTS–
WHEREAS THE EARTH OF WHICH IT IS SAID, *AND GOD
CALLED THE DRY LAND EARTH,* IS THE ELEMENT
EARTH ALONE. THIS IS NOW CLEAR. [*Guide*, p. 351]

The fourth item [*Guide*, p. 351] continues as a commentary on the second verse of the book of Genesis, identifying the four elements in them.

> And the *earth* was unformed and void,
> and *darkness* was on the face of the deep;
> and the *spirit* of God hovered
> over the face of the *waters*. [Genesis 1:2]

After announcing another item,

AMONG THE THINGS YOU OUGHT TO KNOW IS [*Guide*, p. 351]

he states,

THE FOUR ELEMENTS ARE THE FIRST TO BE MEN-TIONED AFTER THE HEAVEN. FOR, AS WE HAVE SAID, THE TERM *EARTH*, MENTIONED IN THE FIRST PLACE, APPLIES TO THEM. FOR HE MENTIONS *EARTH, WA-TER, SPIRIT*, AND *DARKNESS*. [*Guide*, p. 351]

For Maimonides these are the elements earth, water, air, and darkness. Earth and water are seemingly apparent. However, it is necessary for him to provide explanations for identifying spirit as air, and darkness as fire. This he does. He proceeds first with an explanation of darkness, and how it can be identified as fire. This is remarkably lacking in obviousness. Maimonides defends the identification of darkness and fire by invoking the principle of parallelism, that in scriptural poetry the same idea is recited in parallel lines with different words.

He first asserts the identity:

NOW *DARKNESS* IS THE ELEMENTAL FIRE; DO NOT THINK ANYTHING ELSE. [*Guide*, p. 351]

He provides one defense in terms of remote lines taken by him as being parallels:

HE SAYS: [*Guide*, p. 351]

The first line:

AND THOU DIDST HEAR HIS WORDS OUT OF THE MIDST OF THE FIRE (Deuteronomy 4:36). [*Guide*, p. 351]

Maimonides continues:

AND HE SAYS [*Guide*, p. 351]

And he cites a verse from the next chapter of Deuteronomy:

WHEN YE HEARD THE VOICE OUT OF THE MIDST OF THE DARKNESS (Deuteronomy 5:20). [*Guide*, p. 351]

He then provides another parallel, this time with an example of contiguous lines:

AND IT ALSO SAYS:

ALL DARKNESS IS LAID UP FOR HIS TREASURES;

A FIRE NOT BLOWN [BY MAN] SHALL CONSUME HIM, (Job 20:26). [*Guide*, p. 351]

After this scriptural argument based on the principle of parallelism, Maimonides provides yet another argument as to why fire may be represented by darkness. The reason is in the nature of elemental fire.

THE ELEMENTAL FIRE WAS DESIGNATED BY THIS TERM [DARKNESS], BECAUSE IT IS NOT LUMINOUS, BUT ONLY TRANSPARENT. [*Guide*, p. 351]

And then, in anticipation of the the association between darkness and night, and to distinguish the two meanings of darkness:

FOR IF THE ELEMENTAL FIRE HAD BEEN LUMINOUS, WE SHOULD HAVE SEEN AT NIGHT THE WHOLE ATMO-SPHERE IN FLAME LIKE FIRE. [*Guide,* p. 351]

Which, of course, we do not.

Thus, by these means, Maimonides indicates to the reader how the *Maaseh Bereshit,* which Maimonides clearly considers under the heading of prophecy, entails the recognition of the theory of the four elements as constituting matter. He then states that the order as presented in Scripture is in accordance with the natural order of the elements.

THE ELEMENTS ARE MENTIONED ACCORDING TO THEIR NATURAL POSITION; NAMELY, FIRST THE EARTH, THEN THE WATER THAT IS ABOVE IT, THEN THE AIR THAT ADHERES TO THE WATER, THEN THE FIRE THAT IS ABOVE THE AIR. [*Guide,* p. 351]

That is, a sequence of earth, water, air, and fire (darkness).

Now we have been prepared to recognize that there are two kinds of order. It is patent that the order being alluded to is not simply sequential. The sequence as found in Scripture is otherwise: earth, fire (darkness), air (spirit), and water[s] (Genesis 1:2).

Maimonides makes an argument that the natural order of the elements, earth, water, air, fire, is to be found in Scripture in three steps, the last being implicit.

First, air is over water.

FOR IN VIEW OF THE SPECIFICATION OF THE AIR AS BEING *OVER THE FACE OF THE WATERS* (Genesis 1:2). [*Guide,* p. 351]

Second, fire is over air.

DARKNESS THAT IS *UPON THE FACE OF THE DEEP* (Genesis 1:2) IS UNDUBITABLY ABOVE THE *SPIRIT.* [*Guide,* p. 351]

He makes an argument that spirit means air:

IT WAS IMPELLED TO USE THE EXPRESSION, *THE SPIRIT OF GOD,* IN ORDER TO DESIGNATE THE AIR IN VIEW OF THE FACT THAT THE LATTER IS SUPPOSED TO BE IN MOTION, I MEAN TO SAY *MERAHEPHET* (MOVING), AND THAT THE MOTION OF THE WIND IS ALWAYS ASCRIBED TO GOD. THUS: *AND THERE WENT FORTH A WIND FROM THE LORD; THOU DIDST BLOW WITH THY WIND; AND THE LORD TURNED A WEST WIND.* THIS OCCURS FREQUENTLY. [*Guide,* p. 351]

Third, the implicit point is that the other three elements are above the earth. Thus, we have the order earth, water, air, and fire, as represented in Scripture.

Last, within this fourth item associated with the *Maaseh Bereshit,* Scripture now goes to the other meaning of darkness, away from its meaning as fire, to darkness in a more literal sense.

IN VIEW OF THE FACT THAT THE TERM *DARKNESS (HOSHEKH),* AS EMPLOYED AFTERWARDS IN THE SIG-NIFICATION OF OBSCURITY, IT BEGINS TO EXPLAIN AND TO DIFFERENTIATE, SAYING: AND THE DARK-NESS (*HOSHEKH*) HE CALLED NIGHT (Genesis 1:5), AS WE HAVE EXPLAINED. CONSEQUENTLY THIS IS NOW CLEAR. [*Guide,* p. 351]

The fifth item explaining "And He divided between the waters . . ." (Genesis 1:7) and the sixth item explaining the failure of Scripture to say about the work of the second day "it was good," as it does with respect to other days of creation, need to be considered together.

In the fifth item, the distinction is drawn between the waters above and the waters which are below the firmament, providing the possibility of a theater for the action of God's creativity above. At the same time, the lack of a statement that "it was good" is interpreted as meaning that God's creative work is unfinished. The result of this is an interpretation of the work of creation on the second day as having left the provision for the continued work of creation on the subsequent days.

The connection between the second day of creation and the vision of Ezekiel, and hence the connection between the *Maaseh Bereshit* and the *Maaseh Merkabah*, is specifically made in *Pirke de Rabbi Eliezer*, a work Maimonides refers to several times in *The Guide of the Perplexed*. In *Pirke de Rabbi Eliezer* it is written:

> On the second day the Holy One, Blessed be He, created the firmament. . . . Which firmament was created on the second day? Rabbi Eliezer said: It was the firmament which is above the heads of the four living creatures [referred to by Ezekiel, for it is said] And over the heads of the living creatures there was the likeness of a firmament. . . . (Ezekiel 1:22) [Chapter 4].

Special attention needs to be drawn to the fifth item, because in it Maimonides indicates a ground for dividing and reconciling the world of sensory perception and another world.

AMONG THE THINGS YOU OUGHT TO KNOW IS THAT THE WORDS, *AND HE DIVIDED BETWEEN THE WATERS, AND SO ON* (Genesis 1:7), DO NOT REFER MERELY TO A DIVISION IN PLACE IN WHICH ONE PART IS LOCATED ABOVE AND ONE BELOW, WHILE BOTH HAVE THE SAME NATURE. [*Guide*, p. 352]

It is not an ordinary distinction as among physical things.

THE CORRECT INTERPRETATION OF THESE WORDS IS THAT HE MADE A NATURAL DIVISION BETWEEN BOTH OF THEM [*Guide*, p. 352]

The division is part of natural science, part of the *Maaseh Bereshit*, which includes form.

I MEAN WITH REGARD TO THEIR FORM [*Guide*, p. 352]

He then describes the difference. With respect to the first, the water which is above

THAT WHICH HE FIRST CALLS WATER, INTO ONE PARTICULAR THING BY MEANS OF THE NATURAL FORM WITH WHICH HE INVESTED IT [*Guide*, p. 352]

The second is water more literally:

AND BESTOWING UPON THE OTHER PART A DIF-
FERENT FORM, THE LATTER PART BEING WATER
PROPER. HENCE IT SAYS: AND THE GATHERING OF
THE WATERS HE CALLED SEAS. [Guide, p. 352]

The first water is not such water.

IN THIS WAY IT MAKES CLEAR TO YOU THAT THE
FIRST WATER OF WHICH IT IS SAID, OVER THE FACE
OF THE WATERS, IS NOT WATER THAT IS IN THE SEAS
[Guide, p. 352]

Maimonides then makes what we take to be an allusion. He states that
the first water is "above the air."

BUT THAT PART OF THE WATER SITUATED ABOVE
THE AIR [WHICH] WAS DIFFERENTIATED BY MEANS OF
A CERTAIN FORM. [Guide, p. 352]

We take this as a double allusion. It is, in the first place, an allusion
to fire, in that that which is above air, in the scheme of earth, water,
air, and fire, is fire. Second, it is an allusion to the notion, which is to
be found in the Talmud and in the Pirke de Rabbi Eliezer as well, that
God created man out of fire, eish. He added the yod of his name to eish
and formed ish, meaning "man," and he added the heh to eish, to form
ishah, meaning "woman" (Sotah 17a, Pirke de Rabbi Eliezer 12).

WHEREAS ANOTHER PART IS THIS WATER HERE.
[Guide, p. 352]

We note another hint that we should take that which is above the
air as meaning fire from that which follows immediately.

THUS THE PHRASE, AND HE DIVIDED BETWEEN THE
WATERS WHICH WERE UNDER THE FIRMAMENT,
AND SO ON, IS ANALOGOUS TO THE PHRASE, AND
GOD DIVIDED BETWEEN THE LIGHT AND THE DARK-

NESS, IN WHICH THE DIVISION IS IN RESPECT OF A CERTAIN FORM. [*Guide*, p. 352]

We have already been told that darkness means fire.
With respect to the firmament:

THE *FIRMAMENT* ITSELF WAS PRODUCED FROM WA-TER. [*Guide*, p. 352]

As Maimonides presently notes, there is a water which is a first matter which gets divided into three forms, one of which is the firmament.

AS [THE SAGES] SAY: *THE MIDDLE GROUP CON-GEALED.* [*Guide*, p. 352]

Maimonides then proceeds to indicate that the word "heaven" is equivocal:

THE WORDS, *AND GOD CALLED THE FIRMAMENT HEAVEN,* IS INTENDED, ACCORDING TO WHAT I HAVE EXPLAINED TO YOU, TO MAKE CLEAR THAT THE TERM [HEAVEN] IS EQUIVOCAL AND THAT THE *HEAVEN* MENTIONED IN THE FIRST PLACE, IN THE WORDS *THE HEAVEN AND THE EARTH,* IS NOT WHAT IS GENER-ALLY NAMED *HEAVEN.* IT HAS RENDERED THIS SIGNI-FICATION EVEN MORE CERTAIN BY THE USE OF THE WORDS *IN THE FACE OF THE FIRMAMENT OF HEAVEN,* WHEREBY IT MEANT TO MAKE CLEAR THAT THE *FIR-MAMENT* IS NOT THE *HEAVEN.* [*Guide*, p. 352]

And even interchangable with the word *firmament.*

BECAUSE OF THIS EQUIVOCALITY OF THE TERMS, THE TRUE *HEAVEN* IS SOMETIMES LIKEWISE CALLED *FIR-MAMENT, JUST AS THE TRUE FIRMAMENT IS CALLED HEAVEN. THUS IT SAYS AND GOD SET THEM IN THE FIRMAMENT OF THE HEAVEN.* [*Guide*, p. 352]

Maimonides presents us with a clear statement of his own belief in this connection. There is, first, the physical structure of the world:

IN THESE WORDS THERE IS LIKEWISE A CLEAR INDICA-
TION OF WHAT HAS ALREADY BEEN DEMONSTRATED,
NAMELY, OF THE FACT THAT ALL THE STARS AS WELL
AS THE SUN AND THE MOON ARE SITUATED WITHIN
THE SPHERE–AS THERE IS NO VACUUM IN THE
WORLD–AND THAT THEY ARE NOT LOCATED UPON
THE SURFACE OF A SPHERE, AS THE VULGAR IMAG-
INE. THIS APPEARS FROM HIS SAYING: *IN THE FIRMA-
MENT OF HEAVEN*, AND NOT: *UPON THE FIRMAMENT
OF THE HEAVEN*. [*Guide*, p. 352]

The firmament constitutes the spatial matrix within which the earth and all the heavenly bodies exist. The allusion to the vulgar is to an idea that all the heavenly bodies are displayed on the inner surface of a sphere–as in a modern planetarium. That firmament is some-times referred to as heaven.

Maimonides then returns to the subject of the creation. As he has already suggested:

THUS IT HAS BECOME CLEAR THAT THERE WAS A
CERTAIN COMMON MATTER, WHICH IT NAMES *WA-
TER*. AFTERWARDS IT WAS DIVIDED INTO THREE
FORMS; A PART OF IT TURNED INTO ONE THING,
NAMELY, THE *SEAS*; ANOTHER PART OF IT TURNED
INTO ANOTHER THING, NAMELY, THE *FIRMAMENT*; A
THIRD PART TURNED INTO A THING THAT IS ABOVE
THE *FIRMAMENT*. [*Guide*, p. 352]

Of these three parts, the first two are commonplace in our experi-ence. One is water in the literal sense, as that comprising the seas. The other is the physical space of the created world within which earth and all the heavenly bodies abide. But there is a third part which, while still part of the world God created, is somehow beyond space itself.

We take it that for Maimonides there is a region beyond both time and space within the created world. Referring to that third part ". . . above the firmament," Maimonides says:

THE LATTER IS ENTIRELY BEYOND THE EARTH. [*Guide*, p. 353]

That is the realm of concern in *The Guide of the Perplexed*, the realm of the secrets of the Torah.

WITH REGARD TO THAT SUBJECT, HE CHOSE A DIF-FERENT METHOD OF APPROACH LEADING TO EX-TRAORDINARY SECRETS. [*Guide*, p. 353]

It is the content of the study of Rabbi Akiva, Elisha Aher, Ben Zoma, and Ben Azzai, the four who sought to enter PaRDeS, the *Maaseh Bereshit* and the *Maaseh Merkabah*.

WITH REGARD TO THE FACT THAT THAT WHICH IS ABOVE THE *FIRMAMENT* IS CALLED WATER IN NAME ONLY AND THAT IT IS NOT THE SPECIFIC WATER KNOWN TO US, A STATEMENT SETTING THIS FORTH HAS ALSO BEEN MADE BY THE SAGES. . . . THEY MADE IT IN THE FOLLOWING PASSAGE: *FOUR ENTERED PAR-ADISE, AND SO ON. RABBI AKIVA SAID TO THEM: WHEN YOU COME TO THE STONES OF PURE MARBLE, DO NOT SAY WATER, WATER, FOR IT IS WRITTEN: HE THAT SPEAKETH FALSEHOOD SHALL NOT BE ESTAB-LISHED BEFORE MY FOUNTAINS.* [*Guide*, p. 353]

Having revealed so much of what he has to say in the discussion in this item, Maimonides then engages in one of his misdirection maneuvers, which will divide his readers between those who are addressed as follows:

REFLECT, IF YOU ARE ONE OF THOSE WHO REFLECT, TO WHAT EXTENT HE HAS MADE CLEAR AND REVEALED THE WHOLE MATTER IN THIS STATEMENT, PROVIDED THAT YOU CONSIDER IT WELL [*Guide*, p. 353]

And as for those who are not one of those who reflect, who, say, have been impelled by pedantic motives to have read so far in Maimonides' book, but who do not comprehend:

UNDERSTAND ALL THAT HAS BEEN DEMONSTRATED IN THE *METEOROLOGICA* AND EXAMINE EVERY-THING THAT PEOPLE HAVE SAID ABOUT EVERY POINT MENTIONED IN THAT WORK. [*Guide*, p. 353]

The person who has read carefully within this item would know that the water of the *Meteorologica*, a book by Aristotle on weather, is precisely not the water intended.

The sixth item: Maimonides then deepens his explanation of the creation of the second day with the indication that the work of the second day was not completed:

AMONG THE THINGS YOU OUGHT TO KNOW AND HAVE YOUR ATTENTION AROUSED TO IS THE REASON WHY IT IS NOT SAID REGARDING THE WORK OF THE SECOND DAY *THAT IT WAS GOOD.* [*Guide*, p. 353]

He here again draws attention to the need for nonliteral interpretation. This is especially noteworthy after his misdirection in connection with Aristotle.

YOU ALREADY KNOW WHAT THE *SAGES* . . . HAVE SAID ABOUT THIS ACCORDING TO THE METHOD OF *NONLITERAL INTERPRETATION.* [*Guide*, p. 353]

He then states that:

THE BEST STATEMENT OF THIS KIND THEY HAVE MADE ABOUT THIS IS THEIR SAYING THAT THIS WAS SO *BECAUSE THE WORK OF THE WATER HAD NOT BEEN TERMINATED.* [*Guide*, p. 353]

Thus the lack of the statement that it was good means that it represented unfinished work of the water. We understand that water to be the water above. And we understand it to be significant when taken in a nonliteral manner.

TO MY MIND ALSO THE REASON IN QUESTION IS VERY CLEAR. [*Guide*, p. 353]

It is clear to him, and, at the same time, it is secret. Our hypothesis with respect to his thought is that it is of a primal scene involving the generation of human souls. That would be both clear and secret. He is enjoined not to expound on the secrets except in the sense of providing the "chapter headings."

We take the following as "chapter headings" of that which to him is "very clear."

FOR WHENEVER IT MENTIONS A THING AMONG THOSE THAT EXIST, HAVING BEEN PRODUCED IN TIME AND SUBSISTING IN DURABLE, PERPETUAL, AND PERMANENT FASHION, IT SAYS WITH REFERENCE TO IT *THAT IT WAS GOOD*. [*Guide*, p. 353]

This refers to all the permanent things of world created in the days of creation prior to the first Sabbath. It refers to that which is already created, and not what is yet to be created.

But here, it does not say that it was good, and therefore the reference has to be to something which is not among the things which had already been created. And that is "something hidden."

BUT THERE IS SOMETHING HIDDEN, AS YOU WILL SEE, WITH REGARD TO THE FIRMAMENT AND THE THING ABOVE IT, WHICH IS CALLED *WATER*. [*Guide*, p. 353]

We are referred to the vision of Ezekiel, the firmament above the heads of the living creatures, and the water above it, the water that Rabbi Akiva said not to refer to as water.

And while the water exists as product of creation in the first days of creation, we would be in error to think of it as being the same order of creation as the things that are more common to us.

FOR IF THE MATTER IS CONSIDERED ACCORDING TO ITS EXTERNAL MEANING AND WITH A RECOURSE ONLY TO SUPERFICIAL SPECULATION, IT DOES NOT EXIST AT ALL. [*Guide*, p. 353]

We are again reminded that this should not be taken in a literal manner.

And we would make a mistake were we to understand this in terms of the physical things of creation.

FOR BETWEEN US AND THE LOWEST HEAVEN, THERE EXISTS NO BODY EXCEPT THE ELEMENTS, AND THERE IS NO WATER ABOVE THE AIR. [*Guide*, p. 353]

The physical water is clearly not intended.

THIS JUDGMENT APPLIES ALL THE MORE IF SOMEONE IMAGINES THAT THIS *FIRMAMENT* AND WHAT IS ABOVE IT ARE ABOVE THE HEAVEN. [*Guide*, p. 353]

If we were to take it in a physical sense

IN THAT CASE THE THING WOULD BE EVEN MORE IMPOSSIBLE AND REMOTE FROM APPREHENSION. [*Guide*, p. 353]

For Maimonides, and the philosophical climate in which he lived, the idea of permanent nonphysical entities was not at all strange. Within this class would be included the permanencies of the forms of Plato, and the permanencies of the Pythagorean type of mathematical relationships of the neo-Platonists. His concern here is not with such nonphysical entities; his concern is rather with the generation of new living souls.

He continues only to tell the reader:

IF, ON THE OTHER HAND, THE MATTER IS CONSID-ERED ACCORDING TO ITS INNER MEANING AND TO WHAT WAS TRULY INTENDED, IT IS MOST HIDDEN. [*Guide*, p. 353]

We understand the representation in terms of sexual activity such as may occur in the dreams and visions of the prophets, which he would want to conceal.

FOR IN THAT CASE IT WAS NECESSARY FOR IT TO BE ONE OF THE CONCEALED SECRETS SO THAT THE VULGAR SHOULD NOT KNOW IT. [*Guide*, p. 353]

If the representation be sexual, then it should be concealed from the vulgar.

Aware of this as a sexual act, Maimonides states next, in a moralistic vein,

HOW THEN COULD IT BE PROPER TO SAY OF SUCH A MATTER *THAT IT WAS GOOD?* [*Guide*, pp. 353-354]

What is good is of open and permanent value.

FOR THE MEANING OF THE WORDS, *THAT IT WAS GOOD,* IS THAT THE THING IN QUESTION IS OF EXTERNALLY VISIBLE AND MANIFEST UTILITY FOR THE EXISTENCE AND PERMANENCE OF THAT WHICH EXISTS. [*Guide*, p. 354]

But here it would not be useful to indicate to the people the nature of the representation.

BUT IN A MATTER WHOSE MEANING IS HIDDEN AND THAT, UNDERSTOOD IN ITS EXTERNAL MEANING, DOES NOT EXIST IN SUCH A WAY AS TO APPEAR USEFUL, WHAT UTILITY EXTERNALLY VISIBLE TO THE PEOPLE AT LARGE COULD THERE BE SO THAT THE WORDS, *THAT IT WAS GOOD,* COULD BE SAID WITH REFERENCE TO IT? [*Guide*, p. 354]

He then adds a final thought about the matter. Sex, while being important to existence, is not an end with respect to permanence.

I CANNOT HELP ADDING FOR YOU THE FOLLOWING EXPLANATION: THE THING IN QUESTION, THOUGH IT REPRESENTS A VERY GREAT PART OF THE EXISTENTS, DOES NOT CONSTITUTE THE PURPOSED END FOR THE PERMANENCE OF THAT WHICH EXISTS; AND THEREFORE THE WORDS, *THAT IT WAS GOOD,* COULD NOT BE SAID WITH REFERENCE TO IT. [*Guide*, p. 354]

And at this point Maimonides puts in an important hint for the interpretation of the vision of Ezekiel, as we will presently note. This is that the word *galgal* in the vision of Ezekiel is to be taken as in the sense of uncovering, as in the euphemism for sexual activity, the uncovering of nakedness. Since this refers to the creation of the world, it is permanent, albeit still in the Platonic mode of creation as the adding of form to matter, as Maimonides indicates in Chapter I:17. Thus Maimonides, here discussing the creation of souls as the unfinished work of creation, puts in a note that the sexual imagery could also be used in connection with the creation of the earth, in the first place, in the first days of creation. Maimonides devotes a chapter to this in his explication of the *Maaseh Merkabah*, Chapter III:4, which we will deal with below.

THIS COULD RATHER OCCUR WITH REFERENCE TO A COMPELLING NECESSITY THAT THE EARTH BE UN-COVERED. UNDERSTAND THIS. [*Guide*, p. 354]

The seventh, eighth, and ninth items are about the natural world. The seventh item is on the dependency of growth on water:

... THE SAGES HAVE MADE IT CLEAR THAT GOD ONLY MADE GRASS AND TREES GROW FROM THE EARTH AFTER HE HAD CAUSED RAIN TO FALL UPON THEM, AND THAT ITS SAYING, *AND THERE WENT UP A MIST FROM THE EARTH, AND SO ON*, IS A DESCRIPTION OF THE FIRST STATE OF MATTERS OBTAINING BEFORE THE COMMAND: *LET THE EARTH PUT FORTH GRASS.* FOR THIS REASON ONQELOS TRANSLATES: *AND THERE HAD GONE UP A MIST FROM THE EARTH.* THIS IS ALSO CLEAR FROM THE TEXT ITSELF BECAUSE OF ITS SAYING: *AND NO SHRUB OF THE FIELD WAS YET IN THE EARTH.* THIS IS CLEAR BY NOW. [*Guide*, p. 354]

The eighth item is on the dependency of natural events on light:

AFTER THE FORCES OF THE SPHERE, THE FIRST OF THE CAUSES PRODUCING GENERATION AND PASSING AWAY ARE LIGHT AND DARKNESS—BECAUSE OF THE

HEAT AND COLD CONSEQUENT UPON THEM. THE EL-
EMENTS INTERMIX IN CONSEQUENCE OF THE MOTION
OF THE SPHERE, AND THEIR COMBINATIONS VARY BE-
CAUSE OF LIGHT AND DARKNESS. THE FIRST COMBI-
NATION THAT IS PRODUCED BY THEM IS CONSTI-
TUTED BY TWO EXHALATIONS, WHICH ARE THE FIRST
CAUSES OF ALL THE METEOROLOGICAL PHENOMENA
AMONG WHICH RAIN FIGURES. THEY ARE ALSO THE
CAUSE OF THE MINERALS AND, AFTER THEM, OF THE
COMPOSITION OF THE PLANTS AND, AFTER THOSE, OF
THAT OF THE LIVING BEINGS; THE FINAL COMPOSI-
TION BEING THAT OF MAN. [*Guide*, p. 354]

Including human beings. Light produces change. Darkness maintains
things as they are:

DARKNESS IS THE NATURE OF THE EXISTENCE OF THE
WHOLE LOWER WORLD, LIGHT SUPERVENING IN IT. IT
SHOULD BE SUFFICIENT FOR YOU TO KNOW THAT
WHEN THERE IS NO LIGHT, THE STATE OF MATTERS
REMAINS PERMANENT. THE [SCRIPTURAL] TEXT
ABOUT THE *MAASEH BERESHIT* GOES EXACTLY IN
THIS ORDER, LEAVING OUT NOTHING. [*Guide*, p. 354]

The ninth item highlights excellence:

THEIR SAYING ... *ALL THE WORKS OF THE BEGIN-
NING WERE CREATED ACCORDING TO THEIR [PER-
FECT] STATURE, [PERFECT] REASON, AND [PERFECT]
BEAUTY (LE-SIBYONAM).* HE MEANS THAT EVERY-
THING THAT WAS CREATED, WAS CREATED AC-
CORDING TO THE PERFECTION OF QUANTITY, THE
PERFECTION OF FORM, AND WITH THE MOST BEAU-
TIFUL ACCIDENTS. THIS IS EXPRESSED IN THE WORD
LE-SIBYONAM (ACCORDING TO THEIR BEAUTY),
WHICH DERIVES FROM THE WORD *SEBI* (BEAUTY) AS
USED, FOR INSTANCE, IN THE PHRASE: WHICH IS *THE
SEBI (BEAUTY) OF ALL LANDS.* KNOW THIS, TOO, FOR
IT IS A GREAT PRINCIPLE, WHICH HAS BEEN ESTAB-
LISHED AS TRUE AND HAS BECOME CLEAR. [*Guide*, pp.
354–355]

Maimonides begins the tenth item as follows:

AMONG THE THINGS ON WHICH YOU OUGHT TO RE-FLECT CAREFULLY [*Guide*, p. 355]

This is a grade above that of enjoining the reader that an item is for him to "know," consistent with the distinction in the Mishnaic law between knowledge and understanding one's own knowledge. It is, as we have indicated, at a dividing point, beginning a treatment of human beings.

Prefatory to our consideration of this item we draw attention to two observations: First, the Hebrew word "know" is both intransitive and transitive. Especially in its transitive sense, it means sexual intercourse. We consider this in connection with the Mishnaic law. The Mishnaic law states that the person who is eligible to study the secret topics is one who understands his own knowledge. That may then be taken to mean the understanding of one's sexuality; and we take it that Maimonides so interpreted the Mishnaic law. Thus the understanding of sexuality, especially what is autogenic in sexuality, corresponding to what the human being is endowed with by virtue of his or her nature as a human being, and corresponding to what the human being is as a result of the creation in the days prior to the first Sabbath, is entailed. Second, by conjoining this that Maimonides cites from Genesis with the words that immediately precede, the text reads: "And God created man in His own image, in the image of God created He him: male and female created He them" (Genesis 1:27), we get the result that the characteristic by which man is made in the image of God is his or her sexuality, and that thus sexuality is attributed to the "Godhead," as Leo Strauss put it, as we have noted above. More accurately with respect to Maimonides' understanding, it is that God is conceived of in the *imagery* of human sexuality in the prophetic apprehensions. And we cannot properly understand the prophetic process without an understanding of the entailment of human sexuality in it.

It is useful to identify four themes within this item. The first is the connection between the two creation stories in Scripture. The second is the connection between what is before and after the first Sabbath. The third is Maimonides learning these things and engaging in exposition with respect to them. And the fourth is of the bisexuality of the human being that was created within the first six days of creation. The last can be considered to be the substantive part of the item, with the first three being introductory.

That which we consider to be the first part of the tenth item:

IS THE FACT THAT IT MENTIONS THE CREATION OF MAN IN THE *SIX DAYS OF THE BEGINNING* [*Guide*, p. 355]

This is to stress the distinction between that which transpires prior to the first Sabbath, and that which transpires after the first Sabbath.

AND SAYS: *MALE AND FEMALE CREATED HE THEM* (Genesis 1:27). [*Guide*, p. 355]

He cites the verse from the first creation story in Scripture. We are alerted that this item is about sexuality. This ties in with the second creation story in Scripture. It is the major topic of the item. Maimonides then says:

IT THEN CONCLUDES ITS ACCOUNT OF CREATION, SAYING: *AND THE HEAVEN AND THE EARTH WERE FINISHED, AND ALL THE HOST OF THEM* (Genesis 2:1). [*Guide*, p. 355]

This identifies the substantive termination of the first account of creation in Scripture.

There is an additional observation to be made here. We have cited the translation as it is given by Pines, referring to "hosts," which is a common translation of the word in Scripture. However, *sevaam* is more appropriately taken in the sense of *desire* or *pleasure* (Jastrow, p. 1258), and was probably so understood by Maimonides. Thus what we have is the conclusion of the creation to include its desires and pleasures, including those associated with sexuality. This may be one of the things on which we are enjoined to "reflect carefully."

The second part:

**THEN HE MAKES A NEW START REGARDING THE CRE-
ATION OF EVE FROM ADAM [*Guide*, p. 355]**

This announces the second account of the creation and introduces
the enumeration of the more substantive portion of item 10, and items
11 to 16 as follows:

THEN IT MAKES A NEW START [*Guide*, p. 355]

Maimonides provides a listing:

**REGARDING THE CREATION OF EVE FROM ADAM
[*Guide*, p. 355]**

This we identify as the substantive matter of item 10, especially with
the explanation which is to come.

AND MENTIONS THE TREE OF LIFE [*Guide*, p. 355]

This we identify as item 13.

AND THE TREE OF KNOWLEDGE [*Guide*, p. 355]

This we identify as item 14.

**AND THE TALE OF THE SERPENT AND ALL THAT
STORY [*Guide*, p. 355]**

This we identify as items 11, 12, and 16.

**AND IT MAKES OUT THAT ALL THIS HAPPENED AFTER
ADAM HAD BEEN PLACED IN THE GARDEN OF EDEN.
[*Guide*, p. 355]**

Adam being placed in the garden is in the fifteenth item.

After so identifying these items, Maimonides proceeds to clearly
assert that these are of the six days of creation prior to the first
Sabbath. In this way he leaves open the matters of the seventeenth
and the eighteenth items to refer in some way to that which takes place

after the six days of creation and after the first Sabbath. He thus writes:

> NOW ALL THE SAGES ... ARE UNANIMOUS IN THINK-
> ING THAT ALL THIS STORY OCCURRED ON FRIDAY,
> AND THAT NOTHING WAS CHANGED IN ANY RESPECT
> AFTER THE *SIX DAYS OF THE BEGINNING.* FOR THIS
> REASON, NONE OF THESE THINGS SHOULD BE JUDGED
> INCONGRUOUS; FOR, AS WE HAVE SAID, UP TILL THEN
> NO PERMANENTLY ESTABLISHED NATURE HAD COME
> ABOUT. [*Guide,* p. 355]

Maimonides interrupts this with some remarks concerning how he has learned of these things, and how he expresses them. This we take as the third part:

> WITHAL THEY HAVE MENTIONED THINGS THAT I
> WILL LET YOU HEAR, HAVING GLEANED THEM IN
> THEIR VARIOUS PLACES, AND I SHALL GIVE YOU
> POINTERS TO CERTAIN THINGS, JUST AS THEY...
> HAVE GIVEN US POINTERS. KNOW THAT THOSE
> THINGS THAT I SHALL MENTION TO YOU FROM THE
> DICTA OF THE SAGES ARE SAYINGS OF THE UTMOST
> PERFECTION; THEIR ALLEGORICAL INTERPRETATION
> WAS CLEAR TO THOSE TO WHOM THEY WERE AD-
> DRESSED, AND THEY ARE UNAMBIGUOUS. HENCE I
> WILL NOT GO TOO FAR IN INTERPRETING THEM, AND
> I WILL NOT SET FORTH THEIR MEANING AT LENGTH.
> FOR I WILL NOT BE *ONE WHO DIVULGES A SECRET.*
> HOWEVER, IT WILL SUFFICE FOR SOMEONE LIKE YOU IF
> I MENTION THEM IN A CERTAIN ORDER AND BY
> MEANS OF SLIGHT INDICATIONS. [*Guide,* p. 355]

Then, what we take as the fourth part: After this note to alert us, he presents the substantive part of item 10, explaining the bisexuality of "Male and female created He them," mentioned at the beginning of the item.

> ONE OF THESE DICTA IS THEIR SAYING THAT ADAM
> AND EVE WERE CREATED TOGETHER, HAVING THEIR

BACKS JOINED, AND THAT THIS BEING WAS DIVIDED AND ONE HALF OF IT, NAMELY EVE, TAKEN AND BROUGHT UP TO [ADAM]. [*Guide*, p. 355]

Maimonides explains how we might understand what is written in Scripture so as to yield the result that the human being was created as an androgyne in the first place.

THE EXPRESSION, *ONE OF HIS RIBS*, MEANS ACCORDING TO THEM ONE OF HIS SIDES. THEY QUOTE AS PROOF THE EXPRESSION, *A RIB OF THE TABERNACLE*, WHICH [THE ARAMAIC VERSION] TRANSLATES: *A SIDE OF THE TABERNACLE*. IN ACCORDANCE WITH THIS, THEY SAY THAT ["OF HIS RIBS"] MEANS: *OF HIS SIDES*. [*Guide*, pp. 355–356]

The notion that the human being was created first as an androgyne and then divided into two parts is to be found in Plato's *Symposium* in the speech of Aristophanes. [Jowett, vol. 2, pp. 189ff]. The idea of an original androgyne is also found in both the Midrash:

When the Holy One, Blessed be He created Adam, He created him an androgyne . . . He created him double faced, then He split him and made him of two backs, one back on this side and one back on the other side. [*Bereshit Rabbah* 8:1]

and in the Talmud:

God created two countenances in the first man, as it says *Behind and before hast Thou formed me* (Psalms 139:5). [*Berakot* 61a]

At first He had the idea to create two, and in the end one was created. [*Ketubot* 8a; *Erubin* 18a]

In the Greek story the division of human beings has its origin as a punishment for insolence with respect to the gods.

Terrible was their might and strength . . . and they made an attack upon the gods. . . . Doubt reigned in the celestial councils. Should they kill them and annihilate the race with thunderbolts . . . then there would be an end of sacrifices and worship which men offered to them; but, on the other hand, the gods could not suffer their insolence unrestrained. At last, after a good deal of reflection, Zeus discovered a way. He said: "... I have a plan which will humble their pride and improve their manners; men shall continue to exist, but I will cut them in two. ..."

... After the division the two parts of man, each desiring the other half, came together, and throwing their arms about one another, entwined in mutual embraces, longing to grow into one. ... [Zeus] turned the parts of generation round to the front ... and they sowed ... in one another; and after the transposition the male generated in the female in order that by the mutual embraces of man and woman they might breed, and the race might continue. ... So ancient is the desire of one another which is implanted in us, reuniting our original nature, making one of two, and healing the state of man. Each of us when separated, having one side only ... is but the indenture of a man, and he is always looking for his other half. ... And when one of them meets with his other half ... the pair are lost in an amazement of love and friendship and intimacy. ... [Jowett, vol. 2, pp. 190–191]

We take it that Maimonides intimates that the sexes are differentiated by their sex organs:

UNDERSTAND IN WHAT WAY IT HAS BEEN EX-PLAINED THAT THEY WERE TWO IN A CERTAIN RE-SPECT AND THAT THEY WERE ALSO ONE; AS IT SAYS: BONE OF MY BONES, AND FLESH OF MY FLESH. [*Guide*, p. 356]

The intimation is, perhaps, of bone as male and flesh as female, yet as a unity, as flesh and bone comprise a single organism.

THIS HAS RECEIVED ADDITIONAL CONFIRMATION THROUGH THE FACT THAT IT SAYS THAT BOTH OF THEM HAVE THE SAME NAME; FOR SHE IS CALLED 'ISHSHAH (WOMAN), BECAUSE SHE WAS TAKEN OUT OF 'ISH (MAN). [*Guide*, p. 356]

And their union is confirmed.

IT ALSO CONFIRMS THEIR UNION BY SAYING: *AND SHALL CLEAVE UNTO HIS WIFE, AND THEY SHALL BE ONE FLESH.* [*Guide*, p. 356]

Maimonides concludes his discussion of this item on the bisexuality of man by saying

HOW GREAT IS THE IGNORANCE OF HIM WHO DOES NOT UNDERSTAND THAT ALL THIS IS NECESSARY WITH A VIEW TO A CERTAIN NOTION. THIS THEN HAS BECOME CLEAR. [*Guide*, p. 356]

We take it that the point Maimonides is intimating is that this very sexuality of man, this bisexuality of man, is that which is involved in prophetic apprehension, the explanation of which is the purpose of *The Guide of the Perplexed*.

Items 11, 12, 15, and 16 bear on a scenario that Maimonides indicates or intimates concerning sexual conduct in the Garden of Eden prior to the acquisition of the knowledge of good and evil. In that scenario Eve has sexual intercourse with Satan and gives birth to Cain and Abel. Adam at that time begets devils. It was only after they were out of the Garden of Eden that they had Seth, who is the only true human being from Adam and Eve. It is also an allegory concerning the nature of human sexual and moral development.

As a preliminary to dealing with this directly, it is necessary to bring to bear the sharp distinction Maimonides makes between the knowledge of true and false, man's original endowment, and the knowledge of good and evil, later acquired by virtue of the events that transpired in the Garden.

> . . . one expresses in our language the notions of truth and falsehood by means of the terms *emet* and *sheqer*, and those of fine and bad by means of *tov* and *ra*. Now man by virtue of his intellect knows *truth* from *falsehood*. Accordingly, when man was [first] in his most perfect and excellent state, in accordance with his inborn disposition and possessed of his intellectual cognitions . . . he had no faculty that was engaged in any way in the consideration of generally accepted [valuative] things, and he did not apprehend them. So among these generally accepted [valuative] things even that which is most manifestly bad,

namely, uncovering the genitals, was not bad according to him, and he did not apprehend that it was bad. [*Guide*, p. 25]

Thus, for Maimonides, the example of the absence of the ability to judge good and bad was the uncovering of the genitals. We take Maimonides to mean the uncovering of the genitals not only in the sense of sheer nakedness, but also in the euphemistic scriptural sense, of engaging in deviant sexual conduct—as, for example, in the listing in Leviticus 18.

Sexuality and intellect in the sense of knowing truth and falsity constitute the original endowment of the human being. And the knowledge of good and evil is to be distinguished from that, coming later, in the allegory, and in human development, which this is an allegory of.

Let us first consider the fifteenth item:

AMONG THE THINGS YOU OUGHT TO KNOW IS THEIR DICTUM: *AND THE LORD GOD TOOK THE MAN— [THAT IS,] RAISED HIM—AND PUT HIM [VAYANI- CHEIHU] INTO THE GARDEN OF EDEN—[THAT IS,] HE GAVE HIM REST.* [*Guide*, p. 357]

This particular verb gets special attention from Maimonides in an earlier chapter, in which he offers a relatively lengthy lexicographical explanation to defend the idea that the word means to set, or establish, in the sense of making something to endure [*Guide*, p. 162]. Thus, we take Maimonides to be intimating that the qualities of intellect and sexuality are basic and primary in the human endowment. Such an understanding is consistent with the remainder of item fifteen.

THUS THEY DO NOT MAKE OUT THAT THIS TEXT MEANS THAT HE TOOK HIM AWAY FROM ONE PLACE AND PUT HIM IN ANOTHER, BUT THAT HE RAISED THE RANK OF HIS EXISTENCE AMONG THE EXISTENTS THAT COME INTO BEING AND PASS AWAY AND ESTAB- LISHED HIM IN A CERTAIN STATE. [*Guide*, p. 357]

We consider item 11 identifying Sammael as Satan, and he as the one "who led Eve astray" [*Guide*, p. 356]. The item begins:

AMONG THE THINGS YOU OUGHT TO KNOW IS THE FOLLOWING EXPLANATION, WHICH THEY GIVE IN THE *MIDRASH*. [*Guide*, p. 356]

The reference appears to be to *Pirke de Rabbi Eliezer*:

THEY MENTION THAT THE *SERPENT* HAD A RIDER, THAT IT WAS THE SIZE OF A CAMEL, THAT IT WAS THE RIDER WHO LED *EVE* ASTRAY, AND THAT THE RIDER WAS SAMMAEL. [*Guide*, p. 356]

Sammael is the leader of the troop of fallen angels.

Sammael was the great prince in heaven . . . He took his band and descended, and saw all the creatures [God] had created . . . and found among them none so skilled to do evil as the serpent. . . . Its appearance was something like that of the camel and he mounted it. The Torah began to cry aloud, saying, Why, O Sammael! now that the world is created, is it the time to rebel against [God]? Is it like a time when thou shouldst lift up thyself on high? [God] will laugh at the horse and its rider (Job 39:18). [*Pirke de Rabbi Eliezer*, p. 92]

Maimonides proceeds to make an argument for the identity of Sammael and Satan.

THEY APPLY THIS NAME TO SATAN. THUS YOU WILL FIND THAT THEY SAY IN A NUMBER OF PASSAGES THAT SATAN WANTED TO TEMPT *ABRAHAM OUR FATHER* NOT TO AGREE TO OFFER ISAAC AS A SACRIFICE, AND THAT HE ALSO WANTED TO TEMPT ISAAC NOT TO OBEY HIS FATHER. AND WITH REFERENCE TO THAT STORY, I MEAN TO SAY THE BINDING [OF ISAAC], THEY SAY LIKEWISE: *SAMMAEL CAME TO OUR FATHER ABRAHAM AND TOLD HIM: WHAT, OLD MAN! HAVE YOU LOST YOUR SENSES, AND SO ON.* THUS IT HAS BECOME CLEAR TO YOU THAT SAMMAEL IS SATAN. [*Guide*, p. 356]

At this point Maimonides includes an indication that we should be prepared for some form of word play.

THIS NAME IS USED WITH A VIEW TO A CERTAIN SIG-NIFICATION [*Guide*, p. 356]

We are invited to speculate on the possible meanings word play may open. But perhaps more important, Maimonides also invites speculation by means of word play on the word for serpent.

JUST AS THE NAME SERPENT (*NAHASH*) IS USED WITH A VIEW TO A CERTAIN SIGNIFICATION. [*Guide*, p. 356]

Our thought goes to *hashmal* and *nehoshet qalal* to be found in the scriptural account of the vision of Ezekiel. We take this as a hint by Maimonides of the sexuality associated with the *Maaseh Merkabah*. In connection with that, we identify two preliminary invitations by Maimonides to engage in word play with these words. We will only cite them at this point and reserve comment until later.

With regard to the same principle [of derivation of watch over from rod of an almond tree], in a reference to the Merkabah [the words] *hashmal* . . . *regel egel*, and *nehoshet qalal*. [*Guide*, p. 348]

Through this method [of derivation] very strange things appear, which are likewise secrets, as in its dictum with regard to the Merkabah: *nehoshet* . . . *qalal* . . . *regel* . . . *egel* . . . *barak*. . . . [*Guide*, p. 393]

And then Maimonides continues with the citation from the *Pirke de Rabbi Eliezer* we cited above:

WHEN THEY SPEAK OF ITS COMING TO DECEIVE EVE, THEY SAY: SAMMAEL WAS RIDING UPON IT; AND THE HOLY ONE, BLESSED BE HE, WAS LAUGHING AT BOTH THE CAMEL AND ITS RIDER. [*Guide*, p. 356]

Maimonides develops the idea of a primordial sexuality in that which we are identifying as item 12 among these items on the *Maaseh*

Bereshit. As a preliminary to this item we need to take note of Maimonides' indication of a primordial sexuality in connection with Adam which Maimonides includes among the very early chapters of *The Guide of the Perplexed*. In Chapter I:7 Maimonides indicates that

> ... none of the children of [Adam] born before [Seth] had been endowed with true human form. ... The authors of the Midrash say ... : *During the entire period of a hundred and thirty years ... Adam begot spirits*; they mean *devils*. [*Guide*, pp. 32–33]

Item 12 begins:

AMONG THE THINGS YOU OUGHT TO KNOW AND HAVE YOUR ATTENTION AROUSED TO IS THE FACT THAT THE *SERPENT* HAD IN NO RESPECT DIRECT RE-LATIONS WITH *ADAM* AND THAT IT DID NOT SPEAK TO HIM, AND THAT SUCH A CONVERSATION AND RE-LATION ONLY TOOK PLACE BETWEEN HIM AND *EVE*; IT WAS THROUGH THE INTERMEDIATION OF *EVE* THAT *ADAM* WAS HARMED AND THAT THE *SERPENT* DESTROYED HIM. [*Guide*, p. 356]

Maimonides, at this point, takes the sexist interpretation of the fall from Scripture at its word. We need also to note that Maimonides accepts the notion that form is to matter as male is to female, which we have already discussed. This is to be qualified.

In the remainder of this item, he indicates a view of sexual morality:

EXTREME ENMITY ONLY COMES TO BE REALIZED BE-TWEEN THE *SERPENT* AND *EVE* AND *ITS SEED AND HERS*. [*Guide*, p. 356]

We take it that Maimonides is taking the serpent as representative of deviant sexuality.

ON THE OTHER HAND *HER SEED* IS INDUBITABLY THE SEED OF *ADAM*. [*Guide*, p. 356]

Then, with what we take in the sense of higher and lower morality, the former associated with the head, the latter with the heel, he says:

EVEN MORE STRANGE IS THE TIE BETWEEN THE SER-
PENT AND EVE, I MEAN BETWEEN ITS SEED AND HERS,
A TIE THAT IS IN THE HEAD AND THE HEEL; SHE
BEING VICTORIOUS OVER IT THROUGH THE HEAD
AND IT OVER HER THROUGH THE HEEL. THIS IS ALSO
CLEAR. [Guide, p. 356]

Maimonides then goes on to indicate sexual deviation. Maimonides
says that Eve had sexual intercourse with the serpent, making the
meaning of his saying that Eve had been led astray more particular, on
the one hand, and more suggestive with respect to the imagery of the
Maaseh Merkabah, which this can be interpreted as preparatory
instruction for. He states:

AMONG THE AMAZING DICTA WHOSE EXTERNAL
MEANING IS EXCEEDINGLY INCONGRUOUS, BUT IN
WHICH – WHEN YOU OBTAIN A TRUE UNDER-
STANDING OF THE CHAPTERS OF THIS TREATISE –
YOU WILL ADMIRE THE WISDOM OF THE PARABLE
AND THEIR CORRESPONDENCE TO WHAT EXISTS
[Guide, pp. 356-357]

We note three things: First, it refers to something patently sexual;
second, Maimonides makes an announcement of this as having
significance for the understanding of the treatise as a whole; third, he
makes an announcement that the sexual which is being expressed is a
parable. This clearly identifies the two-step method of Rabbi Akiva –
the recognition of the sexual, and the recognition of the sexual as
allegorical – which is indicated in the section in Hagigah in the discussion of the Maaseh Bereshit and the Maaseh Merkabah, as we have
discussed above.

IS THEIR STATEMENT: WHEN THE SERPENT CAME TO
EVE, IT CAST POLLUTION INTO HER. THE POLLU-
TION OF [THE SONS OF] ISRAEL, WHO HAD BEEN
PRESENT AT MOUNT SINAI, HAS COME TO AN END.
[AS FOR] THE POLLUTION OF THE NATIONS WHO
HAD NOT BEEN PRESENT AT MOUNT SINAI, THEIR
POLLUTION HAS NOT COME TO AN END. [Guide, p. 357]

The idea of the serpent, Satan, or Sammael, having had sexual intercourse with Eve is variously found in the traditional literature. The idea that she conceived is explicitly stated in *Pirke de Rabbi Eliezer*: "[Sammael] riding on the serpent came to her, and she conceived . . ." (Friedlander, p. 150).

Maimonides here, invoking the connection with Mount Sinai from the Talmud (*Shabbat* 146a; *Yebamot* 103b), makes it clear that the project at Mount Sinai was that of overcoming the primordial kind of sexuality indicated by these interpretations of the scriptural account of creation. Thus he says:

THIS TOO YOU SHOULD FOLLOW UP IN YOUR THOUGHT. [*Guide*, p. 357]

In item 16 Maimonides completes the scenario with the declaration about the different status of Cain and Abel, on the one hand, and Seth, on the other, as he does in Chapter I:7.

AMONG THE THINGS YOU OUGHT TO ALSO TO KNOW AND HAVE YOUR ATTENTION AROUSED TO IS THE MANIFESTATION OF WISDOM CONSTITUTED BY THE FACTS THAT THE TWO CHILDREN OF *ADAM* WERE CALLED *CAIN* AND *ABEL*; THAT IT WAS *CAIN* WHO SLEW *ABEL IN THE FIELD*; THAT BOTH OF THEM PERISHED, THOUGH THE AGGRESSOR HAD A RESPITE; AND THAT ONLY *SETH* WAS VOUCHSAFED A TRUE EXISTENCE: *FOR GOD HATH APPOINTED (SHAT) ME ANOTHER SEED*. THIS HAS ALREADY BEEN SHOWN TO BE CORRECT. [*Guide*, p. 357]

Maimonides invites the reader to engage in a word-play exercise with respect to meanings that might be entailed in the names Cain and Abel, to correspond to the scriptural indication of the derivation of the name of Seth. While some more specific indications might well be found in *The Guide of the Perplexed*, it may also be the case that in these instances Maimonides leaves the reader on his own. Our thought is brought to the general question that is raised by our enterprise. That is, how far can we go in our speculations concerning that which is intimated without specific indicators making it highly likely that our speculations correspond to the intentions Maimonides had as he wrote? In a way, this item represents the limit.

We turn now to the two items that we skipped over as we addressed the items in connection with the primordial sexual scenario. These are two items that give indications concerning the two trees mentioned in Scripture, the Tree of Life and the Tree of Knowledge of Good and Evil. We take Maimonides to understand the trees as corresponding to the *Maaseh Bereshit* and the *Maaseh Merkabah*, as part of the creation itself.

Item 13 concerns the Tree of Lfe, corresponding to the *Maaseh Bereshit*:

AMONG THE THINGS YOU OUGHT TO KNOW IS THEIR DICTUM: [THE SIZE OF] THE TREE OF LIFE [CORRE-SPONDS] TO A WALK OF FIVE HUNDRED YEARS [*Guide*, p. 357]

We take this to mean that a walk of five hundred years indicates that whatever is being referred to is unreachable by human beings, who do not live five hundred years.

AND ALL THE WATERS OF THE BEGINNING SPRING FROM BENEATH IT. [*Guide*, p. 357]

Identifying it with *Bereshit*.

THEY MAKE IT CLEAR THERE THAT THIS MEASURE IS MEANT TO APPLY TO THE THICKNESS OF ITS BODY AND NOT TO THE DIMENSIONS OF ITS BOUGHS. THEY SAY: THE OBJECT OF THIS SAYING IS NOT ITS BOUGHS, BUT ITS TRUNK, [WHOSE SIZE CORRE-SPONDS] TO A WALK OF FIVE HUNDRED YEARS. THE INTERPRETATION OF ITS TRUNK IS: THE THICKNESS OF ITS UPRIGHT TIMBER. THEY ADD THE SUPPLEMEN-TARY REMARK IN ORDER TO COMPLETE THE EXPLA-NATION AND THE EXPOSITION OF THE MEANING. THIS THEN IS CLEAR. [*Guide*, p. 357]

The boughs are the manifestations of nature, which are readily available and which, we have seen, are associated with the argument for the existence of God. This is also consistent with Maimonides' indication that the *Maaseh Bereshit* corresponds to natural science [*Guide*, p. 6].

Item 14, which we are taking as being an intimation by Maimonides concerning the *Maaseh Merkabah*, is extraordinarily laconic. However, it is consistent with Maimonides' understanding of the *Maaseh Merkabah* as most secret.

> AMONG THE THINGS YOU OUGHT ALSO TO KNOW IS THEIR DICTUM: *AS FOR THE TREE OF KNOWLEDGE, THE HOLY ONE, BLESSED BE HE, HAS NEVER REVEALED THAT TREE TO MAN AND WILL NEVER REVEAL IT.* THIS IS CORRECT INASMUCH AS THE NATURE OF WHAT EXISTS REQUIRES IT. [*Guide*, p. 357]

The essence of God, approachable by prophets only through their dreams and visions, and never even frontally revealed to Moses, representing the ultimate creativity of God, will never be revealed.

Maimonides' presentation of the two trees is at variance with the manifest content of Scripture. For in Scripture, human beings are said to have eaten from the Tree of Knowledge: "And when the woman saw that the tree was good for food . . . she took of the fruit thereof and did eat; and she gave also unto her husband with her, and he did eat" (Genesis 3:6) and are banished from Eden to prevent them from eating from the Tree of Life: "And the Lord God said: 'Behold the man is become as one of us, to know good and evil; and now, lest he put forth his hand, and take also of the tree of life, and eat, and live for ever.' Therefore the Lord God sent him forth from the garden of Eden . . ." (Genesis 3:22–23).

However, he links absolute inaccessibility with the Tree of Knowledge, and technical inaccessibility with the Tree of Life, the reverse of what we might expect from the external meanings of Scripture. The gradation of accessibility does, however, correspond to the gradation of the *Maaseh Bereshit* and the *Maaseh Merkabah*, as indicated in the Mishnaic law.

We turn now to consider the remaining two items, those we have designated as 17 and 18. Item 17 deals with language. Item 18 deals with words which Maimonides describes as those that "occur with reference to the relation between the heaven and God." We find that these allude to creativity.

The item we designate as 17 is as follows:

AMONG THE THINGS YOU OUGHT TO KNOW AND HAVE YOUR ATTENTION AROUSED TO IS THE DIC-TUM: *AND MAN GAVE NAMES, AND SO ON.* [*Guide*, p. 357]

Maimonides here refers to: "And the man gave names to all the cattle, and to the fowl of the air, and to every beast in the field; but for Adam there was not found a helpmeet for him" (Genesis 2:20). The important point is that language is artificial.

IT INFORMS US THAT LANGUAGES ARE CONVEN-TIONAL AND NOT NATURAL, AS HAS SOMETIMES BEEN THOUGHT. [*Guide*, pp. 357–358]

Language is a human product for Maimonides. In this discussion of the creation, of the creation of the world by God, he finds it necessary to make it clear that language is not something made by God, but is something made by human beings. This has important theological ramifications, being counter to all views that center on the "word" or even the "name" of God.

This leads into the indications concerning creativity that are to be found in the last item, item 18.

AMONG THE THINGS YOU OUGHT TO REFLECT UPON [*Guide*, p. 358]

As we have noted this form of punctuation of the item, using "reflect" rather than "know," places this item in parallel with item 10, which is the beginning of the discussion of human sexuality. This item patently refers to words used in Scripture with respect to God's creativity.

ARE THE FOUR WORDS THAT OCCUR WITH REFER-ENCE TO THE RELATION BETWEEN THE HEAVEN AND GOD. [*Guide*, p. 358]

Let us begin with the thought that "the relation between the heaven and God" is that the latter created the former. It is important to take note of the classical three-way formulation of God's creativity as given in Isaiah, ". . . created (*berativ*) . . . formed (*yezartiv*) . . . made (*asitiv*)" (Isaiah 43:7), in terms of the three words, *baro*, *yazar*, and *assoh*. As will become evident, the purpose of this item is to single out *yazar* as the special word for God imparting a soul to the human being. Maimonides gives a list of four words:

THESE WORDS ARE BARO' (TO CREATE) AND ASSOH (TO MAKE) AND QANOH (TO ACQUIRE, POSSESS) AND EL (GOD). [*Guide*, p. 358]

He exemplifies. With respect to *baro*:

IT SAYS: *GOD (ELOHIM) CREATED (BARA') THE HEAVEN AND THE EARTH.* [*Guide*, p. 358]

With respect to *assoh*:

AND IT SAYS; *IN THE DAY THAT THE LORD GOD MADE (ASSOT) EARTH AND HEAVEN.* [*Guide*, p. 358]

With respect to *qanoh*:

IT SAYS ALSO: *POSSESSOR (QONEH) OF HEAVEN AND EARTH.* [*Guide*, p. 358]

With respect to *El*:

AND IT SAYS: *GOD (EL) OF THE WORLD. AND: THE GOD (ELOHE) OF THE HEAVEN, AND THE GOD (ELOHE) OF THE EARTH.* [*Guide*, p. 358]

We take it that the Isaiah list is the reference list for Maimonides. Two words are in common with the Isaiah list, *baro* and *assoh*. One word, *yazar*, is not included in his list. Two words, *El* and *qanoh*, are additional.

Grammatically the word *El* is different from the others. It is a noun. The other words are verbs. However, the examples clearly suggest that if we allow *El* to have the meaning "creator," the effect is that of a verb. His examples then become "Creator of the world" and "The creator of the heaven, and the creator of the earth." The meaning is still of "the relation between heaven and God." If *El* is understood in the sense of angel, then it is with reference to the ongoing relation between heaven and God.

As far as the word *qanoh* is concerned, Maimonides makes sure that the careful reader will dismiss it.

> WITH REFERENCE TO THEM [HEAVEN AND EARTH] IT SAYS QANOH [ACQUIRE, POSSESS], BECAUSE HE . . . HAS DOMINION OVER THEM JUST AS A MASTER HAS OVER HIS SLAVES. FOR THIS REASON HE IS ALSO CALLED THE LORD ('ADON) OF ALL THE EARTH AND THE LORD (HA-'ADON). HOWEVER, AS THERE IS NO LORD ('ADON) WITHOUT THERE BEING SOMETHING POSSESSED (QIN-YAN) BY HIM, THIS TENDS TOWARD THE ROAD OF THE BELIEF IN THE ETERNITY OF A CERTAIN MATTER. [*Guide*, p. 358]

If the word *qanoh* leads to the belief in the eternity of matter, the objectionable assumption made by Aristotle, it is to be rejected. Rather,

> THE TERMS BARO' [CREATE] AND 'ASSOH [MAKE] ARE USED WITH REFERENCE TO [HEAVEN AND EARTH]. [*Guide*, p. 358]

While rejecting *qanoh* for the reason that it opens the door to the Aristotelian assumption, the word *El*, in the sense of creator, is to be looked upon more favorably.

> AS FOR THE EXPRESSIONS, THE GOD (ELOHE) OF THE HEAVEN AND ALSO GOD OF THE WORLD (EL OLAM), THEY ARE USED WITH RESPECT TO HIS PERFECTION. AND THEIRS. [*Guide*, pp. 358–359]

We pause to comment on the peculiarity of "theirs." To appreciate this fully, we go back to Maimonides' understanding that the creation was of three things, "the *Elohim* with the heaven and with the earth." The *Elohim* are the abiding creative forces within history. They are that whereby God's creativity is exerted in history. Continuing, Maimonides says,

> HE IS *ELOHIM*–THAT IS, HE WHO GOVERNS–AND THEY ARE THOSE GOVERNED BY HIM, NOT IN THE SENSE OF DOMINATION–FOR THAT IS THE MEANING OF *QONEH* [POSSESSOR]. [*Guide,* p. 359]

Qoneh is rejected because it suggests the Aristotelian eternity. An additional reason for rejecting it is given; it has a connotation of domination. We take special note of the implicit distinction Maimonides makes for God's role between that of creator and that of dominator, accepting the former and rejecting the latter.

> BUT WITH RESPECT TO HIS RANK . . . IN BEING AND IN [THE] RELATION [OF HIS BEING] TO THEIRS. FOR HE IS THE DEITY AND NOT THEY. [*Guide,* p. 359]

We take this in the sense of the first sentence of Scripture as understood by Maimonides, that God created the Elohim with the heaven and with the earth. God, the original creator, is the deity, and not the Elohim.

> I MEAN HEAVEN. KNOW THIS. WE TAKE THIS TO MEAN, *I MEAN [AS THE] HEAVEN [WAS CREATED BY HIM, SO WERE THEY]. KNOW THIS.* [*Guide,* p. 359]

Maimonides distinguishes between the meanings *baro* and *assoh*, in the sense of the difference between the first instant of the creation of the universe out of nothing, in the sense of the creation of the Elohim with the heaven and with the earth, on the one hand, and the formative action presumed to have taken place in the subsequent days of creation, on the other.

HOWEVER, WITH REGARD TO THE EXISTENCE PROPER TO THE WHOLE OF THE WORLD, WHICH IS CONSTI-TUTED BY THE HEAVEN AND THE EARTH, THE TERM BARO' (CREATE) IS USED. FOR ACCORDING TO US IT SIGNIFIES BRINGING INTO EXISTENCE OUT OF NON-EXISTENCE. IT ALSO SAYS 'ASSOH (TO MAKE), WHICH IS APPLIED TO THE SPECIFIC FORMS THAT WERE GIVEN TO THEM—I MEAN THEIR NATURES. [*Guide*, p. 358]

Maimonides identifies three words that occur in Scripture with respect to what God does, but that are to be subsumed under the heading of *assoh*.

REGARDING THE DICTA: *WHICH THOU HAST ESTAB-LISHED (KONANTA); HATH SPREAD OUT (TIPPHAH) THE HEAVENS; WHO STRETCHEST OUT (NOTEH) THE HEAVENS,* THE TERMS USED THEREIN ARE INCLUDED IN THE VERB *TO MAKE (ASSOH).* [*Guide*, p. 358]

However, these are to be distinguished from *yazar*:

AS FOR THE WORD *YEZIRAH* (FORMING), IT DOES NOT OCCUR IN THIS SENSE; FOR IT SEEMS TO ME THAT *YEZIRAH* IS ONLY APPLIED TO SHAPING AND FORMING A CONFIGURATION OR TO ONE OF THE OTHER ACCIDENTS, FOR SHAPE AND CONFIGURATION ARE ALSO ACCIDENTS. FOR THIS REASON IT SAYS; *WHO FORMETH (YOZER) THE LIGHT*—FOR LIGHT IS AN ACCIDENT—AND; *THAT FORMETH (YOZER) THE MOUNTAINS*—THAT IS WHO SHAPES THEM. SIMI-LARLY: *AND THE LORD GOD FORMED (VA-YIZER),* AND SO ON. [*Guide*, p. 358]

The "and so on" is revealing. For it refers to the ensoulment of Adam, what God will ever continue to do in history: "And the Lord God formed (*vayezer*) the man from the dust of the earth and He breathed the soul of life into his nostrils . . ." (Genesis 2:7;) [*Guide*, p. 358]. What the item then succeeds in doing is to identify *baro* and *assoh* with the *Maaseh Bereshit*, and *yazar* with the *Maaseh Merkabah*.

After thus providing this itemized presentation with respect to the *Maaseh Bereshit*, including the indications in it that bridge it to the *Maaseh Merkabah*, Maimonides ends the chapter by drawing attention to the place of these items in the whole of his argument. He tells the reader to take the items together:

THE SUM OF THE OBSERVATIONS GIVEN HERE [*Guide, p. 359*]

And add them to what he has said in *The Guide of the Perplexed* before and after, letting us know that the whole of it is an integrated argument:

TOGETHER WITH WHAT HAS BEEN STATED BEFORE AND WHAT WILL BE STATED AFTER WITH REGARD TO THIS SUBJECT. [*Guide*, p. 359]

The subject is the meaning of prophecy. Scripturally this is primarily represented by the *Maaseh Bereshit* and the *Maaseh Merkabah*, the accounts that refer to God's creativity. Maimonides has "stated before" the meaning of terms associated with prophecy and the arguments for the existence, in contrast with essence, of God, including what he takes to be the excellent arguments of Aristotle and the less than excellent arguments of the Mutakallimum; albeit Aristotle's arguments are faulted for their failure to accept the creation out of nothingness. The reach of the prophets toward essence is greater than that of the philosophers. The essence is ultimately unreachable. And the reach of the prophets other than Moses is only through dreams and visions.

What is yet to be "stated after with regard to this subject" comprises three things. First, there is the discussion of the Sabbath and its significance for its being after the *Maaseh Bereshit* and before the *Maaseh Merkabah* in substance — and in the presentation in *The Guide of the Perplexed*. Second, the treatise on the psychology of prophecy, the psychology of dreams and visions. Third, the explication of the *Maaseh Merkabah* in as explicit a manner may be permitted.

What has been "stated before and what will be stated after" are exhaustive with respect to the topic. There are pages in *The Guide of the Perplexed* following the discussion of the *Maaseh Merkabah*. They,

however, will be of "other subjects," as he mentions after he has
completed his discussion of the *Maaseh Merkabah* [*Guide*, p. 430].

IS SUFFICIENT CONSIDERING THE PURPOSE OF THIS TREATISE [*Guide*, p. 359]

And again reminding the reader that the addressee should have
certain talent, background, and the afflictions of heartache and
perplexity.

AND CONSIDERING HIM WHO STUDIES IT. [*Guide*, p. 359]

III

A Commentary on Chapter II:31,
on the Sabbath, with Some
Further Commentary on
Chapters I:67–70

W̲e consider Chapter II:31, on the Sabbath. The chapter is very short. However, as we have already pointed out, it is placed between the explicit discussions of the *Maaseh Bereshit* and the *Maaseh Merkabah*, after Chapter II:30 and before the Introduction to Part III and Chapters III:1–7. We take this physical arrangement of the text of *The Guide of the Perplexed* as an indication of Maimonides' substantive thought of the relationship of the Sabbath to the *Maaseh Bereshit* and the *Maaseh Merkabah* as referring back to the former and ahead to the latter. The chapter on the Sabbath is the substantive center of *The Guide of the Perplexed*.

As a preliminary to the discussion of Chapter II:31, we consider Chapters I:67–70, four extraordinarily explicit theological chapters. As we will note, the first and fourth of these chapters are with respect to prophetic apprehension, while the second and third are with respect to philosophical apprehension.

In Chapter I:67 Maimonides alludes to a critical verse: "[He] rested (*shabbat*) and ensouled (*vayyinaphash*)" (Exodus 31:17) saying ". . . the verb *vayyinaphash* . . . derive[s] from the word *nephesh* (soul) [*Guide*, p. 162], permitting the translation "ensouled."

We consider the structural place of Chapter I:67 within the pages of

The Guide of the Perplexed relative to the three chapters, Chapters I: 68, 69, and 70, that follow it. Let us make an outline of the contents of these four chapters.

Chapter I:67: The chapter appears as a lexicographical one dealing, in the first instance, with what Scripture means when it says of God that "He said." In the second instance, within this chapter Maimonides speaks of the Sabbath and brings in the verb *vayyinaphash,* as we have indicated.

Chapter I:68: A summary of the Aristotelian notion of God as "intellect . . . intellectually cognizing subject . . . intellectually cognized object" [*Guide,* p. 163].

Chapter I:69: A summary of the notion that God may be conceived of in terms of three of the Aristotelian four causes, the efficient, formal, and final causes, and leaving out the material cause: "Now one of the opinions of the philosophers, an opinion with which I do not disagree, is that God . . . is the efficient cause . . . of the world . . . , that He is the form, and that He is the end" [*Guide,* p. 167].

Chapter I:70: A chapter in which we identify two critical notions: First, that God is "the rider," *rokeb.* We have already indicated how Maimonides leads us to take this as derivative from the word *kerub,* cherub, making this word to have the meaning "the cheruber," allowing the sense "the maker of cherubim." "Know that this expression, *the rider of the heavens* (Deuteronomy 33:26) is figuratively used of Him . . ." [*Guide,* p. 172]. Second, that God provides souls in Araboth. Maimonides cites and discusses the passage from *Hagigah* 12b which describes Araboth, Araboth of the expression *The rider in Araboth* (Psalms 68:5) [*Guide,* p. 172]: "*Araboth—that in which [exist] . . . the souls and the spirits that shall be created in the future . . .*" (*Hagigah* 12b) [*Guide,* p. 173].

From the substantive point of view, Chapters I:67 and I:70 go together. One indicates that God is the ensouler in history. The other describes the process as taking place in Araboth. These chapters relate to prophetic apprehension—in the sense of the *Maaseh Merkabah* and the reach toward the essence of God, which is involved.

Chapters I:68 and I:69 go together as the description of God from the Aristotelian point of view, as intellect and as cause. These chapters relate to the philosophic arguments for the existence of God. We have already noted how, in the view of Maimonides, the philosopher is inferior to the prophet, possessed only of an excellent rational faculty, prevented from apprehending God's creativity by his view of the eternity of time, while the prophet is possessed of excellence in the imaginative faculty as well, and is not impeded with respect to apprehending the creativity of God because he accepts the creation out of nothingness.

It is patent that the two philosophical chapters sandwiched between the prophetic chapters are to be understood literally, however abstractly, while the other two chapters are to be understood figuratively.

Chapters I:68 and I:69 represent a serious theological problem. In *The Guide of the Perplexed*, Maimonides argues at length that God may not be described in positive attributes. Yet it would appear, at least superficially, that his description of God in terms of intellect in one chapter, and cause in another, is in violation of this principle. Yet if we fully allow the distinction between existence and essence, the difficulty is resolved. For the description in terms of intellect and cause goes only to the proof of the existence of God, not to the essence of God.

In putting in these two chapters, Chapters I:68–69, seemingly giving a description of God in positive terms, intellect and cause, Maimonides set himself up for criticism from some of his coreligionists as having defected from piety—as indeed happened in subsequent history. For there were those who regarded Maimonides as having transgressed, like Aher, by becoming enchanted by Greek texts. However, the criticism would have cogency only for the reader who had not sufficiently understood the significance of the distinction between existence and essence. And for those who failed to appreciate the distinction, these chapters constitute a kind of misdirection. Insofar as some readers were thus misdirected, Maimonides was successful in keeping that which he had to communicate concealed in accordance with the Mishnaic law.

As for the content of the other chapters, I:67 and I:70, insofar as they appeared to entail ascription of positive attributes to God, they were of another order. Those ascribed attributes were, as Maimonides made amply clear, figurative. They were subject to interpretation in accordance with the principle of Rabbi Akiva.

After this preliminary concerning the description of God in the four chapters, Chapters I:67–70, we approach Chapter II:31 with the expectation that Maimonides will both intimate and conceal the creations before and after the first Sabbath.

Maimonides opens with an indication that he expects the reader to have been informed concerning the Sabbath already. We take it that he means this in the sense of the two meanings associated with the Sabbath, the *Maaseh Bereshit* and the *Maaseh Merkabah*, that before and that after the first Sabbath.

PERHAPS IT HAS ALREADY BECOME CLEAR TO YOU WHAT IS THE CAUSE OF THE LAW'S ESTABLISHING THE SABBATH SO FIRMLY [*Guide*, p. 359]

So firmly that the death penalty was invoked for violating it.

AND ORDAINING DEATH BY STONING FOR BREAKING IT. THE MASTER OF THE PROPHETS HAS PUT PEOPLE TO DEATH BECAUSE OF IT. [*Guide*, p. 359]

He draws attention to its rank in the Decalogue:

IT COMES THIRD AFTER THE EXISTENCE OF THE DEITY AND THE DENIAL OF DUALISM. [*Guide*, p. 359]

His saying "denial of dualism" is extraordinary. The commandment that he refers to as "the denial of dualism" is the commandment "Thou shalt have no other gods before me," with no special reference to "dualism."

We take this as an intimation by Maimonides with respect to the dualism of male and female. The meaning of this is that the prophetic vision entails the apprehension of what seems to be a dual deity, comprising male and female personages. As we have said, for Maimonides this does not constitute a violation of the commandment because the vision is a figurative expression and arises out of a dream or a vision of the prophets other than Moses, and has no other veridicality. Indeed, when Maimonides explicates the vision of the dual "divided man" in Ezekiel, he makes a special point to deny that the vision of Ezekiel is the apprehension of the deity. He states: ". . . the likeness of a man that was on the throne and that was divided is not a parable referring to Him . . . but to a created thing" [Guide, p. 430].

That which the Talmud contains concerning what Aher apprehended refers specifically to a dualism, and is thus a major hint that such a dualism is the content that is apprehended: "[Aher] saw that permission was granted to Metatron to sit . . . Forbearance and peace! Could there be two powers?" (Hagigah 15a).

We may also look upon this as a particularly revealing example of the way in which Maimonides takes himself to be interacting with the reader. The chapter gives indications concerning the dual significance of the Sabbath. Thus, a reader who reads syncretically might see "dualism" in a context discussing dualism and think no further about it, believing that the dualism referred to is the same as the dualism the chapter as a whole is devoted to. However, a careful reading indicates that the dualism referred to is the dualism associated with the second commandment and not the commandment associated with the Sabbath. We take the remainder of Maimonides' comments partly as an effort to cover his characterization of the commandment "Thou shalt have no other gods before me" as the "denial of dualism," by stressing the dualism of the Maaseh Bereshit and Maaseh Merkabah.

FOR THE PROHIBITION OF THE WORSHIP OF ANY-THING EXCEPT HIM ONLY AIMS AT THE AFFIRMATION OF BELIEF IN HIS UNITY. [Guide, p. 359]

This returns the reader to allowing the alternative as possibly plural, which could not be the case with "dualism."

Our attention is then further drawn away from the issue of one or more than one alternatives, to the question of action supporting the opinion that there is only one god.

YOU KNOW FROM WHAT I HAVE SAID THAT OPINIONS DO NOT LAST UNLESS THEY ARE ACCOMPANIED BY

ACTIONS THAT STRENGTHEN THEM, MAKE THEM
GENERALLY KNOWN, AND PERPETUATE THEM
AMONG THE MULTITUDE. [*Guide*, p. 359]

Our attention is then drawn by Maimonides to consider the *Maaseh
Bereshit* rather than the *Maaseh Merkabah*, the latter being where the
issue of dualism in the prophetic apprehension is important.

FOR THIS REASON WE ARE ORDERED BY THE LAW TO
EXALT THIS DAY, IN ORDER THAT THE PRINCIPLE OF
THE CREATION OF THE WORLD IN TIME BE ESTAB-
LISHED AND UNIVERSALLY KNOWN IN THE WORLD
THROUGH THE FACT THAT ALL PEOPLE REFRAIN
FROM WORKING ON ONE AND THE SAME DAY. . . . IF IT
IS ASKED: WHAT IS THE CAUSE OF THIS? THE ANSWER
IS: *FOR IN SIX DAYS THE LORD MADE* [*Guide*, p. 359]

And were we to stop reading at this point, it is as though the matter
were completely indicated. Yet, he cannot leave it at that. For him, the
significance of the Sabbath is with respect to both the *Maaseh Bereshit*
and the *Maaseh Merkabah*. And it is important that he tell us that in
The Guide of the Perplexed. He therefore goes on:

FOR THIS COMMANDMENT TWO DIFFERENT CAUSES
ARE GIVEN, CORRESPONDING TO TWO DIFFERENT EF-
FECTS. [*Guide*, p. 359]

And we understand that this means that the Sabbath has reference to
both the *Maaseh Bereshit* and the *Maaseh Merkabah*. So now we get
two sets of citation.

IN THE FIRST *DECALOGUE* THE CAUSE FOR EXALTING
THE SABBATH IS STATED AS FOLLOWS: *FOR IN SIX
DAYS THE LORD MADE, AND SO ON.* [*Guide*, p. 359]

and

IN DEUTERONOMY, ON THE OTHER HAND, IT IS SAID:
AND THOU SHALT REMEMBER THAT THOU WAST A

SLAVE IN EGYPT. THEREFORE THE LORD THY GOD COMMANDED THEE TO KEEP THE SABBATH DAY. [*Guide*, p. 359]

One refers backward, and the other refers forward from the first Sabbath.
He then goes on to differentiate them.

THIS IS CORRECT. FOR THE EFFECT, ACCORDING TO THE FIRST STATEMENT, IS TO REGARD THAT DAY AS NOBLE AND EXALTED. AS IT SAYS: *WHEREFORE THE LORD BLESSED THE SABBATH DAY, AND HALLOWED IT.* THIS IS THE EFFECT CONSEQUENT UPON THE WORDS: *FOR IN SIX DAYS, AND SO ON.* [*Guide*, pp. 359–360]

The backward reference is with respect to nobility and exaltation. Then, with respect to the forward reference:

HOWEVER, THE ORDER GIVEN US BY THE LAW WITH REGARD TO IT AND THE COMMANDMENT ORDAINING US IN PARTICULAR TO KEEP IT [*Guide*, p. 360]

That is, to rest on the Sabbath days in days following the first Sabbath.

ARE AN EFFECT CONSEQUENT UPON THE CAUSE THAT WE HAD BEEN *SLAVES IN EGYPT* WHERE WE DID NOT WORK ACCORDING TO OUR FREE CHOICE AND WHEN WE WISHED AND WHERE WE HAD NOT THE POWER TO REFRAIN FROM WORKING. [*Guide*, p. 360]

And furthermore, to exercise freedom of choice, an essential feature of the souls generated in connection with the *Maaseh Merkabah*. Referring again to the backward and forward reference of the Sabbath,

THEREFORE WE HAVE BEEN COMMANDED INACTIVITY AND REST SO THAT WE SHOULD CONJOIN THE TWO THINGS: [*Guide*, p. 360]

Backward,

THE BELIEF IN A TRUE OPINION – NAMELY THE CRE-
ATION OF THE WORLD IN TIME [*Guide,* p. 360]

That is, the *Maaseh Bereshit,* the extant world.

WHICH, AT THE FIRST GO AND WITH THE SLIGHTEST
OF SPECULATIONS, SHOWS THAT THE DEITY EXISTS
[*Guide,* p. 360]

That is, that which provides the ground for the belief in the existence
of God.
    And forward,

AND THE MEMORY OF THE BENEFIT GOD BESTOWED
UPON US BY GIVING US REST *FROM UNDER THE BUR-
DENS OF THE EGYPTIANS.* [*Guide,* p. 360]

And then still another version.

ACCORDINGLY THE SABBATH IS, AS IT WERE, OF UNI-
VERSAL BENEFIT, BOTH [*Guide,* p. 360]

First,

WITH REFERENCE TO A TRUE SPECULATIVE OPINION
[*Guide,* p. 360]

Second,

AND TO THE WELL-BEING OF THE STATE OF THE
BODY. [*Guide,* p. 360]

IV

A Commentary on the Introduction to the Third Part, and Chapters III:1–7, on the Maaseh Merkabah

Maimonides' explicit commentary on the *Maaseh Merkabah* is made in the Introduction to Part III and Chapters III:1–7 [*Guide*, pp. 415–430]. We will begin our commentary with a brief statement of what the nature of the prophetic vision is: The vision is of the generation of the cherubim or the living creatures. These are the souls of human beings.

The vision consists of three parts. First, the living creatures in the center; second, below them, the *ophannim*. These comprise the matter with which the soul is joined in becoming a living human being; and third, above the living creatures, the united male and female powers— themselves the product of God's creation—that generate the living creatures.

With respect to Scripture, Isaiah presents the most laconic statement, and Ezekiel the most detailed. There is a debate in the Talmud with respect to whether the strong ban on exposition is with respect to all three parts, or only with respect to the third. The explication with respect to the living creatures provides information concerning the endowment of human beings with respect to developmental sequence, and with respect to the functions, cognition, skill, and sexuality represented in the vision of Ezekiel by face, wings-and-hands together, and feet, respectively.

The explication of the materialization of the human being is through form being added to the matter of the earth, represented by the sexual metaphor.

The ultimate nature of the generational process is contained and concealed in the words *hashmal* and *mashmalah*.

With this summary before us, we can proceed to a close examination of Maimonides' presentation of the *Maaseh Merkabah*.

The Introduction to the Third Part of *The Guide of the Perplexed* again, as at the beginning [*Guide*, p. 3] and at the beginning of the second part [*Guide*, p. 235], contains the words from the story of Abraham's dealings with a Gentile, in which the latter acknowledges the existence of God.

IN THE NAME OF THE LORD, GOD OF THE WORLD (Genesis 21:33). [*Guide*, p. 415]

Maimonides reminds the reader that his purpose is to explain the *Maaseh Bereshit* and the *Maaseh Merkabah*.

WE HAVE ALREADY MADE IT CLEAR SEVERAL TIMES THAT THE CHIEF AIM OF THIS TREATISE IS TO EXPLAIN WHAT CAN BE EXPLAINED OF THE *MAASEH BERESHIT* AND THE *MAASEH MERKABAH* [*Guide*, p. 415]

We note that *Maaseh Bereshit* and *Maaseh Merkabah* are taken by Maimonides as the same as prophecy.

WITH A VIEW TO HIM FOR WHOM THE TREATISE HAS BEEN COMPOSED [*Guide*, p. 415]

For him who is qualified by talent, education, and by being afflicted with heartache or perplexity, who can understand that which he knows, who can transcend the concrete and the literal, and who can come to understand the dreams and visions of the prophets.

WE HAVE ALREADY MADE IT CLEAR THAT THESE
MATTERS BELONG TO *THE MYSTERIES OF THE TO-
RAH*, AND YOU KNOW THAT [THE SAGES] . . . BLAME
THOSE WHO DIVULGE *THE MYSTERIES OF THE TO-
RAH*. [*Guide*, p. 415]

For the matter is discussable only in sexual terms, and one is morally
constrained not to do that.

THEY . . . HAVE ALREADY MADE IT CLEAR THAT THE
REWARD OF HIM WHO CONCEALS THE MYSTERIES OF
THE TORAH, WHICH ARE CLEAR AND MANIFEST TO
THE MEN OF SPECULATION, IS VERY GREAT. [*Guide*,
p. 415]

At this point, Maimonides puts in a major clue that the matter is
sexual, with a verse from Isaiah and a comment on it from the
Talmud.

AT THE CONCLUSION OF [THE TRACTATE] *PESAHIM*,
WHEN SPEAKING OF THE DICTUM—*FOR HER GAIN
SHALL BE FOR THEM THAT DWELL BEFORE THE
LORD, TO EAT THEIR FILL, AND LIMEKHASSE ATIK
(COVER [THE NAKEDNESS OF] THE ANCIENT ONE)*
(Isaiah 23:18). [*Guide*, p. 415]

Pines—for whatever reasons—withdraws from translating *limekhasse atik* [*Guide*, p. 415].
We have inserted "the nakedness of" with respect to the word for
"cover" consistent with the usage to be found, for example, in the story
of how Shem and Japheth took a garment, and walking backward,
"covered the nakedness of their father" Noah, who was lying exposed
(Genesis 9:23).
Continuing then, from what appears to be an unusual version of
the Talmud, Maimonides says:

THEY SAY: FOR HIM WHO COVERS THE THINGS RE-
VEALED (*DEVARIM SHEGILIN*) [*Guide*, p. 415]

Pines translates this as "the things revealed." But equally, the genitals—literally, that is, the things for uncovering, as of nakedness, euphemistically, for things associated with sexual intercourse. Maimonides specifically indicates the possible meaning of *shegal* in this sense in Chapter III:8 [*Guide*, p. 436]. Indeed, as will be noted below, this has more direct significance in connection with the vision of Ezekiel.

OF THE ANCIENT OF DAYS, NAMELY, THE MYSTERIES OF THE TORAH [*Guide*, p. 415]

Contemporary versions of the Talmud have *devarim shekisah* (*the things concealed*) *of [or by] the Ancient of Days*. Thus even the current Talmud is different from the version cited by Maimonides. The different versions of the Talmud show up interestingly in the English translations as follows: The Soncino translation, from current versions, is ". . . the things which the Ancient . . . of days concealed." (*Pesahim* 119a, p. 613 of Soncino). Pines, translating from Maimonides' citation, gives an opposite translation: ". . . the things revealed by the Ancient of Days . . ." [*Guide*, p. 415].

While Pines translates literally, the important point is that the version of the Talmud Maimonides appears to be citing permits the meaning in the sense of a sexual euphemism. Maimonides follows this with his pointer, as it were.

UNDERSTAND THE EXTENT OF THAT TOWARD WHICH THEY GIVE GUIDANCE, IF YOU ARE OF THOSE THAT UNDERSTAND. THEY HAVE ALREADY MADE IT CLEAR HOW SECRET THE *MAASEH MERKABAH* WAS AND HOW FOREIGN TO THE MIND OF THE MULTI-TUDE. AND IT HAS BECOME CLEAR THAT EVEN THAT PORTION OF IT THAT BECOMES CLEAR TO HIM WHO HAS BEEN GIVEN ACCESS TO THE UNDERSTANDING OF IT, IS SUBJECT TO A LEGAL PROHIBITION AGAINST ITS BEING TAUGHT AND EXPLAINED EXCEPT ORALLY TO ONE MAN HAVING CERTAIN STATED QUALITIES, AND EVEN TO THAT ONE ONLY THE CHAPTER HEAD-INGS MAY BE MENTIONED. [*Guide*, p. 415]

The foreignness comprises the sexual imagery, the allegoricalness in the philosophical sense, and the allegoricalness in the prophetic sense. Maimonides then discusses his own plight with respect to his project of speaking and remaining silent at the same time:

THIS IS THE REASON WHY THE KNOWLEDGE OF THIS MATTER HAS CEASED TO EXIST IN THE ENTIRE RELIGIOUS COMMUNITY, SO THAT NOTHING GREAT OR SMALL REMAINS OF IT. AND IT HAD TO HAPPEN LIKE THIS, FOR THIS KNOWLEDGE WAS ONLY TRANSMITTED FROM ONE CHIEF TO ANOTHER AND HAS NEVER BEEN SET DOWN IN WRITING. IF THIS IS SO, WHAT STRATEGEM CAN I USE TO DRAW ATTENTION TOWARD THAT WHICH MAY HAVE APPEARED TO ME AS INDUBITABLY CLEAR, MANIFEST, AND EVIDENT IN MY OPINION, ACCORDING TO WHAT I HAVE UNDERSTOOD IN THESE MATTERS? [Guide, p. 415]

We draw attention to the fact that this appears late within the pages of The Guide of the Perplexed. We have to refer to the grades of secrecy that are of such concern to Maimonides. This writing is immediately before the more secret of the two, the Maaseh Bereshit and the Maaseh Merkabah. Indeed, we will see presently how Maimonides even notes grades of secrecy within the Maaseh Merkabah, the living creatures and the ophannim being less secret than the man sitting on the throne. Then he shifts:

ON THE OTHER HAND, IF I HAD OMITTED SETTING DOWN SOMETHING [Guide, p. 415]

At least something?

OF THAT WHICH HAS APPEARED TO ME AS CLEAR, SO THAT THAT KNOWLEDGE WOULD PERISH WHEN I PERISH, AS IS INEVITABLE [Guide, pp. 415–416]

In the Epistle Dedicatory he indicates that circumstances forced the separation from his student, the one he considered qualified to receive these teachings. One might presume that Maimonides did not have another student so qualified and available for oral instruction in the time left in his life as he judged it:

I SHOULD HAVE CONSIDERED THAT CONDUCT AS EX-TREMELY COWARDLY WITH REGARD TO YOU AND EV-ERYONE WHO IS PERPLEXED. [*Guide*, p. 416]

However Maimonides may have come to it, *The Guide of the Perplexed* is clearly written for publication, for copying and open distribution. Indeed, it was even available for translation, as this took place within Maimonides' lifetime and with his cooperation.

IT WOULD HAVE BEEN, AS IT WERE, ROBBING ONE WHO DESERVES THE TRUTH OF THE TRUTH, OR BE-GRUDGING AN HEIR HIS INHERITANCE. AND BOTH OF THESE TRAITS ARE BLAMEWORTHY. [*Guide*, p. 416]

Thus the writing of *The Guide of the Perplexed* is an obligation. Shifting back to the constraint obligations:

ON THE OTHER HAND, AS HAS BEEN STATED BEFORE, AN EXPLICIT EXPOSITION OF THIS KNOWLEDGE IS DE-NIED BY A LEGAL PROHIBITION, IN ADDITION TO THAT WHICH IS IMPOSED BY JUDGMENT. [*Guide*, p. 416]

Open discussion of sexuality can be disturbing of thought, emotion, and conduct, especially in the young, the immature, and the uneducated.

He shifts again:

IN ADDITION TO THIS THERE IS THE FACT THAT IN THAT WHICH HAS OCCURRED TO ME WITH REGARD TO THESE MATTERS, I FOLLOWED CONJECTURE AND SUPPOSITION; NO DIVINE REVELATION HAS COME TO ME TO TEACH ME THAT THE INTENTION IN THE MATTER IN QUESTION WAS SUCH AND SUCH, NOR DID

I RECEIVE WHAT I BELIEVE IN THESE MATTERS FROM
A TEACHER. [*Guide*, p. 416]

As we have previously pointed out, the allusion here is to the
tradition of Kabbalah, literally the "received" in the sense of secrets
orally transmitted from one to the other. Not, as it were, having
"received" in confidence, he has no obligation to maintain confidence.
What he indicates he gets directly from the open writings, with respect
to which he speculates.

BUT THE TEXTS OF THE PROPHETIC BOOKS AND THE
DICTA OF THE SAGES, TOGETHER WITH THE SPECULA-
TIVE PREMISES THAT I POSSESS, SHOWED ME THAT
THINGS ARE INDUBITABLY SO AND SO. [*Guide*, p. 416]

Thus, he expresses his confidence in his intellectual powers, yet,
recognizes that he could be wrong:

YET IT IS POSSIBLE THAT THEY ARE DIFFERENT AND
THAT SOMETHING ELSE IS INTENDED. [*Guide*, p. 416]

Again, he asserts his confidence in his intellectual powers:

NOW RIGHTLY GUIDED REFLECTION [*Guide*, p. 416]

and conviction with respect to divine aid, as contrasted with divine
revelation mentioned above:

AND DIVINE AID IN THIS MATTER HAVE MOVED ME
TO A POSITION, WHICH I SHALL DESCRIBE. [*Guide*, p.
416]

Maimonides then states that he will expound in a certain way about
Ezekiel.

NAMELY, I SHALL INTERPRET TO YOU THAT WHICH
WAS SAID BY *EZEKIEL THE PROPHET* [*Guide*, p. 416]

which is commonly referred to as the *Maaseh Merkabah*

IN SUCH A WAY [*Guide*, p. 416]

as to obscure it

THAT ANYONE WHO HEARD THAT INTERPRETATION
WOULD THINK THAT I DO NOT SAY ANYTHING OVER
AND BEYOND WHAT IS INDICATED BY THAT TEXT
[*Guide*, p. 416]

thus stating that he does say things over and beyond what is indicated
by the text

BUT THAT IT IS AS IF I TRANSLATED WORDS FROM ONE
LANGUAGE TO ANOTHER OR SUMMARIZED THE
MEANING OF THE EXTERNAL SENSE OF THE SPEECH.
[*Guide*, p. 416]

He refers to the distinction between the external and the internal
meaning. He says that the internal meaning will be indicated while
giving the appearance that only the external meaning is indicated. We
have here a patent admission of dissemblance.

ON THE OTHER HAND, IF THAT INTERPRETATION IS
EXAMINED WITH A PERFECT CARE BY HIM FOR WHOM
THIS TREATISE IS COMPOSED AND WHO HAS UNDER-
STOOD ALL ITS CHAPTERS–EVERY CHAPTER IN ITS
TURN [*Guide*, p. 416]

If *The Guide of the Perplexed* is examined very carefully by one qualified
to understand it, then

THE WHOLE MATTER, WHICH HAS BECOME CLEAR
AND MANIFEST TO ME, WILL BECOME CLEAR TO HIM
SO THAT NOTHING IN IT WILL REMAIN HIDDEN FROM
HIM. [*Guide*, p. 416]

This is as far as he can go in achieving the purposes of explication and
remain in conformity with the Mishnaic law.

THIS IS THE ULTIMATE TERM THAT IT IS POSSIBLE TO ATTAIN IN COMBINING UTILITY FOR EVERYONE WITH ABSTENTION FROM EXPLICIT STATEMENTS IN TEACHING ANYTHING ABOUT THIS SUBJECT – AS IS OBLIGATORY. [*Guide*, p. 416]

Maimonides then says:

AFTER THIS INTRODUCTION HAS PRECEDED, APPLY YOUR MIND [*Guide*, p. 416]

We are enjoined to engage in intellectual effort of a kind that will produce awareness of the internal meanings of texts when we are presented with what seem to be external meanings.

TO THE CHAPTERS THAT WILL FOLLOW [*Guide*, p. 416]

on the topic

CONCERNING THIS GREAT, NOBLE AND SUBLIME SUB-JECT ... WHICH IS A STAKE UPON WHICH EVERY-THING HANGS [*Guide*, p. 416]

the unity of God

AND A PILLAR UPON WHICH EVERYTHING IS SUP-PORTED. [*Guide*, p. 416]

the existence of God [*Yesodei Hatorah* I:1,6].

We turn now to consider Chapter III:1 [*Guide*, p. 417]. In this chapter Maimonides deals with the representation of the faces of the living creatures referred to in the Book of Ezekiel. One of the ways by which we can come to understand what Maimonides is intimating is to take note of seeming liberties that he may take with texts, especially the texts of Scripture. One such instance is in the way that Maimonides speaks of the faces of the living creatures as they are mentioned in the account by Ezekiel. We can assume that Maimonides understands that his reader knows Scripture well enough to note such liberties. And we can assume that the taking of the liberty is itself a pointer.

It will be helpful to state what we take Maimonides to be intimating in Chapter III:1. We take it that Maimonides is attempting to characterize the developmental sequence with which the human being is endowed.

Two prior notions are relevant. One of them is the Aristotelian teleological notion expressed in the example of the oak tree being contained in the acorn. The other is that associated with the riddle of the Sphinx, the stages of life that are intrinsic to the human being, expressed allegorically in terms of the number of feet at each stage. We take it that Maimonides is attempting to find such a set of stages of life in Ezekiel's animal figures of the faces. However, the text is not fully obliging for Maimonides. And thus we find him straining the text to make it accommodate the idea that he would find in it concerning human development.

As a preliminary to looking at the way in which Maimonides treats the animal faces in Ezekiel in Chapter III:1, we note an earlier reference to the animal faces in Ezekiel in Chapter I:49: "Nor should you be led into error by what you find especially in *Ezekiel* with regard to *the face of an ox* and *the face of a lion* and *the face of an eagle* and *the sole of the foot of a calf (kaf egel regel)*" [*Guide*, p. 110].

As we will presently learn, Maimonides takes ox and cherub as the same and as both referring to "human being of tender age." We take lion as walking on four legs and eagle as walking on two legs. Also, as we will presently be led to understand, the sole of the foot of a calf (*kaf egel regel*) may be taken to represent a mature man. Thus the sequence as Maimonides gives it in Chapter I:49 may be taken to represent the stages of an infant in arms, a child walking on all fours, a child walking on two feet, and a mature man.

Let us here note what is to be found in the text in Scripture. First, *The sole of the foot of a calf (kaf egel regel)* appears nowhere in such a direct conjunction with the description of the faces. It appears as follows:

> And I saw, and, behold, a stormy wind came out of the north, a great
> cloud, with a fire flashing up, so that a brightness was round about it;
> and out of the midst thereof as a fountain of *hashmal*, out of the midst

of the fire. And out of the midst thereof came the likeness of four living creatures. And this was their appearance: they had the likeness of a man. And every one had four faces, and every one of them had four wings. And their feet were straight feet; and the sole of their feet was like the sole of the foot of a calf (*kaf egel regel*); and they sparkled like burnished brass (*nehoset kalal*). [Ezekiel 1:4–7]

Second, the text continues, and we do find one mention of the animal faces, but in a different order than that mentioned in Chapter I:49:

And they had the hands of a man under their wings on their four sides; and as for the faces and wings of the four, their wings were joined together as a woman to her sister; they turned not when they went; each went in the direction of his face. As for the likeness of their faces, they had the face of a *man*; and they four had the face of a *lion* on the right side; and they four had the face of an *ox* on the left side; they four had also the face of an *eagle*. Thus were their faces. . . . [Ezekiel 1:8–11]

That is, the text provides the sequence *man, lion, ox, and eagle* (Ezekiel 1:10).

Third, the faces are also described in the tenth chapter of Ezekiel: "And every one had four faces: the first face was the face of the cherub, and the second face was the face of a man, and the third the face of a lion, and the fourth the face of an eagle" (Ezekiel 10:14). This too does not correspond precisely to what Maimonides has in I:49.

If we substitute the corresponding stages, Maimonides' sequence presented in I:49 is:

> infant in arms, crawling child, walking child,
> man.

The sequence in Ezekiel 1:7 is

> crawling child, infant in arms, walking child.

And the sequence in Ezekiel 10:14 is

infant in arms, man, crawling child, walking
child.

Thus, if it were his intention to read out his stages from the text, the text is not so obliging. We note, though, that Maimonides warns:

Nor should you be led into error by what you
find especially in *Ezekiel* with regard [to the
faces]. [*Guide*, p. 110]

After this preliminary, let us turn to a more direct consideration of Chapter III:1. What we find is that it mostly constitutes an effort on the part of Maimonides to make the text indicate a developmental sequence, infant in arms, crawling child, walking child, and man.

The chapter begins by letting us know that the human being is intended, albeit animals are mentioned:

IT IS KNOWN THAT THERE ARE MEN THE FORM OF WHOSE FACES RESEMBLES THAT OF ONE OF THE OTHER ANIMALS, SO THAT ONE MAY SEE AN INDI-VIDUAL WHOSE FACE RESEMBLES THAT OF A LION AND ANOTHER INDIVIDUAL WHOSE FACE RESEMBLES THAT OF AN OX AND SO FORTH. IT IS ACCORDING TO THE SHAPES THAT TEND TO HAVE A LIKENESS TO THOSE ANIMALS THAT PEOPLE ARE NICKNAMED. [*Guide*, p. 417]

Maimonides then presents a sequence that he attributes to Ezekiel, but that does not exist in Scripture.

THUS HIS SAYING: THE FACE OF AN OX AND THE FACE OF A LION AND THE FACE OF AN EAGLE. [*Guide*, p. 417]

This does conform to infant in arms, crawling child, and walking child. But it is not to be found in *Ezekiel!*

Maimonides then explains that all of these refer to man:

ALL OF THEM MERELY INDICATE THE FACE OF A MAN THAT TENDS TO HAVE A LIKENESS TO FORMS BE-LONGING TO THESE SPECIES. [*Guide*, p. 417]

He mentions "two proofs":

TWO PROOFS INDICATE THIS TO YOU. [*Guide*, p. 417]

The first proof:

ONE OF THEM IS HIS SAYING WITH REGARD TO THE LIVING CREATURES IN GENERAL: AND THIS WAS THEIR APPEARANCE; THEY HAD THE LIKENESS OF A MAN (Ezekiel 1:5). [*Guide*, p. 417]

We take him to mean a proof that these are allegorical and refer to human beings.

There is an interruption at this point, and Maimonides inserts another version of his own listing.

THEREAFTER HE DESCRIBES EVERY LIVING CREATURE AMONG THEM AS HAVING THE FACE OF A MAN AND THE FACE OF AN EAGLE AND THE FACE OF A LION AND THE FACE OF AN OX. [*Guide*, p. 417]

It is the same sequence that is given in I:49 but in reverse order and with *man* substituted for the *sole of the foot of the calf (kaf egel regel)*. That is, the sequence is man, walking child, crawling child, infant in arms.

Maimonides then goes on to present "the second proof." Again, we ask, what is it a proof of?

THE SECOND PROOF IS HIS EXPLANATION IN THE SECOND *MERKABAH*, WHICH HE SET FORTH IN ORDER TO EXPLAIN THINGS LEFT OBSCURE IN THE FIRST *MERKABAH*. HE SAYS IN THE SECOND *MERKABAH*: AND EVERY ONE HAD FOUR FACES: THE FIRST FACE WAS THE FACE OF THE CHERUB, AND THE SECOND FACE WAS THE FACE OF A MAN, AND THE THIRD THE

FACE OF A LION, AND THE FOURTH THE FACE OF AN
EAGLE (Ezekiel 10:14). [*Guide*, p. 417]

He explains that this is a proof that ox and cherub are the same, and
that cherub refers to what we have been calling an infant in arms.

THUS HE EXPLICITLY INDICATES THAT WHAT HE
HAD CALLED THE FACE OF AN OX IS THE FACE OF THE
CHERUB. NOW CHERUB DESIGNATES A HUMAN BEING
OF TENDER AGE. [*Guide*, p. 417]

He continues by saying:

WITH REGARD TO THE TWO REMAINING FACES [LION
AND EAGLE], THE ANALOGY LIKEWISE APPLIES. [*Guide*,
p. 417]

We take from this as follows: Just as cherub and ox represent a stage
of human development, so do the "two remaining faces."

These are two "proofs" that take the faces as referring to human
beings, the first in a general sense, the second in the sense of stages of
development.

One of the questions that remains is why Maimonides identifies
man with *regel egel*. This he does by placing them in parallel between
his list of Chapter I:49 and his lists of Chapter III:1. The answer is that
regel egel is a euphemism for the male genitalia. Indeed, the question of
the meaning of *regel egel* is not a minor one within the total context of
The Guide of the Perplexed. For, as we have already pointed out,
Maimonides draws special attention to a set of words as having great
significance in two places. *Regel egel* is among them. Thus:

With regard to the same principle, in reference to the *Merkabah* there
occurs the word *hashmal*, as they have explained, and also *regel egel* (the
foot of a calf) and *nehoshet qalal* (burnished brass). [*Guide*, p. 348]

and

Through this method very strange things appear, which are likewise
secrets, as in its dictum with regard to the *Merkabah*: brass (*nehoshet*)
and burnished (*qalal*) and foot (*regel*) and calf (*egel*) and lightning

(*bazak*). If you carefully examine each passage in your mind, they will become clear to you—after your attention has been aroused—from the gist of what has been set forth here. [*Guide*, p. 393]

We take *regel egel* to be the male genitalia, and *nehoshet qalal* to be the female genitalia, as these characterize living creatures. The indications that this is what is being intimated are presently given by Maimonides. They will be discussed below. However, being aware of this can be helpful in getting some sense of the words with which Maimonides ends Chapter III:1. He writes:

ALSO HE HAS OMITTED IN THIS PASSAGE *THE FACE OF AN OX* IN ORDER TO DRAW ATTENTION TO A CER-TAIN DERIVATION OF WORDS, AS WE HAVE INDI-CATED IN A FLASH. [*Guide*, p. 417]

We take this to mean the following: There are two parts to the intimation. First, there is another interpretation of the discrepancy between the list in the first and tenth chapters of Ezekiel. In the list in the tenth chapter of Ezekiel there is no mention of the face of the ox. The derivation that is involved is that ox and calf are related, so that the absence of mention of the ox is drawing attention to *egel*, calf.

Second, as Maimonides presently indicates, the word *egel*, meaning calf, is the same as the word *agol*, meaning round [*Guide*, p. 418]. Thus, it is round foot. Now, foot is a euphemism for penis. Maimo-nides draws specific attention to that in Chapter III:8 in connection with the expression for urine as waters of the feet, *meme raglayim* [*Guide*, p. 436]. This then provides the license for Maimonides to substitute the *sole of the foot of a calf (kaf regel egel)* for "man" in the listing he provides in Chapter I:49.

At this point Maimonides puts in a hint concerning the sexuality not of the living creatures, but to the vision above the living creatures. As we have already pointed out, Maimonides sees the vision as consisting of three visions, that of the living creatures, the subject of this chapter, Chapter III:1, being in the middle. Above it is the vision of the man on the throne, the generator of the living creatures. It is the sexuality associated with this highest vision that is the subject of the greatest injunction against exposition. We take it that Maimonides alludes to that in saying:

IT IS IMPOSSIBLE TO SAY: PERHAPS THIS WAS AN AP-
PREHENSION OF OTHER FORMS: FOR HE SAYS AT THE
END OF THIS SECOND DESCRIPTION: THIS IS THE
LIVING CREATURE THAT I SAW UNDER THE GOD
(*ELOHE*) OF ISRAEL BY THE RIVER KHEBAR. (Ezekiel
10:20). [*Guide*, p. 417]

If the major point to be clarified is indeed the sexuality of the generating part of the three-part vision, not merely the sexuality that is the heritage of the living creatures, and this is what this second description is about, then he can say:

THUS THAT WHICH WE HAVE BEGUN TO MAKE CLEAR
HAS ALREADY BECOME CLEAR. [*Guide*, p. 417]

Maimonides turns from the discussion of the developmental patterns inherent in the living creatures to a set of indications of their structural and functional characteristics, and from that to a set of indications concerning the materialization of the living creatures in conjunction with the *ophannim*. This elaboration of the structure and function of the living creatures, the *ophannim*, and their conjunction is the subject of the lengthy Chapters III:2 and III:3.

Chapter III:4 challenges the interpretation that was often given concerning the *ophannim* as "wheels" and therefore as representative of the heavenly spheres. It points to the association of "uncovering" with earth, with the word *galgal* meaning both wheel and a derivative of the word "uncover," as in the euphemism for the "uncovering of naked-ness."

Chapter III:5 delineates the three parts of the vision of Ezekiel, the *ophannim*, the living creatures, and the man. It especially identifies the dual nature of the vision of the man on the throne, referring to "the ultimate perception."

Chapter III:6 indicates that Isaiah's laconic statement is the same as Ezekiel's statement.

Chapter III:7 is Maimonides' most explicit statement concerning the vision of the man on the throne, and especially of the sexual imagery involved.

The description of the living creatures in Chapter III:2 is divided into two parts. The first is the "form" of the living creatures, their structure. The second is the "motion" of the living creatures, their function. The discussion of the form of the living creatures begins at the beginning of Chapter III:2 [*Guide*, p. 417] and ends with Maimonides saying: "This is all that he says concerning the form of the living creatures. . . ." [*Guide*, p. 418].

The structure of the living creatures is tripartite. It consists of faces, wings that become transformed into human hands, and feet. These correspond to cognition, craft, and sexuality. Maimonides leads the reader to this as follows:

HE STATES THAT HE SAW FOUR LIVING CREATURES AND THAT EVERY LIVING CREATURE AMONG THEM HAD FOUR FACES, FOUR WINGS, AND TWO HANDS. [*Guide*, p. 417]

At this point Maimonides does not mention feet. However, at the close of this section he indicates that the discussion has included feet: "This is all that he says concerning the form of the living creatures, I mean their shape . . . substance . . . forms . . . [that is, faces, and] wings . . . hands . . . feet [*Guide*, p. 418].

AS A WHOLE, THE FORM OF EACH CREATURE WAS THAT OF A MAN; AS HE SAYS: *THEY HAD THE LIKE-NESS OF A MAN* (Ezekiel 1:5). [*Guide*, p. 417]

Thus he indicates that what is stated about living creatures is of the essentials of human beings:

HE ALSO STATES THAT THEIR TWO HANDS WERE LIKE-WISE THE HANDS OF A MAN, IT BEING KNOWN THAT A MAN'S HANDS ARE INDUBITABLY FORMED AS THEY ARE IN ORDER TO BE ENGAGED IN THE ARTS OF CRAFTSMANSHIP. [*Guide*, pp. 417–418]

In Chapter III:7 Maimonides adds an explanation concerning the transformation of the wings into hands:

> Among the things to which your attention ought to be directed belongs the fact that in the first apprehension he states that the living creatures had both wings and the hands of man; whereas in the second apprehension . . . he apprehended in the first place only their wings, the hands of man appearing in them afterward. . . . [Guide, p. 429]

After this indication concerning the hands, representing human craft, Maimonides proceeds to make indications concerning the feet. In that which follows, Maimonides leads the reader to understand both *regel egel* as referring to male sexuality, and *nehoshet qalal* as referring to female sexuality.

The structure of the following set of comments by Maimonides is to be noted. First, he presents indications with respect to *regel egel*. Second, he presents an indication concerning the bodies of the living creatures. We take this as recognition of the special role of the body in connection with sexuality. Third, he presents the indications with respect to *nehoshet qalal*.

THEN HE STATES THAT THEIR FEET ARE STRAIGHT; HE MEANS THAT THEY HAVE NO ARTICULATIONS. THIS IS THE MEANING OF HIS DICTUM, *STRAIGHT FEET,* ACCORDING TO ITS EXTERNAL SENSE. [Guide, p. 418]

We are alerted to the distinction between external and internal meaning. The external meaning is that feet are meant as feet, literally. We are prepared for finding the word "feet" to have some other meaning:

[THE SAGES] HAVE LIKEWISE SAID: *AND THEIR FEET WERE STRAIGHT FEET – THIS* TEACHES *[US] THAT ABOVE THERE IS NO SITTING.* UNDERSTAND THIS ALSO. [Guide, p. 418]

We take this as an allusion to the story of how Aher perceived Metatron sitting as we have already discussed, "sitting" being a euphemism for sexual activity, as we have previously discussed.

Maimonides continues at this point to emphasize the figurative nature of sexuality, as he characteristically does, following the principle of Rabbi Akiva. He does this by contrasting the discussion of the hands, which are to be understood as more literal, in the sense of indicating human abilities to make and to do, with sexuality, which is more associated with the figurative.

THEN HE STATES THAT THE SOLES OF THEIR TWO FEET, WHICH ARE INSTRUMENTS FOR WALKING, ARE NOT LIKE THE FEET OF A MAN, WHEREAS THEIR HANDS ARE LIKE THE HANDS OF A MAN. [*Guide*, p. 418]

Maimonides at this point gives us the critical indication concerning the interpretation of *regel egel*, by indicating that the word *egel* is to be understood in the sense of *agol*, "round," rather than in the sense of "calf."

FOR THE FEET WERE ROUND, AS A *KAF* OF A *REGEL EGEL*. [*Guide*, p. 418]

With the interpretation of *egel* as round, *regel* is a euphemism for the male organ. And the word *kaf* appears to have the same sense as in the story of Jacob being touched on the *kaf yerech*, characteristically translated as the hollow of the thighbone, but which is also a euphemism for Jacob's genitalia (Genesis 33:26,33).

Maimonides then proceeds to make an interpretation which suggests a distinction between faces and wings [and hands], on the one hand, and feet, on the other. Faces and wings are associated with human individuality. But with respect to sexuality, human beings are bonded to one another.

THEN HE STATES THAT THERE IS NO INTERVAL AND NO SPACE BETWEEN THOSE FOUR *LIVING CREATURES*, EACH OF THEM ADHERING TO THE OTHER; HE SAYS, *COUPLED TOGETHER, A WOMAN TO HER SISTER* (Ezekiel 1:9). [*Guide*, p. 418]

On the separation with respect to whatever is referred to by face and by wings (hands):

THEN HE STATES THAT THOUGH THEY ADHERED TO
ONE ANOTHER, THEIR FACES AND THEIR WINGS WERE
SEPARATED ABOVE; HE SAYS: *AND THEIR FACES AND
THEIR WINGS WERE SEPARATED ABOVE.* [*Guide,* p.
418]

He repeats, this time to mention the bodies:

CONSIDER HIS SAYING *ABOVE.* FOR ONLY THE BODIES
ADHERED TO ONE ANOTHER, WHEREAS THEIR FACES
AND THEIR WINGS WERE SEPARATED, BUT ONLY
FROM ABOVE. THAT IS WHY HE SAYS: *AND THEIR
FACES AND THEIR WINGS WERE SEPARATED ABOVE.*
[*Guide,* p. 418]

We take this in the sense of faces and hands contributing to individuality, while bodies do not.

And then, what we take as Maimonides adding to this his understanding in terms of female sexuality:

THEN HE STATES THAT THEY WERE BRILLIANT *AS A
FOUNTAIN OF NEHOSHET KALAL* (Ezekiel 1:7). [*Guide,* p.
418]

The association of female sexuality with *nehoshet* is indicated in
Scripture in Ezekiel 16:36: ". . . your *nehoshet* [*nehushtaich*] was poured
out, and your nakedness was uncovered through your harlotries with
your lovers. . . ." At this point Maimonides puts in a major indicator
to invite a sexual interpretation:

THEN HE STATES THAT THEY ALSO GAVE LIGHT.
[*Guide,* p. 418]

At this point Maimonides cites Ezekiel 1:13, misciting it slightly and
incompletely. The verse may be translated: And the appearance of the
living creatures was as naked coals of fire [*ke-gachlei eish boarot*,
literally, as coals fire naked] (Ezekiel 1:13).

The word for naked is the word used in the expression "uncover
nakedness."

HE STATES: THEIR APPEARANCE WAS AS COALS OF
FIRE. [*Guide,* p. 418]

By substituting "their" for living creatures, Maimonides leaves an ambiguity as to whether living creatures in the sense of both genders is meant, or whether it refers just to the female, to which the previous sentence can be taken to refer. And by not citing the next word, leaving it, as it were, to the reader, Maimonides thus provides a pointer to the sexuality he is intimating. It is evident that Maimonides drew the notion that they give light from the fact that the text says that the coals of fire were naked.

This part ends with:

THIS IS ALL THAT HE SAYS CONCERNING THE FORM OF THE LIVING CREATURES, I MEAN THEIR SHAPE, THEIR SUBSTANCE, THEIR FORMS, THEIR WINGS, THEIR HANDS, AND THEIR FEET. [*Guide*, p. 418]

Maimonides does not include faces in this enumeration. The discussion of faces follows.

Maimonides divides the discussion of faces into two parts. The first part starts with: "Then he began to describe the manner of the motions. . . ." [*Guide*, p. 418]. The second part starts with: "Then he states that the form of the motion . . ." [*Guide*, p. 418]. Motion for Maimonides includes all change. Thus faces for Maimonides is to be understood as associated with the endowment of the soul with respect to change.

As a preliminary to that which we will take note of in what Maimonides says about the faces, it will be helpful to identify two issues: the question of the literality of God as the generator of human souls, and the question of God's place in the determination of human conduct.

With respect to the first, as we have already indicated, Maimonides regards the expressions in Scripture by the prophets as figurative. On the other hand, the apprehensions of the prophets are not thereby to be regarded as merely autistic. Quite the contrary, as we have indicated, Maimonides shares the Platonic view that human beings may reach toward truth through the use of the imaginative faculty in a way that is not possible by the rational faculty alone. Thus, the prophets apprehend some higher truth in dreams and visions. Second, that which the prophets apprehend in the *Maaseh Merkabah* is the generation of human souls in history. That, of course, gives God an active role in history beyond, say, miracles, or the interventions of the Exodus, or the giving of the Torah at Sinai. What we need to be prepared for is Maimonides' struggle with the issue of how it is that the human being is the agent of his conduct while at the same time being the fulfillment of the will of God. We will understand Maimonides' "chapter headings" the better by keeping these points in mind.

We turn now to his comments on "the manner of the motions" [*Guide*, p. 418].

He finds Ezekiel to have apprehended directionality in the motions of the living creatures:

THEN HE BEGAN TO DESCRIBE THE MANNER OF THE MOTIONS OF THESE *LIVING CREATURES*. REGARDING THESE HE STATES THAT WHICH YOU WILL HEAR. HE SAYS THAT IN THE MOTIONS OF THE *LIVING CREA-TURES* THERE WAS NO TURNING, NO DEVIATION, AND NO CURVE, BUT ONLY ONE MOTION. FOR HE SAYS: *THEY TURNED NOT WHEN THEY WENT*. [*Guide*, p. 418]

These directions are not the same for each living creature. The latter is significant with respect to the notion that each soul is unique, having its own direction:

THEN HE STATES THAT EACH OF THE LIVING CREA-TURES WENT IN THE DIRECTION TOWARD WHICH ITS FACE WAS TURNED. FOR HE SAYS: *EACH GOES IN THE DIRECTION OF ITS FACE*. THUS HE MAKES IT CLEAR THAT EACH *LIVING CREATURE* WENT ONLY IN THE DIRECTION THAT WAS CONTIGUOUS TO ITS FACE. [*Guide*, p. 418]

Then, as we take it, Maimonides finds that the text is not totally obliging with respect to his interpretation of the endowment of each soul with its unique direction. He says:

WOULD ONLY THAT I KNEW TO WHICH FACE, FOR THEY HAD MANY FACES. [*Guide*, p. 418] forcing the idea that there is but one direction. Even though the text indicates many faces, nonetheless such singular and unique direction characterizes the living creatures.

HOWEVER, TO SUM UP, THE FOUR DID NOT ALL OF THEM GO IN ONE DIRECTION. FOR IF IT HAD BEEN SO, HE WOULD NOT HAVE ASSIGNED TO EACH OF THEM A SEPARATE MOTION, SAYING: *EACH GOES IN THE DI-RECTION OF ITS FACE*. [*Guide*, p. 418]

It is at this point that Maimonides ends the argument that each living creature has a unique direction, the argument concerning the "manner" of the motions. He begins a new discussion on the "form" of the motion.

THEN HE STATES THAT THE FORM OF THE MOTION OF THESE LIVING CREATURES WAS RUNNING [*Guide*, p. 418]

We take this in the sense that Maimonides has instructed the reader. There is an external meaning and an internal meaning, and the internal meaning can be arrived at by means of some kind of word play. What is suggested is the changing of the order of the letters as Maimonides indicates with respect to *bahol* and *habol* in Chapter II:43 [*Guide*, p. 393]. This would involve changing the word for run, *raz*, to the word for rock or form, *zur*.

Thus, the form of the motion is formation. And that is in the meaning of *yezirah*. We have already noted that Maimonides intimates that *yezirah* is the word for God's activity in the ongoing creation of the souls of human beings. What we meet here, then, is the idea that *yezirah* also is the endowment of the living creatures:

AND THAT IT WAS LIKEWISE BY RUNNING THAT THEY RETRACED THEIR WAY. FOR HE SAYS: *AND THE LIVING CREATURES RAN AND RETURNED (RAZO VA-SHOB)*. FOR *RAZO* IS THE INFINITIVE OF THE VERB *RAS* (TO RUN) AND *SHOB* IS THE INFINITIVE OF THE VERB *SHAB* (TO RETURN). [*Guide*, pp. 418–419]

We take the second word as *sheb*, from *yosheb*, meaning sit, and having a meaning as a euphemism for sexual activity. Thus we are led to understand that that which is externally running and returning should be understood as God's endowment for forming and for sexual activity.

Maimonides then seeks to give further direction to our thought by pointing out that other words could have been used, but they would have been words that would not allow such a word-play derivation. He says:

HE DID NOT USE THE VERBS *HALOKH* (TO GO) AND *BO* (TO COME), BUT SAID THAT THEIR MOTION CON-SISTED IN RUNNING AND RETRACING THEIR WAY. [*Guide*, p. 419]

Maimonides then states that he makes it clear by offering a conundrum to clarify it with:

AND HE MADE IT CLEAR IN AN IMAGE, SAYING: *AS THE APPEARANCE OF A FLASH OF LIGHTNING (BAZAQ)*. FOR *BAZAQ* IS ANOTHER WORD FOR *BARAK* (Ezekiel 1:14). [*Guide*, p. 419]

How can Maimonides say of this reference to *bazaq* that thereby Ezekiel "made it clear"? Maimonides does follow this immediately with an "explanation" concerning the appearance of lightning as a going and coming. This, however, is not satisfactory, in that *halokh* and *bo* might have done as well. What needs to be made clear is why precisely he uses the words *raz* and *sheb*.

We will postpone dealing with what Maimonides says immediately after the above to suggest that there is another explanation to which Maimonides wishes to draw our attention. It will be recalled that Maimonides presents, in earlier pages, two lists of words of special significance with respect to the *Maaseh Merkabah*. These are: "hashmal . . . regel egel . . . nehoshet kalal" [Chapter II:29; *Guide*, p. 348], and "nehoshet . . . kalal . . . regel . . . egel . . . bazak" [Chapter II:43; *Guide*, p. 393].

We thus note a parallel between *hashmal* and *bazak*. We have suggested that Maimonides would have us take *nehoshet kalal* as female sexuality, and *regel egel*—or as he indicates, *regel agol* (round foot)—with male sexuality. What we then understand is that both *hashmal* and *bazak* represent sexual union in some way. *Hashmal* is the word associated with sexual union in connection with the higher of the three visions, which Maimonides deals with in detail in Chapter III:7; *bazak* represents sexual union in connection with the middle level of the three visions, involving the living creatures.

The notion we then have is that there is a parallelism of represented sexual imageries in the prophetic vision. *Yezirah* is at both the upper level and the level of the living creatures. Maimonides then cites Jonathan ben Uziel's interpretation of *baraq* as meaning lightning literally. However, Maimonides disagrees with Jonathan ben Uziel's astronomic-physical interpretation of the vision of Ezekiel, devoting Chapter III:4 to an explanation of how Jonathan ben Uziel was misled.

ACCORDINGLY HE SAYS THAT IT IS LIKE *LIGHTNING (BARAQ)*, WHOSE MOTION APPEARS TO BE THE SWIFTEST OF MOTIONS AND WHICH STRETCHES OUT RAPIDLY AND AT A RUSH FROM A CERTAIN PLACE AND THEN WITH THE SAME RAPIDITY CONTRACTS AND RETURNS TIME AFTER TIME TO THE PLACE WHENCE IT MOVED. *JONATHAN BEN UZIEL* . . . INTER-PRETED THE WORDS *RASO VA-SHOB* AS FOLLOWS: *THEY WENT ROUND THE WORLD AND RETURNED [AS] ONE CREATURE AND RAPID AS THE APPEAR-ANCE OF LIGHTNING.* [*Guide,* p. 419]

We presume that he intends his objection to Jonathan ben Uziel and gives an alternative explanation:

THEN HE [EZEKIEL] STATES THAT THE MOTION TAKES PLACE, NOT BECAUSE OF THE DIRECTION TOWARDS WHICH THE LIVING CREATURE MOVES [*Guide,* p. 419]

That is, not in the direction of the face, not by virtue of the "manner" of the motion, as has been indicated above.

IN THIS MOTION OF RUNNING AND RETRACING ONE'S
WAY, BUT BECAUSE OF SOMETHING ELSE, I MEAN THE
DIVINE PURPOSE. [*Guide*, p. 419]

That is, there is a divine purpose, indicated by Ezekiel's words in
indicating running and retracing, which is given to the living creature,
and which is not implicit in the unique direction associated with the
face. Stating this clearly:

ACCORDINGLY HE SAYS THAT IT IS IN THE DIRECTION
WHICH THE *LIVING CREATURE* SHOULD MOVE [*Guide*,
p. 419]

According to a moral sense.

ACCORDING TO THE DIVINE PURPOSE [*Guide*, p. 419]

He puts in two things, the first in accordance with Jonathan ben Uziel,
and the physical sense, which we know to ignore.

THAT IT ACCOMPLISHES THIS RAPID MOVEMENT
[*Guide*, p. 419]

The second, which we are to credit in accordance with the instructions given by Maimonides in *The Guide of the Perplexed*,

WHICH IS A *RUNNING AND RETURNING (RASO VA-
SHOB)*. [*Guide*, p. 419]

This allows the word play which is the key to understanding the
meaning. That is, we can understand the divine purpose which is in
the living creatures in the sense of forming and sexual relations.
Ezekiel lets us know about the divine purpose in the living creature:

FOR HE SAYS CONCERNING THE *LIVING CREATURES*:
*WHITHER THE AIR (RUAH) WILL BE (YIHYEH) THEY
WILL GO; THEY TURNED NOT WHEN THEY WENT*
(Ezekiel 1:12). *RUAH* HERE DOES NOT MEAN WIND, BUT
PURPOSE, AS WE HAVE MADE CLEAR WHEN SPEAKING
OF THE EQUIVOCALITY OF *RUAH*. HE SAYS ACCORD-

INGLY THAT THE *LIVING CREATURE* RUNS IN THE
DIRECTION IN WHICH IT IS THE DIVINE PURPOSE
THAT THE LIVING CREATURE RUN. [*Guide*, p. 419]

We take this in the sense that the living creature forms in accordance
with the divine purpose.

While Jonathan ben Uziel may be off in his physical interpretation,
his understanding is not divergent with respect to the role of the
divine will, especially insofar as he pays attention to the meaning of
terms. He interprets in a "similar way" based on his interpretation of
the Hebrew word for "was" (*yihyeh*), showing that God's determination
by putting the divine purpose into the living creature is not in the
simple sense of physical determination.

*JONATHAN BEN UZIEL ... HAS ALREADY INTER-
PRETED THIS TOO IN A SIMILAR WAY, SAYING: THEY
WENT WHEREVER THE WILL WAS THAT THEY
SHOULD GO, AND THEY DID NOT TURN WHEN GO-
ING.* NOW INASMUCH AS HIS SAYING READS,
WHITHER THE AIR WILL BE THEY WILL GO, AND
CONSEQUENTLY ITS OUTER MEANING SIGNIFIES
THAT SOMETIMES GOD WILL WISH IN THE FUTURE
THAT THE LIVING CREATURE SHOULD GO IN A CER-
TAIN DIRECTION AND THEN IT WOULD TAKE THAT
DIRECTION AND SOMETIMES AGAIN HE WILL WISH
THAT IT SHOULD GO IN ANOTHER DIRECTION DIF-
FERENT FROM THE FIRST AND IT WOULD GO ACCORD-
INGLY; HE GOES BACK TO THE PASSAGE AND EX-
PLAINS THIS OBSCURE POINT, LETTING US KNOW
THAT THIS IS NOT SO AND THAT *YIHYEH* (WILL BE)
HAS HERE THE MEANING *HAYAH* (HAS BEEN) AS IS
OFTEN THE CASE IN HEBREW. THUS THE DIRECTION
IN WHICH GOD WISHED THE LIVING CREATURE TO GO
HAD BEEN DETERMINED; THE *LIVING CREATURE*
TAKES THE DIRECTION THAT GOD HAD WISHED IT TO
TAKE; AND THE WILL IS CONSTANT IN THIS DIREC-
TION. [*Guide*, p. 419]

Maimonides completes this point about the will of the living
creature being purposed by God, but not the action of the will
determined by God.

IN ORDER TO EXPLAIN THIS MATTER AND TO COM-
PLETE WHAT HE [EZEKIEL] HAS TO SAY ABOUT IT, HE
SAYS IN ANOTHER VERSE: *WITHERSOEVER THE AIR
WILL GO, THEY WILL GO THITHER, AS THE AIR TO GO*
(Ezekiel 1:20). [*Guide,* pp. 419–420]

And he completes this portion of his description of the middle vision
on the living creatures, saying:

UNDERSTAND THIS WONDROUS EXPLANATION. THIS
TOO BELONGS TO HIS DESCRIPTION OF THE FORM OF
THE MOTION OF THE FOUR LIVING CREATURES,
WHICH COMES AFTER THE DESCRIPTION OF THEIR
SHAPES. [*Guide,* p. 420]

Maimonides then turns to provide clues to the understanding of
one of the most obscure items in Scripture, the *ophannim* which are
referred to in the account by Ezekiel. While the meaning of the word
ophan is dubious, it is characteristically translated as "wheel." However, as we will presently see, that word has a different meaning for
Maimonides. For him, it represents matter. And the meaning of the
vision is that of the joining of the living creature, the soul of the
human being, to the matter of the earth in becoming a living human
being.

For Maimonides, the *ophannim* are the lowest third of the vision,
after the man on the throne and the living creatures, the whole of it
making the generation of the living creatures by the man on the
throne, and the union of the soul with the material of the earth.

In approaching Maimonides' explanation of the *ophannim* and the
man on the throne, we need to highlight the following points:

First, the created universe is tripartite, consisting of Elohim,
heaven, and earth.

Second, that ". . . earth is an equivocal term used in a general and
a particular sense. In a general sense it is applied to all . . . four
elements. In a particular sense it is applied to one element . . . the
earth" [*Guide,* p. 350].

Third, the process whereby matter is formed is representable in
terms of a sexual image. Thus, matter is representable as a "married

harlot" [*Guide*, p. 13]. It is even appropriate to say that the earth is "uncovered" [*Guide*, p. 354]. Matter is characterizable in terms of two main characteristics. First, it has no form of its own. Second, it is associated with prurience.

Fourth, that Maimonides does not share the idea, which he identifies with Jonathan ben Uziel, that the *ophannim* should be identified with the heavenly bodies. He takes that up in Chapter III:4.

Maimonides then continues:

THEN HE STARTED UPON ANOTHER DESCRIPTION
[*Guide*, p. 420]

That is, after the description of the living creatures.

SAYING THAT HE HAD SEEN A SINGLE BODY BENEATH THE *LIVING CREATURES* AND ADHERING TO THEM.
[*Guide*, p. 420]

Attached above.

THIS BODY WAS JOINED TO THE EARTH. [*Guide*, p. 420]

That is, attached below as well.

In this vision the graphics, as it were, place the *ophannim between* the physical earth and the living creatures. Yet we must remind ourselves that Maimonides has no thought but that he is describing something figuratively. Even as he rejects the vision as descriptive of the heavens in any literal sense, so is he not taking the earth in the literal sense. The *ophannim* refer to what might be called an "earthenizing" process. But Maimonides does not intend, as would follow from the principle of Rabbi Akiva, a literal process.

AND ALSO FORMED FOUR BODIES AND LIKEWISE FORMED FOUR FACES. [*Guide*, p. 420]

The parallel with the description of the living creatures is important to Maimonides, for he presently notes an attachment of the corresponding parts between the living creatures and the *ophannim*.

HE DOES NOT ASCRIBE TO IT ANY FORM AT ALL. [*Guide*, p. 420]

This is in contrast to his discussion of the living creatures. While the living creatures are described in terms of human beings and animals, there is ascribed to the *ophannim*

NEITHER A MAN'S FORM NOR ANOTHER FORM PER-TAINING TO LIVING BEINGS [*Guide*, p. 420]

Yet matter is great, terrible, and fearful.

. . . BUT STATES THAT THEY WERE GREAT, TERRIBLE, AND FEARFUL BODIES WITHOUT ASCRIBING TO THEM ANY SHAPE AT ALL. [*Guide*, p. 420]

As we will note presently, Maimonides intimates that prurience is indicated by "eyes" in this description. Thus to "great, terrible, and fearful," Maimonides adds the characteristic of prurience.

HE STATES THAT ALL THEIR BODIES WERE EYES. [*Guide*, p. 420]

These formless bodies are the *ophannim*.

THEY ARE THOSE THAT HE CALLS OPHANNIM, SAY-ING: *AND I SAW THE LIVING CREATURE, AND BE-HOLD, ONE OPHAN UPON THE EARTH BY THE LIVING CREATURES, WITH HIS FOUR FACES* (Ezekiel 1:15). ACCORDINGLY HE HAS MADE IT CLEAR THAT IT WAS A SINGLE BODY WHOSE ONE EXTREMITY WAS BY *THE LIVING CREATURES* WHILE THE OTHER WAS ON THE EARTH AND THAT THIS *OPHAN* HAD FOUR FAC-ES [*Guide*, p. 420]

We here take what Maimonides is saying about the one–four matter as corresponding to the one–four matter that he provides in Chapter II:30 as all the elements being called earth, as well as one of the four being called earth. He continues in this vein.

HE SAYS: *THE APPEARANCE OF THE OPHANNIM AND THEIR WORK WAS LIKE UNTO THE COLOR OF BERYL* [*Guide*, p. 420]

Maimonides presently identifies this as one of the things that might have misled Jonathan ben Uziel.

AND THE FOUR HAD ONE LIKENESS. THUS AFTER HAVING SPOKEN OF ONE *OPHAN*, HE GOES ON TO SPEAK OF FOUR. ACCORDINGLY HE MAKES IT QUITE CLEAR THAT THE FOUR *FACES* THAT THE *OPHAN* HAS ARE THE FOUR *OPHANNIM*. [*Guide*, p. 420]

All the elements have one likeness, in that they are all earth, in the more general sense. Thus the four faces that earth, the general, has are the four elements: earth—the particular—and the other three, water, air, and fire:

THEN HE STATES THAT THE SHAPE OF THE FOUR *OPHANNIM* IS ONE AND THE SAME, FOR HE SAYS: *AND THE FOUR HAD ONE LIKENESS.* [*Guide*, p. 420]

Yet they are all earth.

THEN HE EXPLAINS WITH REGARD TO THESE *OPHANNIM* THAT THEY WERE ENCASED ONE WITHIN THE OTHER, FOR HE SAYS: *AND THEIR APPEARANCE AND THEIR WORK WAS AS IT WERE AN OPHAN WITHIN (BE-TOKH) AN OPHAN.* THIS IS AN EXPRESSION THAT IS NOT USED WITH REGARD TO THE LIVING CREATURES; FOR HE DOES NOT USE WITH REGARD TO THE LIVING CREATURES THE WORD *TOKH* (WITHIN). RATHER DO THEY ADHERE TO EACH OTHER; AS HE SAYS: *COUPLED TOGETHER, A WOMAN TO HER SISTER.* AS FOR THE *OPHANNIM*, HE STATES THAT THEY WERE ENCASED ONE WITHIN THE OTHER, *AS IT WERE AN OPHAN WITHIN AN OPHAN.* [*Guide*, p. 420]

The distinction is a distinction between two kinds of union. There is the union which is "like a woman to her sister" and there is the union in which one thing is within (be-tokh) another. The latter, suggestive of sexual intercourse, is the more prurient. Thus, the greater prurience is with respect to the ophannim, while the lesser prurience is with respect to the living creatures.

Maimonides in the very next section provides a critical clue to the idea of prurience. It centers around the meaning to be attributed to the Hebrew word that is ordinarily translated as "eyes." Maimonides raises the question as to what einayim means, continuing as follows:

AS FOR THE WHOLE BODY OF THE OPHANNIM OF WHICH HE SAYS THAT IT WAS FULL OF EYES (EINA-YIM) [Guide, p. 420]

He then presents a list of possibilities concerning the meaning of the word. First,

IT IS POSSIBLE THAT HE MEANT THAT THEY WERE REALLY FULL OF EYES [Guide, p. 420]

Second,

BUT IT IS ALSO POSSIBLE THAT HE MEANT THAT THEY HAD MANY COLORS, AS IN THE PASSAGE: AND THE COLOR THEREOF (VE-EINO) AS THE COLOR OF (KE-EIN) BDELLIUM. [Guide, p. 420]

Third,

IT IS LIKEWISE POSSIBLE THAT HE MEANT THAT THEY WERE LIKENESSES, JUST AS WE FIND THE ANCIENT MASTERS OF THE LANGUAGE SAY, KE-EIN SHE-GANAB, KE-EIN SHE-GAZAL, MEANING: LIKE UNTO WHAT ONE HAS STOLEN, LIKE UNTO WHAT ONE HAS ROBBED. [Guide, pp. 420–421]

And fourth and last:

[THE WORD *EINAYIM* MAY ALSO MEAN] VARIOUS STATES AND ATTRIBUTES, AS IN ITS DICTUM: *IT MAY BE THAT THE LORD WILL LOOK BE-EINI* (II Samuel 16:12). [*Guide*, p. 421]

It is to what Maimonides might be intimating in this fourth and last remark about the meaning of *einayim* that we turn our attention. Maimonides is misciting Scripture. We cannot take it as error when he does that; the nature of the error gives us an even more precise notion of what he is intimating. The error is as follows. The word *eini* (my eye) is not in Scripture. What is in Scripture is a word that would ordinarily be read as *avoni* (my sin, or iniquity). There is a traditional set of marginal notes giving substitutes for certain scriptural words in oral reading. Many of these have the patent aim of avoiding obscenity or blasphemy when Scripture is read orally in the synagogue. This is one of those cases in which there is such a traditional marginal note, the marginal note substituting *eini* for *avoni*.

What Maimonides does here is to give the marginal note rather than Scripture. In the context of finding different meanings for the word, he in effect points out that one of the meanings associated with the word for eye, *ayin*, is that for which *ayin* can be a stand-in, *avon*. In this way, Maimonides suggests that the meaning of the eyes in the vision of Ezekiel is sinfulness. This is consistent with his view of matter as a cause of transgression.

HE MEANS, [ON] MY STATE. [*Guide*, p. 421]

That is, my sinfulness.

THIS IS WHAT HE DESCRIBES WITH REGARD TO THE FORM OF THE *OPHANNIM*. [*Guide*, p. 421]

It is interesting that in one sense matter has no form, and yet in another sense it has. It has no form in the sense that it takes on form. It has form in the sense that sinfulness can be considered to be part of its form.

Maimonides then begins a discussion of the motion of the *ophannim*:

AS FOR THE MOTION OF THE OPHANNIM [*Guide,* p. 421]

This discussion of the motion of the *ophannim* after a discussion of the form of the *ophannim* imitates the discussion of the motion of the living creatures after the discussion of the form of the living creatures [*Guide,* p. 418]. However, this is a mere formality in his rhetoric, for as he explains, the motion of the *ophannim* is only epiphenomenal, deriving from the attachment of the living creatures to the *ophannim.*

HE [EZEKIEL] AGAIN SAYS THAT THERE WAS IN THEIR MOTION NO CURVE, NO TURNING, AND NO DEVIA-TION. [*Guide,* p. 421]

This corresponds to what Maimonides says in connection with the living creatures: "[Ezekiel] says that in the motions of the living creatures, there was no turning, no deviation and no curve, but only one motion" [*Guide,* p. 418].

THERE WERE ONLY STRAIGHT MOTIONS THAT DID NOT VARY. THIS IS HIS SAYING: *WHEN THEY WENT, THEY WENT UPON THEIR FOUR SIDES; THEY TURNED NOT WHEN THEY WENT.* [*Guide,* p. 421]

Then Maimonides indicates that the motion of the *ophannim* is derived from the motion of the living creatures.

THEN HE STATES THAT THESE FOUR *OPHANNIM* DO NOT MOVE ESSENTIALLY, AS DO THE *LIVING CREA-TURES,* FOR THEY HAVE NO ESSENTIAL MOTION AT ALL, MOVING ONLY WHEN MOVED BY SOMETHING OTHER THAN THEMSELVES. HE INSISTENTLY RE-PEATS THIS NOTION AND REAFFIRMS IT SEVERAL TIMES. AND HE MAKES OUT THAT THE MOVERS OF THE *OPHANNIM* ARE NONE OTHER THAN THE *LIVING CREATURES,* SO THAT, TO USE AN IMAGE, THE RELA-TION OF AN *OPHAN* TO A LIVING CREATURE COULD BE LIKENED TO WHAT HAPPENS WHEN ONE TIES AN INANIMATE BODY TO THE HANDS AND FEET OF A

LIVING BEING: EVERY TIME THE LIVING BEING MOVES, THE PIECE OF TIMBER OR THE STONE TIED TO A LIMB OF THAT LIVING BEING MOVES LIKEWISE. [*Guide*, p. 421]

Textual confirmation of this notion is variously provided:

ACCORDINGLY HE SAYS: *AND WHEN THE LIVING CREATURES WENT, THE OPHANNIM WENT BY THEM: AND WHEN THE LIVING CREATURES WERE LIFTED UP FROM THE EARTH, THE OPHANNIM WERE LIFTED UP* (Ezekiel 1:19).

AND HE ALSO SAYS: *AND THE OPHANNIM WERE LIFTED UP FACING THEM* (Ezekiel 1:20).

AND HE EXPLAINS THE CAUSE OF THIS, SAYING: *FOR THE AIR OF THE LIVING CREATURE WAS IN THE OPHANNIM* (Ezekiel 1:20).

HE REPEATS THIS NOTION IN ORDER TO CONFIRM IT AND MAKE IT UNDERSTOOD, SAYING: *WHEN THOSE WENT, THESE WENT; AND WHEN THOSE STOOD, THESE STOOD; AND WHEN THOSE WERE LIFTED UP FROM THE EARTH, THE OPHANNIM WERE LIFTED UP FACING THEM; FOR THE AIR OF THE LIVING CREA-TURE WAS IN THE OPHANNIM* (Ezekiel 1:21). [*Guide*, p. 421]

Maimonides then makes a summary of this relationship between the living creatures and the *ophannim*, bringing up front the two functions of the living creatures that he had identified as the manner or shape [*Guide*, pp. 199, 204] of motions and the form of the motions [*Guide*, p. 199], the latter associated with the divine purpose.

ACCORDINGLY THE ORDER OF THESE MOTIONS IS AS FOLLOWS: THE *LIVING CREATURES* MOVED IN WHAT-EVER DIRECTION IT WAS THE DIVINE PURPOSE THAT THE LIVING CREATURES SHOULD MOVE [*Guide*, p. 421] corresponding to the form of the motions:

AND BY THE MOTION OF THE *LIVING CREATURES*
[*Guide*, p. 421]

corresponding to the manner or shape of the motions

THE OPHANNIM WERE MOVED, FOLLOWING THE FORMER THROUGH BEING BOUND TO THEM. FOR THE OPHANNIM DO NOT OF THEIR OWN ACCORD MOVE THE LIVING CREATURES. [*Guide*, p. 421]

That is, the direction is only from the living creatures to the *ophannim* and not the reverse.

AND HE SETS FORTH THE ORDER OF THAT GRADE
[*Guide*, p. 421]

of the *living creatures* and the *ophannim:*

SAYING: *WHITHERSOEVER THE AIR WILL GO, THEY WILL GO THITHER, AS THE AIR TO GO; AND THE OPHANNIM WERE LIFTED UP FACING THEM; FOR THE AIR OF THE LIVING CREATURE WAS IN THE OPHANNIM* (Ezekiel 1:20). [*Guide*, p. 421]

And then finally, to reaffirm the point about the will of the living creature being intended by God, but not the action of the will determined by God, he refers back to his discussion [*Guide*, pp. 419–420] of that point by mentioning Jonathan ben Uziel.

I HAVE ALREADY MADE KNOWN TO YOU THE TRANS-LATION OF JONATHAN BEN UZIEL: *WHEREVER THE WILL WAS THAT THEY SHOULD GO, AND SO ON.*
[*Guide*, p. 421]

Maimonides then places the foregoing detailed discussion of the vision of the living creatures and the *ophannim* into the larger picture of the three levels of the vision as a whole.

WHEN HE HAD FINISHED THE DESCRIPTION OF THE
LIVING CREATURES, OF THEIR FORMS, AND OF THEIR
MOTIONS, AND HAD MENTIONED THE *OPHANNIM*
THAT ARE BENEATH THE *LIVING CREATURES*, THEIR
BEING BOUND TO THE LATTER AND MOVED WITH
THEIR MOTION, HE STARTS TO SET FORTH A THIRD
APPREHENSION THAT HE HAD AND GOES BACK TO
ANOTHER DESCRIPTION CONCERNING THAT WHICH
IS ABOVE THE *LIVING CREATURES*. [*Guide*, pp. 421–422]

Maimonides here alludes to two descriptions of "that which is
above the living creatures." The second one is clear enough. It is the
description that begins with Ezekiel 1:26: "And above the firmament
that was over their heads was the likeness of a throne. . . ."

What Maimonides leads us to understand is that Ezekiel 1:4 refers
to the same vision. We take it that what is intimated is that we can
read Ezekiel 1:4 and Ezekiel 1:5 as indicative of the generation of the
living creatures from that which is described in Ezekiel 1:4:

And I saw, and behold a stormy wind came out of the north, a great
cloud and fire flashing and brightness surrounding it, and from within,
as a fountain of *hashmal*, from within the fire. [Ezekiel 1:4]

And from within came the likeness of four living creatures. . . . [Ezekiel
1:5]

Explicating Ezekiel 1:26, Maimonides says that

HE [EZEKIEL] SAYS THAT ABOVE THE FOUR *LIVING
CREATURES*, THERE IS A *FIRMAMENT*; UPON THE FIR-
MAMENT, THE LIKENESS OF A THRONE; AND UPON
THE THRONE, A LIKENESS AS THE APPEARANCE OF A
MAN. [*Guide*, p. 422]

And he sums it up:

THIS IS THE WHOLE OF THE DESCRIPTION HE HAS
MADE OF WHAT HE HAS FIRST APPREHENDED *BY THE
RIVER OF KHEBAR*. [*Guide*, p. 422]

By referring to the account in Ezekiel 1 as "first," he alludes to Ezekiel 8–10. Chapter III:3 contains an enumeration of points that Maimonides draws from Ezekiel 8–10. He opens Chapter III:3:

AFTER *EZEKIEL* . . . HAD SET FORTH THE DESCRIPTION OF THE *MERKABAH* AS GIVEN IN THE BEGINNING OF THE BOOK [*Guide*, p. 422]

"Beginning of the book" refers to Ezekiel 1:1ff.

THE SELFSAME APPREHENSION RETURNED TO HIM A SECOND TIME WHEN, *IN A VISION OF PROPHECY*, HE WAS BORNE TO *JERUSALEM*. [*Guide*, p. 422]

This refers to the account of Ezekiel 8–10. That account states at the beginning: "And I saw, and behold the likeness as the appearance of fire from the appearance of his loins and downward fire and from his loins and upward as the appearance of *zohar* as a fountain of *hashmalah*" (Ezekiel 8:2).

This verse contains the critical words "downward" and "upward," wherewith the Mishnaic law refers to this passage. This passage is significant because it identifies *zohar* with the critical word *hashmalah*. *Zohar* was taken by Moses de Leon, who was impressed by Maimonides' *The Guide of the Perplexed*, as the name of the work that was to become influential in Jewish mysticism throughout the subsequent centuries. *Hashmalah* is here to be found with a feminine ending.

By Maimonides mentioning the word "Jerusalem," he clearly identifies this passage. For the very next verse states: "And the form of the hand was put forth, and I was taken by a lock of my head, and a spirit lifted me up between the earth and the heaven, and brought me to Jerusalem. . . ." (Ezekiel 8:3). He makes a set of additional points by referring to the Jerusalem vision.

THEREUPON HE EXPLAINED TO US THINGS THAT AT FIRST HAD NOT BEEN EXPLAINED. [*Guide*, p. 422]

First, the identification of the cherubim with the living creatures:

THUS FOR OUR BENEFIT HE REPLACED THE WORD
LIVING CREATURES BY THE WORD *CHERUBIM* [*Guide*,
p. 422]

In addition they are angels.

MAKING IT KNOWN TO US THAT THE LIVING CREA-
TURES THAT WERE MENTIONED AT FIRST ARE ALSO
ANGELS–I MEAN THE CHERUBIM. [*Guide*, p. 422]

He shows how the word *cherubim* is used in the same way as the *living creatures* as being connected to the *ophannim* and directing the motions of the latter.

HE SAYS: *AND WHEN THE CHERUBIM WENT, THE
OPHANNIM WENT BESIDE THEM; AND WHEN THE
CHERUBIM LIFTED UP THEIR WINGS TO MOUNT UP
FROM THE EARTH, THE SAME OPHANNIM ALSO
TURNED NOT FROM BESIDE THEM* (Ezekiel 10:16). THUS
HE CONFIRMS THE FACT THAT, AS WE HAVE MEN-
TIONED, THE TWO MOTIONS WERE BOUND TO-
GETHER. [*Guide*, p. 422]

He invokes the evidence of the text that it is the same vision:

THEN HE SAYS: *THIS IS THE LIVING CREATURE THAT
I SAW UNDER THE GOD OF ISRAEL BY THE RIVER
KHEBAR; AND I KNEW THAT THEY WERE CHERUBIM*
(Ezekiel 10:20). [*Guide*, p. 422]

He concludes this first item.

ACCORDINGLY HE REPEATS THE DESCRIPTION OF THE
SELFSAME MOTIONS AND MAKES IT CLEAR THAT THE
LIVING CREATURES ARE *CHERUBIM* AND THE *CHER-
UBIM* ARE THE *LIVING CREATURES*. [*Guide*, p. 422]

The second item pertains to the meaning of *galgal*. Maimonides deals with this at some length later, when he discusses the view of Jonathan ben Uziel in Chapter III:4. As we will note, *galgal* is not to be taken in the sense of derivation from *galal* (to roll) but *galah* (to uncover) as in to "uncover the nakedness of."

Here he presents it as a second item very laconically:

THEREUPON HE EXPLAINS IN THIS SECOND DESCRIP-
TION ANOTHER NOTION, NAMELY, THE NOTION
THAT THE *OPHANNIM* ARE THE *GALGALIM*; HE SAYS:
AS FOR THE OPHANNIM, *THEY WERE CALLED IN MY
HEARING HAGALGAL* (Ezekiel 10:13). [*Guide*, p. 422]

The third item deals with the way in which the *ophannim* are compelled by the living creatures:

THEN HE EXPLAINS A THIRD NOTION REGARDING
THE *OPHANNIM*, SAYING WITH REFERENCE TO THEM:
*BUT TO THE PLACE WHITHER THE HEAD LOOKED
THEY FOLLOWED IT; THEY TURNED NOT AS THEY
WENT* (Ezekiel 10:11). THUS HE STATES EXPLICITLY
THAT THE COMPULSORY MOTION OF THE *OPHANNIM*
FOLLOWED *TO THE PLACE WHITHER THE HEAD
LOOKED*. THAT IS TO SAY, AS HE HAS EXPLAINED, IT
FOLLOWED *WHITHER THE AIR WILL BE*. [*Guide*, pp.
422–423]

Maimonides, in the fourth item, draws attention to eyes being mentioned in connection with the *ophannim*. He states nothing, except to point it out. And we take it in the sense that we have already understood, that eyes shall be interpreted to mean sinfulness. This then, in this second account of the *Merkabah* by Ezekiel, confirms the sinfulness associated with the *ophannim*, the materialistic part of the vision.

THEN HE ADDS A FOURTH NOTION REGARDING THE
OPHANNIM; HE SAYS: *AND THE OPHANNIM WERE
FULL OF EYES ROUND ABOUT, EVEN THE OPHANNIM
THAT THEY FOUR HAD*. HE DID NOT MENTION THIS
NOTION AT FIRST. [*Guide*, p. 423]

As a fifth item, Maimonides indicates an identification of the human physical nature with the *ophannim*:

THEN HE SAYS IN THIS LAST APPREHENSION WITH REGARD TO THE OPHANNIM: *THEIR FLESH AND THEIR BACKS AND THEIR HANDS AND THEIR WINGS* (Ezekiel 10:12). AT FIRST HE HAD NOT MENTIONED THAT THE OPHANNIM HAD FLESH OR HANDS OR WINGS, BUT ONLY THAT THEY WERE BODIES. FINALLY, HOWEVER, HE GOES SO FAR AS TO SAY THAT THEY HAVE FLESH, HANDS, AND WINGS [*Guide,* p. 423]

And then, in conformity with his earlier notion of the formlessness associated with the *ophannim*, Maimonides says:

BUT HE DOES NOT ASCRIBE TO THEM ANY FORM WHATEVER. [*Guide,* p. 423]

The last and the sixth item in this chapter provides a view of how the living creatures and the *ophannim* may match as they do. They do match:

IN THIS SECOND APPREHENSION HE ALSO EXPLAINS THAT EVERY OPHAN IS RELATED TO A CHERUB, SAYING: *ONE OPHAN BESIDE ONE CHERUB, AND ANOTHER OPHAN BESIDE ANOTHER CHERUB* (Ezekiel 10:9). [*Guide,* p. 423]

This is possible because of the parallel between them. Of the living creatures, or the cherubim, he says:

HE [EZEKIEL] ALSO EXPLAINS THERE THAT THE FOUR LIVING CREATURES ARE ONE LIVING CREATURE BECAUSE OF THE ADHERENCE OF ALL OF THEM TO ONE ANOTHER; FOR HE SAYS: *THIS IS THE LIVING CREATURE THAT I SAW UNDER THE GOD OF ISRAEL BY THE RIVER OF KHEBAR.* [*Guide,* p. 423]

To this organic unity, as it were, of the living creatures there is a parallel physical unity in the *ophannim*.

SIMILARLY HE CALLS THE *OPHANNIM*, ONE *OPHAN* UPON *THE EARTH*, IN SPITE OF THERE BEING, AS HE ALSO MENTIONS, FOUR *OPHANNIM*; [*Guide*, p. 423]

The latter has two explanations, first

AND THIS IS BECAUSE OF THEIR BEING JOINED TO ONE ANOTHER [*Guide*, p. 423]

We have already noted that the joining together of the *ophannim* is in the physical sense of one being inside another.
And second,

AND OF THEIR HAVING ALL *FOUR ONE LIKENESS*. [*Guide*, p. 423]

And they are united in the sense that the four elements are fundamentally one substance.
Maimonides ends Chapter III:3 by saying:

THESE ARE THE EXPLANATIONS, REGARDING THE FORMS OF THE *LIVING CREATURES* AND THE *OPHAN-NIM*, THAT ARE ADDED, FOR OUR BENEFIT IN THIS SECOND APPREHENSION. [*Guide*, p. 423]

We note that this allows "forms" to apply to the living creatures but not necessarily to the *ophannim*. This idea of the formlessness of the *ophannim* is an important part of the argument yet to come concerning *galgal*, as we will note in connection with the next chapter, Chapter III:4, on Jonathan ben Uziel.

Chapter III:4 deals with the word *hagalgal*. It disputes the interpretation of Jonathan ben Uziel that it is indicative of anything associated with the heavens. The argument resolves itself around the lexicographical question as to whether it should be referred to *galah*, to uncover, or *galal*, to roll. Maimonides prefers the former to the latter.

IT BEHOOVES US TO DRAW YOUR ATTENTION TO A CERTAIN THOUGHT ADOPTED BY JONATHAN BEN UZIEL. [*Guide*, p. 423]

The need to discuss this at this point derives from the fact that Maimonides deals with virtually every other aspect of the *ophannim* before this point, except the stubborn historical fact that *ophannim* have been interpreted as the spheres of the heavenly bodies. That, of course, grossly literalizes the nature of vision of Ezekiel, and takes away the possibility of understanding what the vision truly is. The reader coming to the *Maaseh Merkabah* would have it as an insuperable obstacle, even as it remained an obstacle for students of *The Guide of the Perplexed* afterward who did not pay sufficient attention to Chapter III:4.

The error of Jonathan ben Uziel is as follows:

WHEN HE SAW THE EXPLICIT STATEMENT, *AS FOR THE OPHANNIM, THEY WERE CALLED IN MY HEARING HAGALGAL* (Ezekiel 10:13), HE CATEGORICALLY DECIDED THAT THE *OPHANNIM* ARE THE HEAVENS. ACCORDINGLY HE TRANSLATED IN EVERY CASE *OPHAN* BY *GALGALA* AND *OPHANNIM* BY *GALGALAYA*. [*Guide*, p. 423]

How might he have fallen into this error? Maimonides offers an explanation.

I HAVE NO DOUBT THAT TO HIS MIND . . . THIS INTERPRETATION WAS CORROBORATED BY THE DICTUM OF EZEKIEL . . . REGARDING THE *OPHANNIM* THAT THEY WERE *LIKE UNTO THE COLOR OF BERYL* (Ezekiel 1:16), A COLOR THAT IS ATTRIBUTED TO THE HEAVENS, AS IS GENERALLY KNOWN. [*Guide*, pp. 423–424]

Jonathan ben Uziel then confounded his error, translating erroneously elsewhere to make it consistent with his error of regarding *galgal* as referring to the heavenly spheres.

HOWEVER, WHEN HE FOUND THE TEXT, *NOW AS I BEHELD THE LIVING CREATURES, BEHOLD ONE OPHAN UPON THE EARTH* (Ezekiel 1:15). [*Guide*, p. 424]

which Maimonides takes at its word, as it were,

WHICH INDUBITABLY INDICATES THAT THE OPHANNIM ARE *UPON THE EARTH*, THIS APPEARED TO HIM TO CONSTITUTE A DIFFICULTY WITH REGARD TO THIS INTERPRETATION. [*Guide*, p. 424]

Because if the *ophan* were a sphere, it would not be "upon the earth." Jonathan ben Uziel then stretched the meaning of the word *earth* to make it a part of heaven, as the only way he could reconcile the text to his interpretation of *galgal* as meaning a heavenly sphere.

ACCORDINGLY HE WENT FURTHER IN HIS INTERPRE-TATION, INTERPRETING [THE WORD] *EARTH* IN THIS PASSAGE AS REFERRING TO THE SURFACE OF HEAVEN, [*Guide*, p. 424]

that is, a lower surface of heaven, making it an earth in a somewhat metaphorical sense.

WHICH IS AN *EARTH* WITH RESPECT TO WHAT IS ABOVE IT. . . . ACCORDINGLY HE TRANSLATED: ONE *OPHAN UPON THAT EARTH BENEATH THE HEIGHT OF HEAVEN.* [*Guide*, p. 424]

Maimonides enjoins the reader to try to understand how it could be that Jonathan ben Uziel could be so misled.

UNDERSTAND THIS INTERPRETATION AS IT IS IN RE-ALITY. IT SEEMS TO ME THAT HE WAS LED TO THIS INTERPRETATION BY HIS BELIEF . . . THAT *GALGAL* IS A TERM DESIGNATING IN THE FIRST PLACE THE HEAV-ENS. [*Guide*, p. 424]

It is understandable that he could come to this conclusion, for the following reasons:

IT SEEMS, HOWEVER, TO ME THAT THE MATTER IS AS
FOLLOWS. THE [HEBREW] TERM FOR ROLLING IS GAL-
GEL. THUS: *AND ROLL THEE DOWN* [VE-GILGAL-
TIKHA] *FROM THE ROCKS; AND ROLLED* [VA-YAGEL]
THE STONE. FOR THIS REASON IT IS SAID, *AND LIKE A
ROLLING THING* [U-KHE-GALGAL] *BEFORE THE
WHIRLWIND,* BECAUSE OF ITS ROLLING. FOR THIS
REASON TOO THE CRANIUM IS CALLED *GULGOLET,*
BECAUSE OF ITS BEING NEARLY ROUND. BECAUSE
EVERY SPHERE ROLLS RAPIDLY, EVERY SPHERICAL
THING WAS CALLED *GALGAL.* HENCE THE HEAVENS
WERE CALLED *GALGALLIM* BECAUSE OF THEIR BEING
ROUND—I MEAN, BECAUSE OF THEIR BEING SPHERI-
CAL. ACCORDINGLY [THE SAGES] SAY [WITH REFER-
ENCE TO FATE]: *IT IS A REVOLVING GALGAL [SPHERE].*
FOR THE SELFSAME REASON THEY LIKEWISE CALL A
PULLEY *GALGAL.* [*Guide,* p. 424]

Maimonides, after giving all of these reasons for identifying *galgal* in
the sense of a heavenly body, points out the lack of support for it in the
text. They may then find that:

ACCORDINGLY [EZEKIEL'S] DICTUM—*AS FOR THE
OPHANNIM, THEY WERE CALLED IN MY HEARING:
HAGALGAL*—MAKES THEIR SHAPE KNOWN TO US
[*Guide,* p. 424]

But there is no ground for that.

FOR HE DOES NOT ASCRIBE TO THEM ANY SHAPE OR
FORM EXCEPT BY SAYING THAT THEY ARE *GALGAL-
LIM.* [*Guide,* p. 424]

We recall that for Maimonides the *ophannim* are characterized by
their absent form, by their taking on the forms of the living creatures.
Thus, Maimonides' indication here that there is no indication of form
is to be understood as his rejection of Jonathan ben Uziel's notion.

As we have noted, Maimonides considers two things to have
promoted Jonathan ben Uziel's belief that *galgal* referred to the
heavenly sphere, the word *hagalgal,* and the word *beryl,* taken in the

sense of the heavenly color. Maimonides then proceeds to deal with the interpretation of *beryl*. As we will see, he would show that it does not necessarily indicate the heavenly color.

Maimonides deals with this with a two-step argument distributed over the pages of *The Guide of the Perplexed*: First, that beryl means the same as sapphire, which is mentioned in Exodus 24:10. Second, that sapphire referred to in Exodus 24:10 refers to the primordial earthly matter.

The first part of argument is presented in Chapter III:4. Maimonides says:

WITH REGARD TO HIS [EZEKIEL'S] SAYING ABOUT THEM *LIKE UNTO BERYL*, HE INTERPRETS THIS ALSO IN THE SECOND DESCRIPTION, SAYING WITH REGARD TO THE *OPHANNIM: AND THE APPEARANCE OF THE OPHANNIM WAS AS THE COLOR OF A BERYL STONE.* [*Guide*, p. 424]

Maimonides then brings Jonathan ben Uziel to his own assistance— even in the course of breaking down Jonathan ben Uziel's argument about the meaning of *hagalgal* and even to the confusion of the reader:

JONATHAN BEN UZIEL ... TRANSLATED THIS: LIKE UNTO A PRECIOUS STONE. [*Guide*, p. 424]

It turns out that Onkelos translated sapphire, in Exodus 24:10, in the same way.

NOW YOU KNOW ALREADY THAT *ONQELOS* USED THIS VERY EXPRESSION TO TRANSLATE: *AS IT WERE, A WORK OF THE WHITENESS OF SAPPHIRE STONE* (Exodus 24:10). HE SAYS: *AS THE WORK OF A PRECIOUS STONE.* [*Guide*, p. 424]

From this Maimonides can then conclude:

THERE IS CONSEQUENTLY NO DIFFERENCE BETWEEN ITS SAYING *AS THE COLOR OF A BERYL STONE*

From Ezekiel 10:9:

AND ITS SAYING, *AS IT WERE, A WORK OF THE WHITENESS OF SAPPHIRE STONE.* [*Guide*, p. 424]

From Exodus 24:10: And then Maimonides urges that we

UNDERSTAND THIS. [*Guide*, p. 424]

What there is to understand is that in earlier pages Maimonides has already identified sapphire as earthly matter: "This has made me interpret figuratively the passage . . . *a work of whiteness of sapphire stone* (Exodus 24:10) as meaning that they apprehended in this prophetic vision the true reality of the inferior first matter . . . the whiteness . . . is the terrestrial matter" [*Guide*, p. 331].

Thus Maimonides has an opinion that differs from that of Jonathan ben Uziel, as he proceeds to say.

YOU MUST NOT FIND IT INCONGRUOUS THAT, HAVING MENTIONED THE INTERPRETATION OF JO-NATHAN BEN UZIEL . . . I PROPOUNDED A DIFFERENT INTERPRETATION. YOU WILL FIND THAT MANY AMONG THE SAGES, AND EVEN AMONG THE COMMEN-TATORS, DIFFER FROM HIS INTERPRETATION WITH REGARD TO CERTAIN WORDS AND MANY NOTIONS THAT ARE SET FORTH BY THE *PROPHETS.* HOW COULD THIS NOT BE WITH REGARD TO OBSCURE MAT-TERS? MOREOVER I DO NOT OBLIGE YOU TO DECIDE IN FAVOR OF MY INTERPRETATION. UNDERSTAND THE WHOLE OF HIS INTERPRETATION FROM THAT TO WHICH I HAVE DRAWN YOUR ATTENTION, AND UN-DERSTAND MY INTERPRETATION. GOD KNOWS IN WHICH OF THE TWO INTERPRETATIONS THERE IS CORRESPONDENCE TO WHAT HAS BEEN INTENDED. [*Guide*, pp. 424–425]

Maimonides is clearly aware of how radically different his interpreta-tion is from that of Jonathan ben Uziel. In the face of a clear difference with him, he expresses some diffidence. However, he must reduce

Jonathan ben Uziel's credibility by pointing out that others have differed with Jonathan ben Uziel's interpretations.

In Chapter III:5 Maimonides indicates the textual ground for the tripartate nature of the vision of Ezekiel. He opens by pointing to the plurality:

AMONG THE THINGS TO WHICH YOUR ATTENTION OUGHT TO BE DIRECTED IS HIS [EZEKIEL'S] EXPRESSION: *VISIONS OF GOD* (Ezekiel 1:1). HE DOES NOT SAY *VISION*, IN THE SINGULAR, BUT *VISIONS*, BECAUSE THERE WERE MANY APPREHENSIONS DIFFERING IN SPECIES; [*Guide*, p. 425]

He points to their graphic arrangement, one above the other, *ophannim* as the lowest, the living creatures as next above, and the man above the living creatures.

I MEAN TO SAY THREE APPREHENSIONS, THAT OF THE *OPHANNIM*, THAT OF THE *LIVING CREATURES*, AND THAT OF THE MAN, WHO IS ABOVE THE LIVING CREATURES. [*Guide*, p. 425]

We have been led to understand that the living creatures are the generated souls of human beings. They are generated by the man above, and they become materialized by union with the *ophannim* below.

The three visions, or the three parts of the vision, are identified textually by the word *va-eire* (and I saw). The Hebrew verb is the root of the noun for vision. One could translate this as "And I had a vision" or "And I had a vision of" instead of "And I saw."

WITH REGARD TO EVERY APPREHENSION HE SAYS: *AND I SAW.* [*Guide*, p. 425]

The first, the *living creatures*:

THUS WITH REFERENCE TO THE APPREHENSION OF THE *LIVING CREATURES* HE SAYS: *AND I SAW, AND,*

BEHOLD, A WHIRLWIND, AND SO ON (Ezekiel 1:4-5).
[*Guide*, p. 425]

The second, the *ophannim*:

WITH REFERENCE TO THE APPREHENSION OF THE
OPHANNIM HE SAYS: *AND I SAW THE LIVING CREA-
TURES, AND, BEHOLD, ONE OPHAN UPON THE
EARTH* (Ezekiel 1:15). [*Guide*, p. 425]

The third, the *man*:

AND WITH REFERENCE TO THE MAN, WHO IN DEGREE
IS ABOVE THE LIVING CREATURES, HE SAYS: *AND I
SAW AS A FOUNTAIN OF HASHMAL, AND SO ON,
FROM THE APPEARANCE OF HIS LOINS, AND SO ON*
(Ezekiel 1:27). [*Guide*, p. 425]

Maimonides is doing some stretching here. Ezekiel 1:4 already refers
to the *hashmal* and thus the man. The man is referred to in Ezekiel
1:26, but Maimonides takes verse 1:27, in which the apprehension is of
the *hashmal*, as appropriate to the man. And in verse 1:15, which he
takes as the apprehension of the *ophannim*, the object of the verb "And
I saw" is the living creatures.

Let us here make two observations with respect to the stretching of
texts to fit interpretations. First, they make a distinct contribution to
the esoteric uses of the text. Second, they are useful in determining
what the intentions of the commentator are. Both may be seen to be
involved here. For by so stretching the texts to give meanings that are
not readily yielded by the texts alone, Maimonides essentially stops
many of his pedantic readers at this point. We are here at the fifth of
the seven chapters. Maimonides has expounded in some detail on the
first two visions, and he is on the threshold of expounding on the most
esoteric third vision.

Yet from another point of view, such stretching of the texts is a
method of revealing the intention of the author. For by determining
how the stretch has been made, one can assess the intention of the

author. In this case we are led to appreciate how the author understands the text as the generation of the souls when he clearly puts the generator at the top, the generated souls in the middle, and the connection to materialization at the bottom—and claims that these are the three visions of Ezekiel.

IN THE DESCRIPTION OF THE *MERKABAH,* HE ONLY REPEATS THE WORD *I SAW* THESE THREE TIMES. THE *SAGES OF THE MISHNAH* HAVE ALREADY EXPLAINED THIS MATTER; IN FACT IT IS THEY WHO DREW MY ATTENTION TO IT. [*Guide,* p. 425]

Maimonides takes it that there are three such apprehensions implied in the way in which the Talmud reports discussion on the text to be designated *Maaseh Merkabah.*

FOR THEY SAID THAT IT IS PERMISSIBLE TO TEACH THE FIRST TWO APPREHENSIONS ONLY, I MEAN THE APPREHENSION OF THE *LIVING CREATURES* AND THAT OF THE *OPHANNIM;* WHEREAS ONLY THE CHAPTER HEADINGS MAY BE TAUGHT WITH REGARD TO THE THIRD APPREHENSION, THAT OF THE *HASHMAL* AND OF WHAT IS CONNECTED WITH IT. [*Guide,* p. 425]

We note this as the opinion of Rabbi Isaac, as we will see below.

Maimonides then makes reference to "our holy Rabbi." By this is meant Rabbi Judah, the compiler of the Mishnah, who is characteristically referred to in the Talmud as "Rabbi." We highlight this at this point because it may be that this is an important indicator with respect to Maimonides' method of concealing and revealing. We will note the significance of this presently.

Maimonides presents what he takes as the opinion of Rabbi Judah:

HOWEVER, *OUR HOLY RABBI* BELIEVES THAT ALL THREE APPREHENSIONS ARE CALLED *MAASEH MER-KABAH* AND THAT WITH RESPECT TO NONE OF THEM MAY ANYTHING OTHER THAN THE *CHAPTER HEAD-INGS* BE TAUGHT. [*Guide,* p. 425]

Maimonides cites the Talmudic text.

THEIR TEXT WITH REGARD TO THIS IS AS FOLLOWS: TILL WHERE [DO WE COUNT IT TO BE] THE MAASEH MERKABAH? RABBI MEIR SAYS: [Guide, p. 425]

The text of the Talmud says "Rabbi omer," not "Rabbi Meir omer." We have earlier provided some speculation concerning whether this may be a deliberate error on Maimonides part, Rabbi Meir being the student of both Rabbi Akiva and Aher, the former giving the key to how prophecy should be interpreted, and the latter having been exposed to Greek texts, two key features of Maimonides' *The Guide of the Perplexed.*

This is the first of three opinions in the Talmudic passage, as he cites it.

TILL THE LAST "AND I SAW" [Guide, pp. 425-426]

Thus, according to Maimonides' version of what Rabbi Judah (or Rabbi Meir) believe, all three are under a ban, but all may be taught by means of chapter headings. This appears to be the opinion that Maimonides follows. A second opinion:

RABBI ISAAC SAYS: TILL [THE "AND I SAW" OF] HASHMAL. FROM [THE FIRST] "AND I SAW" TILL [THE "AND I SAW" OF] HASHMAL, [IT IS PERMISSIBLE] TO TEACH; FROM THERE ON THE CHAPTER HEADINGS ARE TRANSMITTED TO [THE DISCIPLE]. [Guide, p. 426]

Rabbi Isaac's opinion allows the open teaching of the first two visions, but puts *hashmal* under the "chapter heading" restriction. The third opinion:

SOME SAY: FROM [THE FIRST] "AND I SAW" TILL [THE "AND I SAW" OF] HASHMAL THE CHAPTER HEADINGS ARE TRANSMITTED TO HIM; FROM THERE ON, [HE MAY BE TAUGHT] IF HE WERE WISE AND UNDER-

STANDING OF HIS OWN KNOWLEDGE; AND [HE MAY]
NOT [BE TAUGHT] IF [HE IS] NOT [THAT]. [*Guide*, p. 426]

This would put the first two visions under the "chapter heading"
criterion and *hashmal* under the original Mishnaic law criterion of
selected persons.

Maimonides asserts that such different opinions are only possible
by the designation of the three "and I saws."

IT HAS THUS BECOME CLEAR TO YOU FROM THEIR
TEXTS THAT THERE WERE VARIOUS APPREHENSIONS
TO WHICH ATTENTION IS DRAWN BY THE EXPRES-
SION: *AND I SAW, AND I SAW, AND I SAW;* THAT
THESE SIGNIFIED DIFFERENT DEGREES; AND THAT
THE LAST APPREHENSION, THAT REFERRED TO IN
THE WORDS "AND I SAW AS A FOUNTAIN OF
HASHMAL" –I MEAN THE APPREHENSION OF THE
FORM OF THE DIVIDED MAN [*Guide*, p. 426]

We take it that Maimonides means two sexes when he speaks of "the
divided man." Thus, as he indicates in connection with Adam and
Eve, ". . . Adam and Eve were created together . . . and that this being
was divided and one half of it, namely Eve. . . ." [*Guide*, p. 355].

OF WHICH IT IS SAID: *FROM THE APPEARANCE OF HIS
LOINS AND UPWARD, AND FROM THE APPEARANCE
OF HIS LOINS AND DOWNWARD* (Ezekiel 1:27; 8:2).
[*Guide*, p. 426]

This is that which is identified in the Mishnaic law: "As for anyone
who should attempt to discern . . . what is upward, what is downward
. . . it were as though he had not come into the world" (*Hagigah* 11b).

IS THE ULTIMATE PERCEPTION AND THE HIGHEST OF
ALL. [*Guide*, p. 426]

With respect to this ultimate third vision, Maimonides says:

THERE IS ALSO A DIFFERENCE OF OPINION AMONG
THE SAGES ABOUT WHETHER IT IS PERMISSIBLE FOR
IT TO BE ALLUDED TO IN ANY WAY THROUGH
TEACHING – I MEAN TO SAY *THROUGH THE TRANS-
MISSION OF THE CHAPTER HEADINGS* – OR WHETHER
IT IS NOT PERMISSIBLE IN ANY WAY THAT AN ALLU-
SION BE MADE TO THE TEACHINGS OF THIS THIRD
APPREHENSION, THOUGH IT BE ONLY *THROUGH THE
CHAPTER HEADINGS; BUT HE WHO IS WISE WILL
UNDERSTAND IN VIRTUE OF HIS OWN INTELLI-
GENCE.* [*Guide*, p. 426]

Then, noting the variation among opinions concerning the *living
creatures* and the *ophannim* as well, he says:

SIMILARLY THERE IS ALSO, AS YOU SEE, A DIFFERENCE
OF OPINION AMONG THE SAGES WITH REGARD TO
THE FIRST TWO APPREHENSIONS LIKEWISE – I MEAN
THOSE CONCERNING THE *LIVING CREATURES* AND
THE *OPHANNIM* – ABOUT WHETHER IT IS PERMIS-
SIBLE TO TEACH EXPLICITLY THE NOTIONS CON-
CERNING THEM, OR WHETHER THIS IS ONLY PER-
MITTED TO BE DONE THROUGH ALLUSIONS AND
ENIGMAS *THROUGH THE CHAPTER HEADINGS.*
[*Guide*, p. 426]

The opinion of Rabbi Judah (or Rabbi Meir), as well as "some," is that
only the chapter headings of the first two visions may be taught. Rabbi
Isaac allows them to be taught openly.

Maimonides ends Chapter III:5 with a comment on the appropriateness of the order in which the three visions are presented:

YOU OUGHT ALSO TO HAVE YOUR ATTENTION DI-
RECTED TO THE ORDER OF THESE THREE APPREHEN-
SIONS. [*Guide*, p. 426]

That is, *living creatures, ophannim,* and *man.* He identifies two things
about the living creatures, nobility and causality.

THUS HE HAS PUT FIRST THE APPREHENSION OF THE
LIVING CREATURES, FOR THEY COME FIRST BECAUSE
OF THEIR NOBILITY AND OF THEIR CAUSALITY – AC-
CORDING TO WHAT HE SAYS: FOR *THE AIR OF THE
LIVING CREATURES WAS IN THE OPHANNIM* – [Guide,
p. 426]

That is, the *living creatures* are noble in being the souls of human
beings, and they are causal as the determiners of the conduct of
human beings.

AND BECAUSE OF OTHER THINGS TOO.

Which we can take as referring to the divine purpose involved in the
living creatures, as he has explained.

AFTER THE *OPHANNIM* COMES THE THIRD APPRE-
HENSION [Guide, p. 426]

Of the man.

WHICH IS HIGHER IN DEGREE THAN THAT OF THE
LIVING CREATURES, AS IS CLEAR. [Guide, p. 426]

Since the man is the cause of the *living creatures* in their very existence.

THE REASON FOR THIS LIES IN THE FACT THAT THE
FIRST TWO APPREHENSIONS NECESSARILY PRECEDE
THE THIRD APPREHENSION IN THE ORDER OF KNOWL-
EDGE, THE LATTER BEING INFERRED WITH THE HELP
OF THE OTHER TWO. [Guide, p. 426]

This is an allusion to the fundamental form of the argument for the
existence of God, being an argument from the existence of the
universe back to the existence of God. Thus, here, analogously, there
is an implicit argument with respect to the existence of the man from
the existence of human beings, beings both materialized and enspir-
ited.

Maimonides is, at the end of Chapter III:5, at the end of where he
can go without extraordinary courage, and even audacity. For he has

been dealing with the living creatures and the *ophannim* in Chapters III:1-4, and only sketched out the tripartite nature of the vision as a whole. He has, in his argument, come, as it were, to the existence but not to the essence of the man. He has dealt largely in chapter headings, and so in conformity with both the opinion of Rabbi Judah and the opinion of some of the sages. And even if his dealing with the subject matter is more open than what the constraint of "chapter headings" would allow, he has the license from Rabbi Isaac that with respect to the living creatures and the *ophannim* there may be open exposition. However, with respect to the highest level, the level of the man, he is obliged by either the "chapter heading" criterion or the Mishnaic law criterion of addressing only those who are wise and understanding of their own knowledge, or both. And this is what he says in Chapter III:5.

We need to give some consideration to what we might consider Maimonides' courage or audacity. In Chapter II:38 he indicates that a prophet needs two characteristics, the characteristic of divination and the characteristic of courage [*Guide*, p. 376]. The need for the prophet having the faculty of divination is obvious. Maimonides describes the faculty of courage:

> [The] faculty of courage varies in strength and weakness . . . so that you may find among people some who will advance upon a lion, while others flee from a mouse. You will find someone who will advance against an army and fight it, and will find another who will tremble and fear if a woman shouts at him. . . . [The] faculties become very greatly strengthened so that this may finally reach the point you know: namely [as in the case of Moses] the lone individual, having only his staff, went boldly to the great king in order to save a religious community from the burden of slavery, and had no fear of dread. . . . Similarly you will find all of [the prophets] to be endowed with great courage. [*Guide*, pp. 376-377]

Beyond courage, Maimonides finds evidence that even audacity is involved in prophecy, in particular the apprehension of the man on the throne. He cites a passage from *Bereshit Rabbah*: "Great is the power of the prophets; for they liken a form to its creator. For it is said: And upon the likeness of the throne was a likeness as the appearance of a man" (Ezekiel 1:26) [*Guide*, p. 103].

Maimonides then identifies Ezekiel's prophecy as being in the same category as the "shocking" act of performing the *halizah* alone and at night. The *halizah* is the ceremony associated with the release from the obligatory marriage between a widow and her husband's brother in which the husband's brother is called before the elders of the city and is made to declare openly that he refuses to marry the widow: ". . . then shall [she] draw nigh unto him in the presence of the elders, and loose his shoe from off his foot, and spit in his face . . ." (Deuteronomy 25:9).

It is patent that the essence of the ceremony is that it should be performed publicly. Maimonides says, however,

> How admirable is their saying "Great is the power," as though [the Sages] considered this matter great. For they always speak in this way when they express their appreciation of the greatness of something said or done, but whose appearance is shocking. Thus they say: "A certain rabbi performed the act [of *halizah*] with a slipper, alone and at night. Another rabbi said thereupon: How great is his strength to have done it alone. . . ." [*Guide*, p. 103]

Thus Maimonides is prepared for allowing what may appear to be outrageous or what may even be outrageous.

Up to this point in our discussion, our comments concerning prurience have been restricted to showing Maimonides pointing toward prurience in the text, as contrasted with his own contribution to prurience. However, in a discussion of the courage that may go to audacity, we would insert here two instances in which it can be judged that Maimonides takes pains to indicate prurience. In one instance Maimonides conjoins two remote texts from Scripture in such a way that there is a prurient result that does not exist until they are so conjoined.

The example occurs in the chapter on touching, Chapter I:18. With what we take as Maimonides' aim in this chapter to indicate the direct sexual meaning of touching as well as the word's meaning as a euphemism for sexuality, he creates a couplet of remote verses, one from Exodus and one from Isaiah, to suggest an extraordinarily prurient image [*Guide*, p. 43]:

> And she caused it to touch his feet. [Exodus 4:25]

And he caused it to touch my mouth. [Isaiah 6:7]

The second is in connection with the word *savav*, meaning to surround, as a transitive verb euphemistic for sexual intercourse, with the female as the subject of the verb.

In Chapter I:26, in which Maimonides speaks of how the Torah speaks in the language of men, he draws attention to *savav* in an interesting manner. He enumerates ten terms that are discussed in the lexicographical section of the *Guide*. However, he adds into it another term, *savav*, placing it in the center of the list.

> . . . when corporeality is abolished, all these predicates are likewise abolished. I mean such terms as *to descend, to ascend, to go, to stand erect, to stand, to surround* [savav], *to sit, to dwell, to go out, to come, to pass*, and all terms similar to these. [*Guide*, p. 57]

The prurient suggestiveness of the term is patent from "Return, oh virgin of Israel. . . . How long will you turn away coyly, oh thou backturning daughter? For the Lord has created a new thing in the earth, that the female shall *surround* [tesoveiv] the male" (Jeremiah 31:21–22).

We will presently note the significance of this contribution on the part of Maimonides for the understanding of Isaiah in Chapter III:6.

The warrant for Maimonides is in what he takes to be the commandment after the commandments with respect to the existence and unity of God, to love God.

> As for the dictum of Scripture: *And thou shalt love the Lord thy God with all thy heart* (Deuteronomy 6:5); I mean to say, with all the forces of the body, for the principle of all of them derives from the heart. Accordingly the intended meaning is, as we have explained in the *Commentary on the Mishnah* and in the *Mishneh Torah*, that you should make His apprehension the end of all your actions. [*Guide*, p. 89]

There are, as Maimonides variously points out, many interferences. There are great interferences that arise out of necessity in connection with what is appropriate with respect to sexual education and with respect to the regulation of conduct. The task is to transcend them without going the way of Ben Azzai, Ben Zoma, and Aher. That is the path of Rabbi Akiva, who openly acknowledged the sexual content of the prophetic apprehensions and who recognized that they were only the representations of something else.

Chapter III:6 is laconic. The quality of being laconic is the subject of the chapter. The thesis is that what Isaiah described briefly is the same as that which Ezekiel described extensively.

KNOW THAT THE GREAT AND SUBLIME NOTION THAT EZEKIEL [Guide, p. 427]

We have identified the great and sublime notion as that of the ongoing generation of human souls in world history after the first Sabbath.

BEING MOVED BY A PROPHETIC FORCE [Guide, p. 427]

Prophecy being in dreams and visions entailing the apprehension by the rational faculty and then by the imaginative faculty, and that overflowing.

THAT INCITED HIM TO LET US KNOW THIS [Guide, p. 427]

That is, to let us know about the generation of human souls

BEGAN TO TEACH US [Guide, p. 427]

What we have even from Ezekiel is only a beginning of instruction.

IN DESCRIBING THE MERKABAH IS THE VERY NOTION THAT ISAIAH . . . LET US KNOW SUMMARILY WITHOUT HAVING TO GO INTO DETAILS. [Guide, p. 427]

The laconic statement by Isaiah is given in Isaiah 6:1, with some further indications in the subsequent text.

FOR HE SAYS: AND I SAW THE LORD SITTING UPON A THRONE HIGH AND LIFTED UP, AND HIS TRAIN FILLED THE TEMPLE. THE SERAPHIM STOOD, AND SO ON (Isaiah 6:1ff). [Guide, p. 427]

What we are prepared to expect is that this sentence, understood properly, represents sexual activity. We need again to note Maimonides saying in Chapter I:46: ". . . we have no intellectual cognition of our bringing somebody other than us to existence except through sexual intercourse" [*Guide*, p. 99]. Albeit we are to understand this in accordance with the principle of Rabbi Akiva, that it is the first of a two-step process.

Maimonides takes this interpretation as the meaning of an allegory about how a country person needed more explanation than a city person with respect to the appearance of the king, the former likely to have seen him riding often. It is an allegory that is located in the Talmud in the discussion of the Mishnaic law concerning the esoteric topics.

THE SAGES HAVE EXPLAINED ALL THIS TO US AND HAVE CALLED OUR ATTENTION TO THE SUBJECT. THEY SAID THAT THE APPREHENSION GRASPED BY EZEKIEL WAS IDENTICAL WITH THAT GRASPED BY ISAIAH.

THEY MADE ABOUT IT A COMPARISON WITH TWO MEN WHO SAW THE RULER WHILE THE LATTER WAS RIDING: ONE OF THEM BELONGED TO THE SETTLED POPULATION AND THE OTHER TO THE DESERT NOMADS. BECAUSE [ISAIAH] KNEW THAT CITY PEOPLE KNOW IN WHAT STATE THE RULER RIDES, HE DID NOT DESCRIBE THAT STATE, BUT SAID ONLY: I SAW THE RULER. [EZEKIEL], HOWEVER, WISHING TO DESCRIBE THIS TO THE DESERT NOMADS, WHO HAVE NO KNOWLEDGE AT ALL REGARDING THE STATE IN WHICH THE RULER RIDES, DESCRIBED TO THEM IN DETAIL THIS STATE AND THE CHARACTERISTICS OF THE RULER'S TROOPS, HIS SERVANTS AND THOSE WHO EXECUTE HIS ORDERS.

AN INTIMATION OF THIS SCOPE IS OF VERY GREAT UTILITY. [*Guide*, p. 427]

By identifying this as an intimation, Maimonides makes an intimation to the reader.

I REFER TO THEIR DICTUM IN *HAGIGAH*: ALL THAT WAS SEEN BY EZEKIEL WAS [LIKEWISE] SEEN BY ISAIAH. ISAIAH IS LIKE UNTO A CITY MAN WHO SAW THE KING; WHEREAS EZEKIEL IS LIKE UNTO A VILLAGER WHO SAW THE KING (*Hagigah* 13b). [*Guide*, p. 427]

At this point Maimonides provides a special intimation to the reader by making a distinction between two ways in which the author of the allegory might have intended it. The first is:

IT IS POSSIBLE THAT THIS TEXT WAS INTERPRETED BY ITS AUTHOR IN ACCORDANCE WITH WHAT I HAVE SAID AT THE BEGINNING [OF THE CHAPTER]: NAMELY, THAT THE CONTEMPORARIES OF ISAIAH HAD NO NEED OF EXPOUNDING THOSE DETAILS TO THEM, IT BEING SUFFICIENT FOR THEM THAT HE SAID: *AND I SAW THE LORD, AND SO ON; WHEREAS THE PEOPLE OF THE EXILE* REQUIRED THESE DETAILS. [*Guide*, p. 427]

If we examine this, it appears to be sufficient with respect to that which Maimonides cites from the Talmud. The next possibility he indicates is more remote from the text. We take it that this second possibility is more consonant with what Maimonides wants to intimate to the reader, although it is less indicated by the Talmudic text.

IT IS ALSO POSSIBLE THAT THE AUTHOR OF THE REMARK BELIEVED THAT ISAIAH WAS MORE PERFECT THAN EZEKIEL [*Guide*, p. 427]

In the sense that Isaiah was more courageous.

AND THAT THE APPREHENSION THAT AMAZED EZEKIEL AND WAS REGARDED BY HIM AS TERRIBLE [*Guide*, p. 427]

And in the sense that Isaiah apprehended in so clear a way that he could speak directly.

WAS KNOWN BY ISAIAH THROUGH A KNOWLEDGE THE EXPOSITION OF WHICH DID NOT REQUIRE EX-TRAORDINARY LANGUAGE, THE SUBJECT BEING WELL KNOWN TO THOSE WHO ARE PERFECT. [*Guide*, p. 427]

This ends Chapter III:6. Let us look carefully at this citation from Isaiah 6:1: *And I saw the Lord sitting upon a throne high and lifted up, and his train filled the temple. The seraphim stood, and so on.*

And I saw. This announces it as a prophetic vision. It corresponds to the "And I saw" of Ezekiel 1:27. We take note that this discussion by Maimonides comes after the characterization of the tripartite nature of the vision, and after the explication of two of the parts. Thus, we expect the reference to be to that which has not yet been discussed, the man on the throne.

The Lord. This appears as the word *adonai* rather than in the form of the Tetragrammaton or abbreviation for it. It occurs the same way in the meeting of Abraham with the angels in Genesis 18:3 in which he clearly addresses men, "And lo, three men stood . . ." (Genesis 18:2), or angels, "And the two angels came . . ." (Genesis 19:1), in which he says "My Lord (*adonai*) if now I have found favor in thy sight . . ." (Genesis 18:2). This is important in that for Maimonides it is not God who is apprehended in these visions.

Sitting upon the throne. We have already indicated that sitting is a euphemism for sexual intercourse. We have also indicated that the Talmud deals with the suggestion that there are two thrones, and we have indicated the opinion of Rabbi Akiva that they are to be understood as "One for Him and one for the beloved" (*Hagigah* 14a).

High. Maimonides has a lexicographical chapter on the words *ram ve-nisa*, which are ordinarily translated as "high and lifted up," Chapter I:20.

In the chapter Maimonides indicates that the word *ram* can be understood in two senses. In the first it means a physical heightening as in "And the ark was made to be high above the earth" (Genesis 7:17). It also, he says, has a second meaning as in "Forasmuch as I have placed thee on high from among the people" (I Kings 14:7). That is, it suggests a heightened status.

We take this as an indication to the reader that when he reads Isaiah he should recognize that whatever rises in the mind of a physical meaning of *ram* should then be interpreted in the second sense, in accordance with the principle of Rabbi Akiva.

He tells the reader specifically, after noting the two senses of the word, that "Every word derived from heightening [*haramah*] has this second meaning when occurring with reference to God. Thus: *Be thou heightened, O God, above the heavens*" (Psalms 57:6) [*Guide*, p. 46]. However, this counsel by Maimonides to the reader against a physical interpretation of *ram* is also a way of suggesting the physical imagery of heightening.

Va-nisa. By putting this word into the same chapter with *ram*, Maimonides achieves the end of making it clear that the *ram va-nisa* of Isaiah 6:1 is understood. Maimonides then proceeds to make the same point as he does with *ram*, that there is a physical and a nonphysical meaning associated with the word *nisa*. Yet at the same time the failure to mention the meaning "to take a wife" is conspicuous in its omission. The word is used to mean "take a wife" variously in Scripture. For example: "And they took as wives (*ve-nasu*) for themselves and their sons from their daughters" (Ezra 9:2). The word is similarly used in Ezra 9:12 and 10:44, Nehemiah 13:25, 2 Chronicles 11:21, 13:21, and 24:3, and Ruth 1:4.

And his train (ve-shulav). And his *shul*. The word has a primary meaning as a hanging (Jastrow, p. 1534). The word appears to have a meaning of skirt or skirts in Scripture. It is used in the description of the fashioning of the robe of priest: "And thou shalt make a robe . . . And thou shalt make on its skirts . . ." (Exodus 28:33–34). To translate as "train" is in the sense of the train of the garment of a king. The verb that follows is in the plural, which would make "skirts" more apt as a translation: *And his skirts. . . .*

Scripture uses the word in connection with sexual impropriety – as, for example, "Her filthiness was in her skirts" (Lamentations 1:9). "For the greatness of thy iniquity are thy skirts uncovered" (Jeremiah 13:22). "Therefore will I also uncover thy skirts upon thy face, and thy shame shall appear. Thine adulteries, and thy neighings, and the lewdness of thy harlotry. On the hills in the fields have I seen thy detestable acts. Woe unto thee O Jerusalem! Thou wilt not be made clean" (Jeremiah 13:26–27)!

Filled (melayim). Maimonides has a chapter on the word for "fill." He opens Chapter I:19: *"To fill (malle)*. This is an equivocal term applied by people speaking the Hebrew language to a body's entering and filling up another body" [*Guide*, p. 45]. He specifically mentions an analogous verse to that of Isaiah 6:1 to say that it should be interpreted in a nonliteral way: ". . . *And the glory of the Lord filled the tabernacle* (Exodus 40:34). Every mention of filling that you will find referring to God is used in this [nonliteral] sense, and not in the sense of there being a body filling a place" [*Guide*, p. 46].

He clearly has the verse from Isaiah 6:1 on his mind in that he specifically interprets from an adjacent verse that it is to be understood in a nonliteral sense: "In this [nonliteral] sense it is said: *The whole earth is filled with His glory* (Isaiah 6:3); the meaning of this verse being that the whole earth bears witness to his perfection, that is, indicates it" [*Guide*, p. 46].

The seraphim stood, and so on. The "and so on" immediately goes to a description of the seraphim, attributing wings to them: "Each one had six wings: with twain he covered his face, and with twain he covered his feet, and with twain he did fly" (Isaiah 1:2).

The Talmud patently identifies the seraphim of Isaiah's vision with the cherubim of Ezekiel's vision:

One verse says *Each one had six wings* (Isaiah 6:2) and another verse says *And everyone had four faces, and everyone had four wings* (Ezekiel 1:6). There is no contradiction. [*Hagigah* 13b]

We now turn our attention to Chapter III:7, the last of the chapters in which Maimonides deals explicitly with the *Maaseh Merkabah*. The chapter consists of seven distinguishable items and a concluding statement announcing the termination of his project, making this chapter the substantive end of *The Guide of the Perplexed*.

The first item takes the opening statement of *Ezekiel* as comprising reverse gematria and anagram. We say "reverse gematria" because gematria is characteristically understood as the taking of letters for their numerical value. Here, numerical values are taken as letters. The result is that Ezekiel's opening is an announcement that the vision is of the generation of the cherubim. We are also thereby led to understand why the *Maaseh Merkabah* is called *Maaseh Merkabah*, for that too is based on an anagram of the word for cherub.

TO THE WHOLE OF THINGS REQUIRING INVESTIGA-TION BELONGS THE TYING OF THE APPREHENSION OF THE *MERKABAH* TO A YEAR, A MONTH, AND A DAY [*Guide*, p. 428]

Maimonides is referring to: "Now it came to pass in the *thirtieth* year, in the *fourth* month, in the *fifth* day of the month" (Ezekiel 1:1). Thirty is *lamed*. Four is *dalet*. Five is *heh*. This makes the word *leidah*, meaning generation. It derives from *yalad*, to bear. The word is found in Hosea, for example, as follows: "There shall be none in birth [*leidah*], none pregnant, and none conceived" (Hosea 9:11).

AND ALSO TO A PLACE. [*Guide*, p. 427]

Maimonides is referring to: ". . . as I was among the exiles by the river *kebar*." *Kebar* is an anagram of *kerub*, cherub. It is also an anagram of *rakab*, to mount or ride, which is the root of the word, *rokeb*, rider, and *merkabah*, chariot.

Maimonides gives a hint concerning *kebar* in an earlier discussion in Chapter I:63. The hint occurs in a discussion of the names of God. Maimonides is explaining the meaning of the word *Shaddai* as a name for God. *Shaddai* is explainable as having been constructed out of two parts, the first part meaning "who" and the second part meaning "sufficient," so that *Shaddai* means "he who is sufficient."

What is to be noted in Maimonides' explanation is the content he attaches to this. Let us note the way in which he makes his presenta-tion carefully. It is the end of the chapter: "The name *Yah* refers similarly to the notion of the eternity of existence, whereas *Shaddai* derives from the word *day*, meaning a sufficiency. . . . The letter *shin* (occurring at the beginning of *Shaddai*) has the meaning *who*, as in *shekbar*" [*Guide*, p. 155].

The letter *shin* before a word as meaning "who" is commonplace. What we take note of is that Maimonides selects *shekbar* from Eccle-siastes 4:2 to exemplify it. The word *kbar* means already, and has the sense of "who already" in the verse: "And I praised the dead *who were already* (*shekbar*) dead . . ." (Ecclesiastes 4:2). While the word does not appear to have any extraordinary significance within the context, it has great significance if Maimonides intended us to understand *kbar* as an anagram of *kerub*. In that case, *shekbar* has the meaning "He who cherubs."

We have already indicated how Maimonides licenses anagrams as a way of determining the internal meaning of prophecy [*Guide*, p. 393]. With respect to these things, Maimonides says:

IT SHOULD NOT BE THOUGHT THAT THIS IS A MATTER WITHOUT SIGNIFICANCE. [*Guide*, p. 428]

In the second item Maimonides puts together a set of verses which, when considered together, constitute a coherent statement. He says:

TO THE THINGS THAT OUGHT TO BE CONSIDERED, FOR IT IS THE KEY TO THE WHOLE, BELONGS HIS SAY-ING: *THE HEAVENS WERE OPENED* (Ezekiel 1:1).

THIS IS SOMETHING THAT FREQUENTLY OCCURS IN THE SPEECH OF THE PROPHETS – I MEAN THE USE OF THE FIGURATIVE EXPRESSIONS OF THE OPENING AND ALSO THE OPENING OF THE GATES [*Guide*, p. 428]

It is important to pause at this point. For Maimonides proceeds to give four citations, one from Isaiah, and three from Psalms. If we allow that Maimonides did not merely put these together as a listing, but put them together in such a way as to intimate a meaning, they comprise an extraordinarily audacious oedipal suggestion:

OPEN THE GATES, AND HE CAME (*PETICHU SHAARIM VA-YAVO*) (Isaiah 26:2).

AND HE OPENED THE DOORS OF HEAVEN (*VADALATO SHAMAIM PATACH*) (Psalms 78:23).

AND HE "MARRIED" THE OPENINGS OF THE WORLD (*VA-SAU PITCHE OLAM*) (Psalms 24:9).

OPEN FOR ME THE GATES OF RIGHTEOUSNESS (*PITCHU LI SHAAREY ZEDEK*) (Psalms 118:18) [*Guide*, p. 428].

Now, Maimonides follows this up immediately with

THIS OCCURS FREQUENTLY. [*Guide*, p. 428]

We might, if we read casually, take the four citations as simply a sampling from a longer possible list that Maimonides might glean from Scripture. Alternatively, the four are chosen and are placed in an order so that together they indicate a meaning.

The last verse continues with: "I will come into them. I will thank the Lord (*yah*). This is the gate that belongs to Lord (the Tetragrammaton); The righteous shall come into it" (Psalms 118:18–20), and we might consider it part of the whole.

It is to be pointed out that the Hebrew word for "come" is given a chapter, Chapter I:22, in the lexicographical section, with the indication that it is a word applied to God and should be read figuratively. It is interesting that in that chapter Maimonides states: "The term, to come, (*bo*) is . . . applied figuratively to certain privations" [*Guide*, p. 52].

Maimonides uses the notion of privation specifically in connection with the use of sexuality as a metaphor:

> Thus Plato and his predecessors designated Matter as the female and Form as the male. Now you know that the principles of the existents subject to generation and corruption are three: Matter, Form, and Particularized Privation, which is always conjoined with Matter. For, were it not for this conjunction with Privation, Matter would not receive Form. It is in this sense that Privation is to be considered as one of the principles. However, when a form is achieved, the particular privation in question, I mean the privation of the form which is achieved, disappears, and another privation is conjoined with matter; and this goes on for ever. . . . [*Guide*, p. 43]

The third item deals with the relative literalness and figurativeness of different parts of the report by Ezekiel.

AMONG THE THINGS TO WHICH YOUR ATTENTION IS TO BE DIRECTED BELONGS THE FACT THAT THOUGH THIS WHOLE DESCRIPTION IS BASED INDUBITABLY ON A VISION OF PROPHECY [*Guide*, p. 428]

Attested to in the text

> FOR HE SAYS: *AND THE HAND OF THE LORD WAS*
> *THERE UPON HIM* (Ezekiel 1:3). [*Guide*, p. 428]

And thus it is a dream or vision, and is to be understood as figurative, nonetheless:

> THERE IS BETWEEN VARIOUS PARTS OF THIS DESCRIP-
> TION A VERY GREAT DIFFERENCE IN EXPRESSION.
> [*Guide*, p. 428]

The differentiation is indicated by the use of the word "likeness."

> FOR WHEN HE SPEAKS OF THE *LIVING CREATURES*, HE
> SAYS *THE LIKENESS OF FOUR LIVING CREATURES,*
> *AND DOES NOT ONLY SAY, FOUR LIVING CREATURES*
> (Ezekiel 1:5). SIMILARLY HE SAYS: *AND THE LIKENESS OF*
> *THE FIRMAMENT WAS UPON THE HEADS OF THE*
> *LIVING CREATURES* (Ezekiel 1:22) AND: *THE LIKENESS*
> *OF A THRONE, AS THE APPEARANCE OF A SAPPHIRE*
> *STONE* (Ezekiel 1:26), AND *THE LIKENESS AS THE AP-*
> *PEARANCE OF A MAN* (Ezekiel 1:26). WITH REGARD TO
> ALL OF THIS HE USES THE EXPRESSION: *LIKENESS.*
> [*Guide*, p. 428]

But such is not the case with respect to the *ophannim*. *Ophannim* are to be understood in the sense of material concretization, and hence not to be described by the word "likeness."

> WITH REGARD TO THE *OPHANNIM*, HOWEVER, HE BY
> NO MEANS SAYS CONCERNING THEM, *THE LIKENESS*
> *OF AN OPHAN* OR *THE LIKENESS OF OPHANNIM*, BUT
> MAKES STATEMENTS REGARDING WHAT THEY RE-
> ALLY ARE IN A FORM EXPRESSIVE OF THAT WHICH
> REALLY EXISTS. [*Guide*, p. 428]

That is, what they are concretely.

There is an instance in which Ezekiel uses the word "likeness" in conjunction with the *ophannim*, but Maimonides indicates to the reader not to take this in the same sense:

BE NOT MISLED BY HIS SAYING, AND *THE FOUR HAD ONE LIKENESS* (Ezekiel 1:16) FOR THIS DICTUM IS NOT ORDERED IN THE SAME WAY AND HAS NOT THE SIGNI- FICATION REFERRED TO. [*Guide*, p. 428]

Maimonides then turns to consider the evidence on this question of what is and is not "likeness" from the tenth chapter of Ezekiel:

IN THE LAST APPREHENSION HE CORROBORATES AND EXPLAINS THIS NOTION. [*Guide*, p. 428]

There is a problem in connection with the concreteness we are to attribute to the firmament:

HE MENTIONS THE FIRMAMENT IN AN ABSOLUTE MANNER, BEGINNING AS HE DOES WITH IT AND SET- TING FORTH THE DETAILS CONCERNING IT, HE SAYS: *THEN I SAW, AND, BEHOLD, IN THE FIRMAMENT THAT WAS ABOVE THE HEAD OF THE CHERUBIM, THERE APPEARED OVER THEM AS IT WERE A SAP- PHIRE STONE, AS THE APPEARANCE OF THE LIKE- NESS OF A THRONE* (Ezekiel 10:1). [*Guide*, p. 428]

This is different from what is said in Chapter 1 of Ezekiel.

THUS HE SPEAKS IN THIS PASSAGE [in Chapter 10] ABOUT THE FIRMAMENT IN AN ABSOLUTE MANNER AND DOES NOT SAY THE *LIKENESS OF THE FIRMA- MENT* AS WAS THE CASE WHEN HE SPOKE OF IT IN CONNECTION WITH *THE HEADS OF THE LIKENESS OF THE LIVING CREATURES.* [*Guide*, pp. 428–429]

This last refers to: "And the likeness over the head of the living creatures was the firmament . . . stretched forth over their heads from above" (Ezekiel 1:22). He then appears to try to turn this difficulty into a proof concerning the sequence of the apprehension of the visions.

AS FOR THE THRONE HE SAYS, *THERE APPEARED OVER THEM THE LIKENESS OF A THRONE,* THIS BEING A PROOF THAT THE APPREHENSION OF THE FIRMAMENT CAME FIRST AND THAT AFTERWARDS *THERE APPEARED TO HIM OVER IT THE LIKENESS OF A THRONE.* [*Guide,* p. 429]

We take it that there is a presumption on the part of Maimonides, that the sequence of apprehension is first the apprehension of the concrete, and then the apprehension of the figurative. This point is one that Maimonides makes throughout *The Guide of the Perplexed.* Thus, we take it that since the firmament is sometimes characterized as likeness and sometimes not, it is intermediary. Nonetheless, the man on the throne is not to be understood as such concrete reality. Indeed, the danger of it being taken as a concrete reality is the major reason for the secrecy associated with it. Thus, what appears at first sight as a difficulty is turned into an indicator of a major point.

UNDERSTAND THIS. [*Guide,* p. 429]

The fourth item again deals with the problem of the division between the literal and the figurative of prophecy. This item consists of two parts. The first relates to the development of hands. The second is a reminder of the more literal character of the *ophannim.* Hands are more concrete than wings. Furthermore, it is with the hands that the human being puts forms into the matter of the universe, thereby creating things; even as the human being, in this vision, is conceived as a soul, as a form, which becomes united with matter to become the human being.

AMONG THE THINGS TO WHICH YOUR ATTENTION OUGHT TO BE DIRECTED BELONGS THE FACT THAT IN THE FIRST APPREHENSION [*Guide,* p. 429]

The reference to Chapter 1 of Ezekiel as the first and Chapter 10 of Ezekiel as the second apprehension needs to be noted. For there is still another apprehension in Chapter 8 of Ezekiel. The latter actually contains a major clue for Maimonides with respect to the notion of the "divided man," the notion of the image representing both male and female elements. We may take his failure to count Chapter 8 of Ezekiel as part of his effort at concealment.

HE STATES THAT THE LIVING CREATURES HAD BOTH WINGS AND THE HANDS OF A MAN [*Guide*, p. 429]

This we take as meaning that the whole process involving the transformation of wings into hands is represented. The step-wise feature of the process is communicated to us in Chapter 10 of Ezekiel:

WHEREAS IN THE SECOND APPREHENSION IN WHICH HE EXPLAINS THAT THE LIVING CREATURES ARE THE CHERUBIM [*Guide*, p. 429]

We are informed of the steps, the steps of the apprehension corresponding to the steps of the transformation. The first step:

HE APPREHENDED IN THE FIRST PLACE ONLY THEIR WINGS [*Guide*, p. 429]

The second step:

THE HANDS OF MAN APPEARING IN THEM AFTER-WARDS IN THE COURSE OF HIS APPREHENSION [*Guide*, p. 429]

The proof being:

FOR HE SAYS: *AND THERE APPEARED IN THE CHER-UBIM THE SHAPE (TABNIT) OF A MAN'S HAND UNDER THEIR WINGS* (Ezekiel 10:8). [*Guide*, p. 429]

Now, we know from Maimonides' chapter on *tabnit*, Chapter I:3, that Maimonides understands that word in a literalistic sense. Thus there is a key in Ezekiel's use of this term when he makes it apply to hands. It is, however, the analogue of the likeness.

HIS SAYING SHAPE [TABNIT] IS ANALOGOUS TO HIS
SAYING LIKENESS [DEMUT]. AND THE PLACE OF THIS IS
UNDER THEIR WINGS. UNDERSTAND THIS. [Guide, p.
429]

This process of the transformation with respect to the hands is part
of the process of materialization in which there is a union of living
creatures with matter that has no form of its own, the ophannim.
Maimonides indicates this, saying:

CONSIDER ALSO HOW HE MAKES AN EXPLICIT STATE-
MENT IN HIS DICTUM, AND THE OPHANNIM WERE
BESIDE THEM (Ezekiel 10:19), THOUGH HE DOES NOT
ASCRIBE A FORM TO THEM. [Guide, p. 429]

The fifth item cites the verse concerning the rainbow from Ezekiel,
Ezekiel 1:28, indicating that it is significant but not indicating what
that significance is:

HE ALSO SAYS: AS THE APPEARANCE OF THE RAIN-
BOW THAT IS IN THE CLOUD IN THE DAY OF RAIN, SO
WAS THE APPEARANCE OF THE BRIGHTNESS ROUND
ABOUT. THIS WAS THE APPEARANCE OF THE LIKE-
NESS OF THE GLORY OF THE LORD (Ezekiel 1:28). [Guide,
p. 429]

While this item is critically placed in this chapter and in this book
as immediately before Maimonides makes his most explicit statement
about the most secret part of the Maaseh Merkabah, his comment is
very laconic.

THE MATTER, THE TRUE REALITY, AND THE ESSENCE
OF THE RAINBOW THAT IS DESCRIBED ARE KNOWN.
[Guide, p. 429]

We are presumed to know it already. Indeed, we are led to the two
places in the Talmud in the discussion of the Maaseh Merkabah that
deal with the rainbow. What is there is described by Maimonides as
follows:

THIS IS THE MOST EXTRAORDINARY COMPARISON
POSSIBLE, AS FAR AS PARABLES AND SIMILITUDES ARE
CONCERNED; AND IT IS INDUBITABLY DUE TO A PRO-
PHETIC FORCE. UNDERSTAND THIS. [*Guide*, p. 429]

What we find in the Talmud is a discussion of the significance of
this verse with some extraordinarily prurient suggestions associated
with it.

The Talmud associates the study of the *Maaseh Merkabah* with a
rainbow in the sky and a wedding:

> Rabbi Joshua and Rabbi Jose . . . were walking by the way. They said:
> Let us expound on the *Maaseh Merkabah.*

> Rabbi Joshua opened the exposition:
>   It was on the day of the summer solstice. The heavens were overcast
> with clouds and there appeared a kind of rainbow in the cloud.
>   And the ministering angels gathered to listen in the way that people
> gather to apprehend the celebration of a groom and bride. [*Hagigah*
> 14b]

A more prurient suggestion is given in connection with the commentary on the part of the Mishnaic law that puts a curse on him who
is careless with the "glory" of his maker:

> *As for anyone who is not forbearing with respect to the glory of his maker, pity*
> *would have been shown to him had he not [been allowed to] come into the*
> *world.* [*Hagigah* 11b, *Hagigah* 16a]
>   What does this mean? Rabbi Abba said: This is one who attempts to
> divine the meaning of (*mistacheil*) the rainbow. [*Hagigah* 16a]

"Rainbow" is clearly being taken as corresponding to "glory." We take
it that Maimonides was cognizant of this correspondence. We note
also that Maimonides takes "glory" to represent the essence of God
[*Guide*, p. 124]: "Then [Moses] asked for the apprehension of His
essence. . . . That is what he means when he says, Show me, I pray
Thee, Thy glory" (Exodus 33:20).

We take it that this section in the Talmud is one of the sources for the idea in Maimonides of the prurient as the expression of the essence. The Talmudic discussion continues:

> Rabbi Joseph said This is one who transgresses in secret, who attempts to divine the meaning of the rainbow. For it is written: *As the appearance of the rainbow that is in the cloud in the day of rain, so was the appearance of the brightness round about. This was the appearance of the likeness of the glory of the Lord* (Ezekiel 1:29). [*Hagigah* 16a]

The Talmud reiterates, and elaborates:

> This is one who transgresses in secret according to Rabbi Isaac. Rabbi Isaac says [furthermore]: Anyone who transgresses in secret is as one who forces the legs of the Shekinah. [*Hagigah* 16a].

Divining the meaning of the rainbow is the divining of the sexual representation of God's creativity. The point that needs to be added to this is the interposition of the individual entertaining such a fantasy in the fantasy in an Oedipal manner. This would allow the Shekhinah to represent the female aspect of the image, the parental image, and the interposition of the fantasier as forcing the legs of the Shekhinah.

The Talmud then indicates a most extraordinary suggestion, strongly intimating that an overt act of sexual deviation might be preferable to the fantasy that brings one into such mental abomination. The text asks: "Is it really so?" That is, is it really so that seeking to divine the meaning of the rainbow is as forcing the legs of the Shekhinah?

And then the text offers an opinion of an old man, seemingly as a voice of wisdom under these circumstances:

> Behold Rabbi Elea, an old man, said: If a man sees that his impulse is overpowering him, let him go somewhere where he is not known, dress in dark clothes and wrap himself darkly, and do what his heart desires, rather than blatantly profane the name of heaven. [*Hagigah* 16a]

We take it that these texts are what Maimonides understands when he says that the essence of the rainbow described is known.

The sixth item is on the word *hashmal*, the most secret part of the vision of Ezekiel. It is of a "divided man."

AMONG THE THINGS TO WHICH YOUR ATTENTION SHOULD BE DRAWN BELONGS TO HIS DIVIDING *THE LIKENESS OF A MAN THAT WAS ON THE THRONE: THE UPPER PART OF THE LIKENESS BEING AS A FOUN-TAIN OF HASHMAL* (Ezekiel 1:27). AND THE LOWER *AS THE APPEARANCE OF FIRE* (Ezekiel 8:2). [*Guide*, p. 429]

Maimonides here makes a pastiche from Ezekiel 1:27 and Ezekiel 8:2. For the texts are not really so obliging in rendering so clear a ground for saying that Ezekiel is the one who divided "the likeness of the man who was on the throne" in the clear bisexual way that Maimonides intimates. However, the fact that the text is not so obliging only makes us more certain of the validity that such is Maimonides' interpretation, which is the object of this exercise.

Maimonides is here citing Ezekiel 8:2 for the "lower."

And I saw and behold the likeness *as the appearance of fire* from the appearance of his loins and downward fire. And from his loins and upward as the appearance of *zohar* like a fountain of *hashmalah*. [Ezekiel 8:2]

We note that in this verse a female form of *hashmal* — *hashmalah* — may be identified. We must also note that in the Jewish tradition, in contrast to the Greek tradition, both males and females are said to emit seed during sexual intercourse (*Berakot* 60a).

Maimonides then draws attention to some intimations concerning the meaning of the word *hashmal*.

THEY HAVE EXPLAINED THAT THE WORD *HASHMAL* IS COMPOSED OF TWO NOTIONS, *HASH* AND *MAL*; THIS MEANS, OF THE NOTION OF RAPIDITY, INDICATED BY *HASH*, AND OF THAT OF CUTTING, INDICATED BY *MAL*, THE INTENTION BEING TO COMBINE THROUGH A SIMILE TWO SEPARATE NOTIONS REGARDING TWO SIDES ABOVE AND BELOW. [*Guide*, p. 429]

By taking *mal* as *cutting*, Maimonides is intimating the circumcision. By taking *hash* as *rapid*, Maimonides intimates speed to emission in sexual intercourse associated with the male, as contrasted with slowness of the female. The Talmud counterbalances male sexual impatience with the notion that boys are more likely to be born if the female emits first (*Berakot* 60a). Maimonides indeed, in the pages of *The Guide of the Perplexed*, cites the Talmud on women's greater sexual pleasure with the uncircumcised [*Guide*, p. 609]. Maimonides then provides a second indication.

THEY ALSO GIVE US A SECOND HINT, SAYING THAT THE WORD DERIVES FROM THE NOTIONS OF SPEECH AND SILENCE, SAYING THAT *THEY SOMETIMES HASHOT (ARE SILENT) AND SOMETIMES MEMALLELOT (SPEAK).* THEY ASCRIBE THE MEANING "SILENCE" (TO HASH) FROM THE VERSE: HEHESHEITI (*I HAVE BEEN SILENT) FOR A LONG TIME* (Isaiah 42:14); THERE IS THUS AN ALLUSION TO TWO NOTIONS THROUGH THE INDICATION OF SPEECH WITHOUT A SOUND. [*Guide*, pp. 429–430]

The key to Maimonides' intimation is in the verse from Isaiah, which he partially cites: "I have been silent for a long time. . . . Now I groan like a woman in labor" (Isaiah 42:14).

We take the "two notions" as the imagery of the two sexes and the imagery of childbirth.

Maimonides then leads into a seventh item of this chapter, that the vision is a created thing:

THERE IS NO DOUBT THAT THEIR DICTUM, *THEY SOMETIMES ARE SILENT (HASHOT) AND SOMETIMES SPEAK (MEMALLELOT),* REFERS TO A CREATED THING. [*Guide*, p. 430]

The seventh item is an item of denial. As a denial it is an intimation of that which requires the denial. We presume that the apprehension is something like what might be regarded as God engaged in sexual activity, which has to be denied. Thus, Maimonides says:

SEE ACCORDINGLY HOW THEY HAVE MADE IT QUITE CLEAR TO US THAT *THE LIKENESS OF THE MAN THAT WAS ON THE THRONE* AND THAT WAS DIVIDED, [*Guide*, p. 430]

"Divided" is as Maimonides speaks of Adam and Eve [*Guide*, p. 355]. We also take it to be indicative of united in the sense that unless there is division, there can be no union to be apprehended. Thus the word "divided" is virtually a euphemism for the union that is apprehended in the dreams or visions of the prophets.

IS NOT A PARABLE REFERRING TO HIM [*Guide,* p. 430]

And the reason for that is that God is one

WHO IS EXALTED ABOVE ALL COMPOSITION [*Guide,* p. 430]

And that which is involved in the apprehension, albeit something objective and true, is that which is a creation of God, and not God Himself.

BUT TO A CREATED THING [*Guide,* p. 430]

Maimonides then refers to the Glory of God.

ACCORDINGLY THE PROPHET HIMSELF SAYS: *THIS WAS THE APPEARANCE OF THE LIKENESS OF THE GLORY OF THE LORD.* NOW *THE GLORY OF THE LORD* IS NOT *THE LORD* AS WE HAVE MADE CLEAR SEVERAL TIMES. [*Guide,* p. 430]

Thus, whatever may appear in the account of Ezekiel, the vision of Ezekiel is not to be understood as being of God. It is in sexual imagery because that is the only way human beings can represent the essence of God, the bringing into being out of nothingness.

ACCORDINGLY EVERYTHING TO WHICH THE PARA-
BLES CONTAINED IN THESE APPREHENSIONS REFER IS
ONLY *THE GLORY OF THE LORD. [Guide,* p. 430]

This is what the Merkabah is.

I MEAN TO SAY THE *MERKABAH,* NOT THE RIDER
(ROKEB), AS HE . . . MAY NOT BE PRESENTED IN A LIKE-
NESS IN A PARABLE. UNDERSTAND THIS. *[Guide,* p. 430]

Not the ultimate creator of the *kerub* (cherub), not the *rokeb* (the
rider), but the *merkabah* – the sexual imagery of dreams and visions.
With the presentation of this last item, Maimonides' project is
complete. The main thought has been presented, the most indicative
intimations in Chapter III:7. He then brings it to a close.

WE HAVE THUS GIVEN YOU ALSO IN THIS CHAPTER
SUCH CHAPTER HEADINGS *[Guide,* p. 430]

Which are to be combined with the intimations which have been
given before.

THAT IF YOU COMBINE THE [CHAPTER] HEADINGS
THERE WILL EMERGE FROM THEM A WHOLE *[Guide,* p.
430]

The tripartite imagery of Ezekiel and the understanding of it as
allegorical in accordance with the principle of Rabbi Akiva.

THAT IS USEFUL WITH REGARD TO THIS THEME.
[Guide, p. 430]

We take this in the sense of that which Maimonides says at the
beginning, that the aim is the understanding of prophecy. If we
understand that of which the prophetic apprehension is we can
understand all, or virtually all, of the terms and parables the prophets
provide in Scripture.

IF YOU CONSIDER ALL THAT WE HAVE SAID IN THE
CHAPTERS OF THIS TREATISE UP TO THIS CHAPTER,
THE GREATER PART OR THE ENTIRETY OF THE SUB-
JECT IN QUESTION, EXCEPT FOR A FEW SLIGHT DE-
TAILS AND REPETITIOUS SPEECH, WHOSE MEANING
REMAINS HIDDEN, WILL BECOME CLEAR TO YOU. PER-
HAPS UPON THOROUGH CONSIDERATION, THIS TOO
WILL BE REVEALED, AND NOTHING OF THIS WILL RE-
MAIN HIDDEN. [*Guide*, p. 430]

And with this, Maimonides' essential *The Guide of the Perplexed* is
finished.

DO NOT HOPE THAT, AFTER THIS CHAPTER, YOU WILL
HEAR FROM ME EVEN A SINGLE WORD ON THIS SUB-
JECT [*Guide*, p. 430]

That is, the prophetic reach to the essence of God through dreams and
visions in sexual imagery of the generation of human souls.

BE IT AS AN EXPLICIT STATEMENT OR IN A FLASHLIKE
ALLUSION [*Guide*, p. 430]

Maimonides expresses a final trepidation:

FOR EVERYTHING THAT IT IS POSSIBLE TO SAY ABOUT
THIS HAS BEEN SAID; I HAVE EVEN PLUNGED DEEP
INTO THIS WITH TEMERITY. [*Guide*, p. 430]

And on to "other subjects."

WE SHALL ACCORDINGLY START UPON OTHER SUB-
JECTS FROM AMONG THOSE THAT, I HOPE, I SHALL
EXPLAIN IN THIS TREATISE. [*Guide*, p. 430]

Having said all that he can about God's creativity, he moves on to
consider the implications for this being, whom he takes to be in the
"*image of God and His likeness*" [*Guide*, p. 431].

References

Aristotle. *De Anima,* trans. R. D. Hicks. Amsterdam: Adolf M. Hakkert, 1965.

Aristotle. *The Basic Works of Aristotle,* ed. R. McKeon. New York: Random House, 1941.

The Babylonian Talmud, trans. I. Epstein et al. (1961). London: Soncino Press.

de Leon, M. (1934). *The Zohar,* trans. H. Sperling et al. London: Soncino Press.

Droge, A. J. (1984). The interpretation of the history of culture in Hellenistic-Jewish historiography. In *Seminar Papers, 1984, Society of Biblical Literature,* ed. K. H. Richards, pp. 136–159. Chico, CA: Scholars Press, 1984.

Freud, S. *The Interpretation of Dreams,* trans. J. Strachey. (1955). New York: Basic Books.

Garfinkle, J. (1912). *Eight Chapters of Maimonides on Ethics.* New York: Columbia University Press.

Jastrow, M. (1903). *A Dictionary of the Targumim, the Talmud Babli and Yerushalmi, and the Midrashic Literature.* Brooklyn, NY: Traditional Press.

Jowett, B., trans. (1937). *The Dialogues of Plato,* vol. 2. New York: Random House.

Maimonides, M. *Mishneh Torah: The Book of Knowledge*, trans. M. Hyamson. (1981). Jerusalem: Feldheim Publishers.

Maimonides, M. *The Guide of the Perplexed*, trans. S. Pines (1974). Chicago: University of Chicago Press.

Maimonides, M. *Introduction to the Talmud, Introduction to Seder Zeraim*, trans. Z. L. Lampel (1975). New York: Judaica Press.

Midrash Rabbah, trans. H. Freedman and M. Simon (1977). London: Soncino Press.

Pirke de Rabbi Eliezer, trans. G. Friedlander (1981). New York: Sepher-Hermon Press.

Scholem, G. G. (1954). *Major Trends in Jewish Mysticism*, 3rd rev. ed. New York: Schocken Books.

Index

281

About the Author

David Bakan received his Ph.D. from Ohio State University and has held numerous teaching positions. He is currently Professor of Psychology at York University in Toronto, Canada. He has served as president of several divisions of the American Psychological Association and gave the Terry Lectures on Science and Religion at Yale University in 1976. Dr. Bakan is the author of several books, including *Sigmund Freud and the Jewish Mystical Tradition* and *The Duality of Human Existence.*